BASIC NEEDS AND THE URBAN POOR:
THE PROVISION OF COMMUNAL SERVICES

The World Employment Programme (WEP) was launched by the International Labour Organisation in 1969, as the ILO's main contribution to the International Development Strategy for the Second United Nations Development Decade.

The means of action adopted by the WEP have included the following:
— short-term high-level advisory missions;
— longer-term national or regional employment teams; and
— a wide-ranging research programme.

Through these activities the ILO has been able to help national decision-makers to reshape their policies and plans with the aim of eradicating mass poverty and unemployment.

A landmark in the development of the WEP was the World Employment Conference of 1976, which proclaimed *inter alia* that 'strategies and national development plans should include as a priority objective the promotion of employment and the satisfaction of the basic needs of each country's population'. The Declaration of Principles and Programme of Action adopted by the Conference have become the cornerstone of WEP technical assistance and research activities during the 1980's.

This publication is the outcome of a WEP project.

BASIC NEEDS AND THE URBAN POOR: THE PROVISION OF COMMUNAL SERVICES

Edited by P. J. Richards and A. M. Thomson

A study prepared for the International Labour Office within the framework of the World Employment Programme

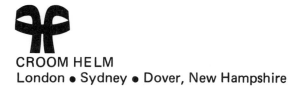

CROOM HELM
London ● Sydney ● Dover, New Hampshire

© 1984 International Labour Organisation
Croom Helm Ltd, Provident House, Burrell Row,
Beckenham, Kent BR3 1AT
Croom Helm Australia Pty Ltd, First Floor, 139 King St.,
Sydney, NSW 2001, Australia

British Library Cataloguing in Publication Data

Basic needs and the urban poor.
   1. Urban poor — Services for — Asia
   I. Richards, P.J.   II. Thomson, A.M.
   362.5'8'095   HV4131.85
   ISBN 0-7099-2281-7

Croom Helm, 51 Washington Street, Dover,
New Hampshire 03820, USA

Library of Congress Catalog Card Number:84-45290
Cataloging in Publication Data Applied For.

10954 9
2212820 8

The responsibility for opinions expressed in studies and other contributions
rests solely with the authors, and publication does not constitute an
endorsement by the International Labour Office of the opinions expressed
in them.

The designations employed and the presentation of material do not imply the
expression of any opinion whatsoever on the part of the International Labour
Office concerning the legal status of any country or territory or of its authorities
or concerning the delimitation of its frontiers.

For permission to reproduce the photograph on p.97, grateful acknowledgement
is due to the Centre international de reportages at d'information culturelle
(CIRIC), Geneva. Other illustrations have been provided by the authors
themselves.

Printed in Great Britain by Biddles Ltd, Guildford, Surrey

CONTENTS

BASIC NEEDS AND THE URBAN POOR

Chapter 5: Health care and the urban poor

Chapter 6: Water supply issues

Chapter 7: Human waste disposal in urban areas

PREFACE

This study is intended to investigate means by which the levels of basic needs satisfaction of the urban poor can be improved by the conscious application of public policies and programmes. It looks at a number of specific fields, including housing policy, building codes, water supply, sanitation, transport, health and education and, for each one, reviews the specific situation of the urban poor and the actual and potential means available to improve their lot. It also includes an overall chapter on the role of the public sector and a short concluding chapter.

The study refers specifically to Asia. However, the contributors have also amassed experience of urban poverty problems, and their possible solutions, in other parts of the world. Thus reference is made to urban poverty problems in other continents. The focus is also mainly on the larger if not primary cities. If their problems can be eased then very probably those of smaller towns can also be solved.

The editors would like to thank R. Szal, E. Gutkind and C. Maldonado to their helpful comments on this study. I. Pearson and T. Viale, who prepared the final typescript, deserve special thanks.

P.J. Richards
A.M. Thomson

Geneva
February 1984

1 INTRODUCTION

by P. J. Richards

The World Employment Conference of the International Labour Organisation, meeting in 1976, adopted a Programme of Action[1] which, under the heading "Basic needs", begins as follows:

1. Strategies and national development plans and policies should include explicitly as a priority objective the promotion of employment and the satisfaction of the basic needs of each country's population.

2. Basic needs, as understood in this Programme of Action, include two elements. First, they include certain minimum requirements of a family for private consumption: adequate food, shelter and clothing, as well as certain household equipment and furniture. Second, they include essential services provided by and for the community at large, such as safe drinking water, sanitation, public transport and health, educational and cultural facilities.

The Conference therefore assumed that basic needs satisfaction would be ensured by a combination of two factors: private consumption expenditure, and the provision of essential services by the community at large.

The Programme of Action of the World Employment Conference does not specify where target levels of basic needs satisfaction should be set (nor, indeed, in what form they should be set) beyond stating that the concept of basic needs is country specific and dynamic.[2] Target levels, must, however, be set at above subsistence levels and, presumably, be revised in the course of economic development. The text of the Programme of Action gives a few directions in setting broad priorities in the operation of government services: thus primary education should be given priority over secondary and tertiary education (paragraph 21) and landless labourers should be assisted in building their own homes (paragraph 12).

1

This volume concentrates on the provision of services for the urban poor, including the special problems attached to carrying out such programmes and the specific characteristics of urban poverty which condition the need of the poor for these services. The volume does not tackle the first component of basic needs identified by the World Employment Conference, namely, the generation of employment at sufficiently productive levels for employment incomes to purchase food and other consumer goods for workers and their dependants. Nevertheless, the division between private consumption on the one hand and essential services on the other is artificial. Essential services also require consumption expenditure and generally households with the highest levels of private consumption enjoy the highest levels of "essential" services. To the list of sectors given above this volume adds housing and subtracts cultural facilities.

The volume concentrates on Asian experience although it draws examples from other continents. Cairo, for example, is frequently drawn on to provide corroboration or illustration of a point. The volume also concentrates on major cities where indeed most knowledge of urban poverty and of the operation of communal services has been acquired. In fact poverty in smaller cities may be as acute and, as the chapter on water supply shows, the level of services provided may be extremely low.

In discussing Asia the volume naturally draws partly on the experience of Hong Kong and Singapore. Of course, their income levels are high and some may feel that the policies they follow now may be of little relevance in India or Bangladesh. Hong Kong and Singapore are also hardly affected by internal migration by the rural poor and what migration flows there are, are controlled. They are thus spared the dilemma that improving the level of urban services may stimulate rural-urban movement. Nonetheless the means which these two city-states have used to solve their problems over the last 25 years are of some general interest. However, the inclusion of wealthier countries in the study does serve to demonstrate that the level of services available must depend largely on average income levels. It is the access to those services and their distribution between income groups which can be changed in all countries.

The reference to services provided by (and for) the community is misleading. As the various chapters show, some services, e.g. some forms of sanitation, are not generally provided by any official agency and require self—help. Schooling and health care are provided by what are usually nation—wide agencies. Water and transport may be provided by urban specific and semi-self-financing bodies.

The object of this study is to provide a knowledge base and recommendations which can serve to upgrade the level of services provided for the urban poor. This may require a change in policy, e.g. on land tenure, or a switch in investment priorities or different means of delivering educational and health care programmes. Action may be taken piecemeal or as part of an overall urban strategy. However, what is likely to be generally necessary is for a better means to be found by which the urban poor can express their own feelings and priorities and be consulted on policies and programmes. A working democratic framework is the first necessity, backed up by other means of educating and mobilising the urban poor.

One problem in using a sectoral approach for this study, apart from the next chapter which examines issues related to poverty and to the role of the government in providing services, is that intersectoral linkages are apparently underemphasised. Clearly better shelter, better sanitation, better health care, etc. all interact and to provide better shelter but ignore sanitation, or more water and ignore sewerage, to quote a real and common example, may be an extravagant means of moving in the right direction. Readers should not therefore feel that treating each subject separately means that inter-sectoral linkages have been forgotten.

There is also the question of the level of basic needs satisfaction to aim for. This has been discussed elsewhere and a few quotations can be made.[3]

> Attempts to set unimpeachably fair, absolute levels are fruitless in all but a minority of cases. In conditions of urban overcrowding there is likely to be a minimum level for sanitary provision (still above certain current levels) below which the achievement of all other targets is threatened. But once this subsistence level is reached it ceases to be useful as a target. In other areas, education for example, target levels

are determined solely by society and not by individual or group subsistence needs.

There are, however, three characteristics which basic needs targets should share: (1) they should be dynamic, i.e. they should be set in a relative manner (see below) although expressed in absolute terms; (2) they should be expressed where possible in terms of outputs rather than inputs (or a mix of the two), and of improvements in personal well-being rather than the coverage provided; (3) they should be the predictable results of programmes which are known to be effective.

A relative concept of basic needs implies that the target level for a given future year should be set in relation to that currently enjoyed by some other population group. This frees policy-makers from a dependence on possibly specious calculations of minimum needs. It also implies (i) that the degree of basic needs satisfaction of all population groups needs to be investigated before setting targets, in order to know how many groups currently fall short of the alternative levels envisaged, and (ii) that equity is a principal consideration in target setting. To what extent equity also implies egalitarianism depends on whether those already enjoying basic needs satisfaction above the target level can make further progress.

The second point is that output targets are far preferable to input targets. Targets should refer, for example, to safe births (not to attended deliveries), to the development of mental abilities (not to a certain number of years of schooling), to mobility (not to the building of so many kilometres of all-weather roads) and to storm-proof housing (not to the production of galvanised sheeting or waterproofed thatch).

The above may seem undeniable. However, the third point concerns precisely the relation between inputs and outputs. Some government programmes are well known to be effective, in the sense that ensuring satisfactory coverage of the population concerned (an input target) practically guarantees a particular level of basic needs satisfaction (an output target). Vaccination campaigns are an example. Other programmes are believed to be effective, some are ineffective.

Where they stand on this scale depends on the number of variables intervening between the inputs and the eventual output. These variables will determine whether greater individual access to inputs will be matched by corresponding improvements in the degree of basic needs satisfaction.

The nature of these intervening variables will differ from one programme to another. They will include home hygiene, exposure to mass media, willingness to undertake home improvements and maintenance, parental education and nutrition. They not only determine the probable effectiveness of a programme; they also, together with income itself, are very important in determining whether complete coverage of the target population can be achieved. Economic and cultural variables of this sort are an essential link in the supplier-consumer partnership which characterises all government programmes.

Can we attempt a basic needs profile of the urban poor? In many ways, as the following chapters show, this cannot be done. The urban poor may live in inner city tenements, or may squat in inner or peripheral areas. As such some may live in areas serviced by centralised water supply and sewerage systems, but at a low standard, while others will not. Their employment, or the employment of the adults and older children, is, however, likely to have common characteristics. It may be intermittent and casual, requiring little skill. Adults are likely to have had little education, children will have difficulty in following full-time studies and are frequently absent from school. Health standards are likely to be low because of poor environmental conditions and malnutrition. The poor will make use of curative health sources in the form of clinics and hospitals but at some cost in terms of time spent waiting and travelling and earnings foregone. When they have to travel they will walk long distances and generally wait a long time for buses. Food storage will always present problems so that purchases must be made daily and probably at a relatively high unit cost. Their votes will be sought at election time but that would be all.

In supplying communal services to the urban poor there will be a number of problems to overcome. By and large the poor will not be able to pay more than a minor sum for e.g. water supplies or transport. Self-financing or profit making agencies will try to pass them by. They will frequently be at a legal disadvantage if squatting on private or unapproved land or be in no position to force private landlords to improve their tenements. As we shall see their children may have problems at school because the school's culture and values are not those they know at home and even because their dialect and means of expression are different. They can do little to escape from their poverty and may become apathetic and over-dependent. They will not keep records, fill up forms and write official letters. All this has to be kept in mind in finding better ways for communal services to reach and aid the poor.

Readers may rightly feel some uneasiness about the imprecision of the term "urban". Unfortunately this lack of precision is unavoidable. There is no alternative to accepting national definitions of what is an urban area. These definitions do not usually combine a measure both of absolute numbers and of population density in the way they probably ideally should. In some countries, Sri Lanka for example, the definition of urban is a legal one and some urban areas contain only a few thousand people. The study, however, deals principally with larger conurbations which usually contain the majority of a country's urban residents.

One final point which is worth making here and is raised also in the next chapter concerns the relation between absolute and relative poverty. In one sense relative poverty is unavoidable if incomes are unequally distributed so that some clearly enjoy a higher standard of living than others, who then feel psychologically deprived. In urban Asia, however, there are clearly large numbers of the absolutely poor by any standard, malnourished and in ill health. Clearly there are proportionately fewer of them in Singapore than in Calcutta. By Singapore standards the vast majority in Calcutta will be poor. In this volume we recognise both that poverty is widespread in the urban areas of low-income Asian countries and that poverty levels do vary nationally. They must have an international component in order for living standards to be compared but still have a national component to take account of local cultural, economic and social norms.

Notes

1. "Declaration of Principles and Programme of Action", in ILO: <u>Meeting basic needs: Strategies for eradicating mass poverty and unemployment</u> (Geneva, 1977)

2. P. Richards and M. Leonor (eds.): <u>Target setting for basic needs</u> (Geneva, ILO, 1982)

3. ibid.

2 URBAN POVERTY AND BASIC NEEDS:
The Role of the Public Sector

by A.M. Thomson

- "The streets themselves are usually unpaved
and full of holes. They are filthy and strewn
with animal and vegetable refuse. Since they
have neither gutters nor drains the refuse
accumulates in stagnant, stinking puddles.
Ventilation in the slums is inadequate owing
to the hopelessly unplanned nature of these
areas".

F. Engels, The condition of the working
class in England

Introduction

These words, written about nineteenth-century
London, could easily apply to many of the large Third
World cities today - Calcutta, Cairo, Manila or
Bombay. Whereas in the nineteenth century large urban
centres were mainly a feature of industrialised
Europe and America, urbanisation has increased until
now over 30 per cent of the population of developing
countries live in urban areas, and by the year 2000
over half the population of the world is expected to
be urban.[1]

Urbanisation rates are by no means uniform. In
regions such as Latin America, which have
proportionally large urban populations, the rate of
urban growth is slowing, whereas in sub-Saharan
Africa the rates are high, and in some cases
increasing. In Asia and the Middle East, the areas
principally under consideration here, the variation
is high, as table 1 shows, though, as might be
expected, an inverse relationship between degree of
urbanisation and rate of urban growth can be
discerned, in extremely general terms.

Prediction is almost always an imprecise art in
the social services, particularly where both
population growth rates and internal migration have
to be considered. However, though there is certainly

9

Table 1:   Rates of urbanisation, in percentages

| Country | Annual growth rate | | | Urban population as per cent of total |
	Total population 1960-79	Urban population 1960-70	1970-80	1980
Low income				
Bangladesh	2.7	6.3	6.8	11
Nepal	2.1	4.3	4.7	5
Burma	2.2	3.9	3.9	27
India	2.2	3.3	3.3	22
Sri Lanka	2.0	4.3	3.6	27
Pakistan	3.0	4.0	4.3	28
Indonesia	2.2	3.6	4.0	20
Sudan	2.4	6.9	6.8	25
Middle income				
Egypt	2.1	3.3	2.8	45
Thailand	2.6	3.5	3.3	14
Philippines	2.8	3.8	3.6	36
Malaysia	2.5	3.6	3.1	29
Hong Kong	2.6	2.6	2.7	90
Singapore	1.9	2.4	1.4	100
Capital surplus oil exporters				
Iraq	3.2	6.2	5.4	72
Saudi Arabia	4.0	8.4	7.6	67
Kuwait	7.9	10.4	7.4	88

Source: World Bank: World development report, (Washington, DC, 1981).

room for argument over the exact size of the urban population at any specific date in the future, or the number of cities over a certain size which will be in existence by then, it is clear that the urban population will be an increasing proportion of a total growing population for virtually all countries over the next few decades. This implies large absolute increases. For example, in the mid-1970s,

Jakarta and Seoul grew by over a quarter of a million
people each year. Nor is it simply a problem of
capital cities. Growth rates in secondary urban
centres are also very high in most countries.

Concern about urban growth generally centres round
two major issues: the growth of employment
opportunities for the urban population and the
ability of the physical and social infrastructure to
accommodate this population growth. The latter is of
particular significance as, up until now, much of
urban growth has been in the form of growth of
squatter or spontaneous settlements, to such an
extent that, for example in the early 1970s, 90 per
cent of the population of Addis Ababa lived in
squatter or slum settlements.[2] In general, the
growth rate of these settlements is much greater than
that of the urban population as a whole. Rates of
natural increase are such that, in many cities, the
absolute increase in numbers will be sufficient to
cause considerable problems, without the additional
factor of rural-urban migration. As table 2 shows,
contrary to what is often supposed, natural
population increase often outweighs internal
migration as a cause of urban growth. Regardless of
what policies are undertaken to affect internal
migration, and their success or failure, governments
will have to come to terms with increasing urban
populations and, in tandem with this, increasing
absolute numbers of the urban poor.

Measuring the extent of urban poverty

Quantifying the urban population per se in a
consistent fashion presents certain problems. Census
definitions vary from country to country; sometimes
settlement size is the only criterion used, in others
a given population density or the existence of
certain institutions are also required for an area to
be considered urban. Figures given here use each
country's own definition of urban areas.

When it comes to quantifying the urban poor,
definitional problems abound at every stage, and data
are often scarce and unreliable. Identifying poverty
in the lowest income groups usually raises few
problems but there is a wide, hazy area in the middle
of the spectrum between poverty and wealth, where it
is difficult to know where to place the cut-off
point. Poverty, absolute poverty, can best be defined
negatively. It is a lack of something. Most commonly,

Table 2:   Sources of intercensal growth of urban populations, in percentages

Country	Intercensal period	Annual population growth rate of urban areas (per cent)	Estimated annual urban rate of natural increase (per cent)	Estimated annual rate of urban growth from internal migration and reclassification (per cent)
Bangladesh	1960-74	6.6	2.9	3.7
India	1961-71	3.2	2.2	1.0
Indonesia	1961-71	3.7	2.4	1.3
Iraq	1957-65	6.4	3.5	2.9
Nepal	1961-71	3.3	2.1	1.2
Republic of Korea	160-70	6.3	2.5	3.8
Sri Lanka	1963-71	4.3	2.2	2.1
Syrian Arab Republic	1960-70	4.9	3.3	1.5

Source: United Nations, Patterns of rural and urban population growth (New York, 1980).

it is taken to be a lack of income, for quantification purposes. This means that some form of poverty line has to be defined. The standard way of doing this is in relationship to food expenditure. Two basic methods are used to set this: either that amount of expenditure which should be sufficient to procure a nutritionally adequate diet is calculated; or the minimum amount of expenditure, shown in household expenditure surveys, actually to provide a nutritionally adequate diet is extracted from the data. Making allowances for non-food expenditure causes difficulties, as there are no equivalents to the recommended dietary intakes, as set by organisations such as the Food and Agricultural Organisation and World Health Organisation, which can be used to identify adequate expenditure on such basic items as fuel, rent or clothing. One way round this problem which is often used is to estimate the percentage of expenditure on non-food items for an appropriate low-income group of the population, and then extrapolate from that, and the level of adequate food expenditure, to get an overall level of expenditure which is then used as a poverty line.

In this volume absolute poverty is viewed within the context of each country. Measures are discussed which each government can take to improve the lot of its poor. Thus, paradoxically, a relative concept immediately enters. The absolutely poor in Hong Kong will probably not be the absolutely poor in Calcutta. Yet no one can deny that in any meaningful sense there are more poor people in Calcutta than Hong Kong. Relying on measures of income distribution will not help much in this context. Incomes in Hong Kong are probably less equally distributed than in Calcutta. Measuring poverty by reference to a local mean income would probably show more poverty in the richer area. Thus poverty measurement requires both an international standard, as in the recommended dietary measurement, and some adjustment to local cultural and social norms. Where average incomes are higher, average consumption levels for all goods and services will be higher. In this way some recognition is given to the existence of relative poverty in richer countries.

Variations on this basic technique of measuring food requirements in terms of international norms and adding an allowance for non-food costs are used in most countries which employ poverty lines to help describe the level of deprivation which exists. In some cases the poverty line is defined on a per capita basis, but most frequently it is defined in terms of a model size of household, to take into account both possible family economies of scale and also variations, particularly in terms of adequate food intake, of standards for men and women, and for different age groups. The degree to which the effect of cultural patterns and tastes in eating are taken into account also varies from country to country. All of these factors will affect the final total of the number of people who are deemed to be "poor".

A continually updated poverty line can be used to show changes in the incidence of poverty over time. Where the construction of a poverty line is impracticable, or politically contentious, other methods have been used. That income level which represents the cut-off point for the lowest 40 per cent of the population in a given year may be taken as a baseline for measuring population movements above or below it, e.g. if, at a future date only 35 per cent of the population had an income which fell, in real terms, below the original cut-off point, this would be seen as a measure of improvement. Alternatively, that income which demarcates the lowest 40 per cent could be measured over time, deflated by an appropriate price index and examined to see whether any real improvement has taken place. Unfortunately, this latter method requires the calculation of a price index appropriate to the consumption pattern of the section of the population concerned, which is frequently not available, nor is the need for it often appreciated. Although these two methods do give information about movement at the lower end of the income distribution, they do not give any notion about the absolute level of poverty.

These kinds of exercise may seem at first glance to have little more practicality or importance than theological arguments about angels on pinheads. The urban poor exist. No one disputes this. How important is it whether their number in any one country is 13.2 million or 14.0 million?

However, numbers can have considerable importance when programmes and politics are being determined and analysed. If the size of the poverty problem is represented as extremely small or extremely large, governments may well ignore it, in the first case as being insignificant and, in the second case, as being beyond their resources to attack effectively. Within these extremes, a relatively small problem is more likely to be approached in a direct and comprehensive fashion by government, whereas with large-scale problems, there will probably be more tendency to try self-help approaches, or to encourage and stimulate the private sector to provide employment opportunities and appropriate basic needs.

¬ Almost as important may be the influence of the degree of breadth in the definition of poverty on the ex-post evaluation of the extent of success of poverty-oriented programmes. As will be discussed at greater length later, one of the major problems in successfully carrying out programmes targeted at the poor is the prevention of diversion of the benefits to other groups in the population. This is particularly the case when the programme provides services which are in short supply for the "non-poor" as well as the poor. The broader the definition of poverty, the less will diversions from the extremely poor be visible. A programme may reach almost entirely the highest band of those defined as "poor" and be regarded as successful without having any impact on real poverty in the society at all.

None of this would be of much importance, if poverty incidence were relatively insensitive to the measures used. However, this is not the case. Scott[3] shows that for rural West Pakistan in 1963-64, the proportion of the population falling below the poverty line can vary between 60 per cent and 79 per cent according to whether the poverty line is defined in terms of households or individuals, income or expenditure and in terms of calorie intake or money. Reducing the expenditure cut-off point by a sixth reduces the proportion below the cut-off point to 43 per cent. It is possible that the sensitivity of poverty incidence to the poverty line is somewhat greater in rural than in urban areas, but incomes at the lower end of the distribution in urban areas are sufficiently clustered, in general, for sensitivity to be rather high.

Given that there are no overwhelming reasons for using one rather than another of these methodologies for quantifying the extent of poverty, when general statements are being made about poverty in the world, or even poverty in a specific country, then it is important to examine the reasons for quantifying poverty and find the method most appropriate for the context. This may not necessarily be a measure based on income alone, or indeed on income at all. Many programmes and policies aimed at alleviating poverty are directed towards specific characteristics of poverty; unemployment, low food consumption, bad housing or poor sanitation. In fact the one policy which is hardly ever considered by developing country governments, both for financial and political reasons, is that of direct income maintenance.

Thus, a useful definition of poverty which can be used for framing national programmes has to include those characteristics which are seen as important in the national context. These may be low food intake, lack of access to water or the necessity to put young children to work rather than send them to school. Most of these factors will be related to income level, but collecting information in these terms, within a basic needs framework, in conjunction with such income data as are available is much more directly relevant to the kinds of programmes which governments are likely to implement. It is also important to have information on income levels and other characteristics of poverty and deprivation for the whole range of persons below the poverty line. This information is needed in order to differentiate between the badly-off and the worst off. If poverty is defined in such a way as to include 80 per cent of the population, then there is little practical difference between a poverty-oriented programme and a national development programme. At the very least, such a broad definition of poverty limits the possibilities of effectively implementing programmes aimed at redistributing resources towards the poor.

Urban and rural poverty
    Most of the discussion above is valid for both urban and rural poverty. When it comes to describing the general characteristics of poverty, however, there are very marked differences. In most countries, welfare in the rural sector is dependent on the distribution of land and the overall prosperity of agriculture. In rather simplified terms, rural people are poor because the overall profitability of agriculture is low. The impact of the poverty is often all the greater as a result of distance from and the inadequacy of services such as health and education, particularly in sparsely populated areas.

Since the late 1970s, more and more emphasis has been put on poverty as largely a rural problem. The failure of development efforts in the 1960s to better the lot of many of the poor in developing countries has been attributed by many to excessive emphasis on industrialisation, and neglect of agriculture. In much broader terms, this has been referred to as "urban bias"[4] i.e. a concentration of resources on the urban sector, not only in terms of the allocation of government expenditure, but, in a more dynamic sense, the distortion of prices to ensure a continual extraction of surplus from the rural sector by the urban sector.

Much of this criticism is undoubtedly justified, and in some areas there is an immediate conflict of interests between the urban poor and the rural poor. The most obvious area is that of food pricing. To quote Lipton:[5] "The urban employer wants food to be cheap, so that his workforce will be well fed and productive. The urban employee wants cheap food too; it makes whatever wages he can extract from the boss go further. Less obviously, the whole interest of the rural community is against cheap food". Although the ultimate beneficiary of a cheap food policy is almost certainly the urban employer, in the short run the urban poor benefit in terms of the effect on their real income at the expense of the rural poor who suffer either directly, in terms of the price for their output, or indirectly, in terms of the rural demand for their labour, or non-farm products. Equally, where there are limited total budgets for health care systems and education, there is a sense in which, whatever the validity of claims for the efficiency of specialisation in areas of concentrated population, of both higher education and complex surgical and hospital care procedures, money spent in urban areas is not being spent in rural areas.

Although urbanisation is increasing, as was indicated above, the majority of the population in developing countries is still rural. The majority of the poor, under whatever definition, still live in rural areas. That this has been recognised by the international agencies is shown by the emphasis on the role of agriculture in development and in numerous publications on, for example, rural primary health care systems and rural water supply. Yet a dichotomy is set up which is oversimplified and misleading. Urban is better off than rural. Urban has

more political power than rural. Urban can influence
government power in its favour. Urban denotes a set
of attitudes, interests and opportunities that are so
dominant and cohesive that rural migrants, whether
they enter into the employment market, the
entrepreneurial market or the political market, can
only succeed by adopting these values, a version of
embourgeoisification.

Urban, however, is not nearly as uniform as this
would suggest. In fact, such quantitative data that
exist indicate that in Asia urban is rather less
uniform than rural. World Bank data cited by
Grimes[6] show that for Asia, income distribution is
less egalitarian in the urban than the rural
population, in contrast to Latin America, where the
opposite is true. In other words, the difference
between the extremes of poverty and wealth may well
be greater in the urban sector. This would suggest
that one of the more useful questions that can be
asked about urban poverty and the provision of basic
needs services to the urban poor concerns the
distribution of the benefits of the existing services
in urban areas among the different income groups. In
this way, one is spared invidious and inconclusive
arguments about the relative severity of urban and
rural deprivation. Urban poverty is significant and
has certain characteristics which are different from
those of rural poverty. To what extent do government
basic services alleviate that poverty and to what
extent do they accentuate it?

Characteristics of the urban poor

There are limits to the degree of generalisation
that one can usefully undertake about the urban poor,
even within one city, far less within a region. The
immediate causes of poverty may vary from
unemployment to ill health to a large number of
dependents in the family. Some of the urban poor come
from families who have lived in cities for a number
of generations; others are recent migrants. Some are
young and single: others belong to large families
which can comprise three generations. There are,
nonetheless, certain possible characteristics of the
urban poor which it is important to examine, because
they affect both the needs of the poor and the
difficulties involved in satisfying those needs.

The most obvious, in fact tautological,
characteristic of the urban poor is that they live in

towns and cities, much closer to one another than do
the rural poor. The population density varies very
much. In some peripheral squatter settlements the
population density may be very similar to that of
middle-income housing areas, and may be under 250
persons per hectare. This compares with a figure for
parts of Central Karachi of over 2,400 persons per
hectare in the late 1960s.[7] Central areas of other
big Asian cities, such as Calcutta, may have
densities which are as high, if not higher. This
level of population pressure compounds the problems
associated with lack of water, sanitation and sewage
disposal systems. This has a marked effect on the
health environment of the population and on the
incidence of disease.

Unlike the rural poor, the urban poor live in an
almost entirely monetised economy. They have, for the
most part, to buy their food, fuel and often drinking
water, though in the less crowded urban areas, some
small livestock may be kept. Employment in the urban
sector, even in the so-called informal sector, tends
to be rather more formalised than in the rural
sector. For example, in Pakistan, Sudan and the
Philippines, the proportion of total income generated
through self-employment was only half in the urban
areas what it was in the rural areas.[8] This
relative inflexibility is consistent with the
evidence on much higher rates of open unemployment in
urban areas than rural, though the incidence of
underemployment is probably the reverse. This also
means that data on money incomes and expenditure give
a more accurate idea of the resources available to
the poor in urban areas than they do in rural areas
(though even in urban areas expenditure data at the
lower end of the distribution are often very dubious).

The characteristic of the urban poor which causes
most concern to governments is their spatial
distribution. Although all who live in inner city
slums and in squatter settlements, whether in the
inner city or the periphery, are not necessarily
poor, almost all the poor live in those areas. This
makes them very visible. They live in predictable
places, and they live together. Inner city slums tend
to consist of old, badly maintained houses, which are
subdivided up and rented out to families, with
resultant overcrowding. What services are provided
are usually totally inadequate for the number of
families living in any one house. Squatter

settlements in the inner cities exhibit similar overcrowding, but because the housing is basically illegal, services are virtually non-existent and housing is often of impermanent material. Much of the housing in squatter settlements is rented, insofar as the "landlord" has put up the original structure. There are also settlements which fall in between these two types, where the landlord owns the land and puts up on it rather impermanent structures for rental. Perhaps the most extreme case of these kinds of settlements is that of the bustees in Calcutta where, in the late 1960s, 30,000 huts were owned by 20,000 individuals and let out to over 700,000 people.[9] Peripheral squatter settlements tend to be less densely populated but again without services. Maps plotting the positions of these outlying squatter settlements indicate the way in which areas close to both transport routes and water sources have been picked. Wegelin[10] shows this nicely for Kuala Lumpur.

It is difficult to find much information on the age and sex structure of the urban poor, as poverty data are taken generally from household expenditure and income distribution studies which are not analysed in such a way as to give this information. For the most part, this has to be inferred from the evidence on the overall urban age and sex structure. Differences in these patterns from those of the rural areas are the result of migration patterns generally. Urbanisation in Asia has resulted in an increase in the male population relative to the female in urban areas. This, however, is not as marked as is the case in Africa, and it is not clear how much this is due to a timelag before families join the migrating male head of households, and how much to temporary migration by the male, who then returns to the rural area. Certainly the older age groups are less present in East Asian urban areas but that is almost certainly a consequence of increased urbanisation in the last 20 years, rather than temporary migration patterns. There is little evidence of urbanisation along the Latin American pattern, which has led to cities which have a relatively high female population.

One factor which is quite clearly documented for a number of countries is the over-representation of large families amongst the urban poor, when poverty is measured in per capita terms. In Indonesia, for example, average household size decreases steadily from 7.35 in the lowest per capita income category to 3.52 in the highest.[11] In the Philippines, over 60 per cent of all families with nine or more members fall below the urban per capita poverty line, as opposed to under 20 per cent of families of three or less.[12] Though some of these additional family members will be adult sons and daughters and grandparents, these figures do imply that the incidence of poverty in urban children will be greater than that in the urban population as a whole.

Some of the literature on urban poverty seems almost to imply that it is, to a large extent, the consequence of rural-urban migration. Such evidence as exists indicates that migrants into cities do not form a disproportionate number of the urban poor. Rural-urban migrants do not usually come from the poorest section of the rural population, and migration often takes place in a stepwise fashion, first to smaller local towns and then on to the larger cities. In Kuala Lumpur, for example, urban-urban migration is by far the most important part of inflows into the city.[13] The reasons for migration are varied. A number of studies in Indonesia, Thailand and the Philippines showed that up to 15 per cent of migration was for the purposes of education. This type of migrant is unlikely to add to urban poverty, though migration may well have an effect on the availability of services for the urban poor.

The kinds of characteristics discussed above belong to a description of urban poverty rather than a theory of urban poverty, whether static or dynamic. They can be useful in determining the environment within which government policy has to operate. Taken in conjunction with figures on existing water supply, housing, use of education facilities, etc., they can be used to help identify factors such as likely need and/or demand for certain basic needs services and geographical areas that should have priority. It would, however, be more satisfying to be able to describe urban poverty in terms of an adequate theory of causation of poverty. Income is the obvious key factor here, but the problems associated with using that to identify poverty have been discussed above. Employment would seem to be another possibility. The conceptualisation of employment in developing country cities as being in either the formal or informal sector has sometimes been taken as a starting point. This has proved to be too simplistic. In Jakarta, a survey showed about a quarter of the low income population to be white-collar workers in the formal sector.[14] Similarly, a study of Davao, in the Philippines, which classified the population by income, put many of the higher income workers in the informal sector into the middle class, whereas it put low-income workers in the formal sector into the lower class. These and other surveys indicate that there is no simple relationship between poverty and whether employment is in the formal or informal sector.

McGee[15] recognises these problems and tries to approach the problem by "emphasising the coping responses of the poor at the individual level". Thus he defines the poor in characteristics such as the following: as many of the household members work as possible, ranging from children to grandparents; the poor seek and engage in a wide diversity of occupations; the poor are forced to seek credit from a wide variety of means. He also discusses the way in which they minimise their expenditure patterns and their attitudes towards birth control and political authority. This approach certainly gives a much more vivid and well-rounded picture of the poor, but there are problems with it. First of all, it is not clear that all of the characteristics itemised are solely characteristics of the poor; some of the strategies mentioned might equally well be carried out by other income groups, but more successfully. For example, a multiplicity of occupations is relatively common at quite high income levels in Cairo. Secondly, although the description of behaviour patterns is useful in identifying potentially negative effects of government policy, e.g. in restricting the opportunities for informal activity in the cities, it gives little positive help in devising programmes to benefit the poor.

Insufficient consideration is given to the possibility that many of the characteristics of the poor result from the attempt to maintain the values and norms of the better off in the face of extremely restricted circumstances. The whole issue of whether a separate culture of poverty exists is extremely contentious, but it is worth noting that at least one study undertaken in Cairo came to the conclusion that the only major difference between the rich and the poor was material resources, and that actions and characteristics which seemed specific to the poor were explicable in terms of their attempts to maintain middle class values.[16] This leads to the conclusion that the only useful programmes for the urban poor are quite simply those that increase their access to resources.

The concept of the culture of poverty implies a self-perpetuation of poverty because of the value systems of the poor. If correct it would imply that anti-poverty programmes are inappropriate until and unless the value systems of the poor have changed. In those parts of Asia where poverty is widespread it is hard to give much meaning to this notion since the values of the poor will be the normal values of the population. Certainly living in abject poverty may well have a destructive effect on human capacities and aspirations. This is precisely what education, health and other programmes have to change. Furthermore there are the Asian success stories of economic growth which seem to show stupendous adjustment to improved economic conditions within one generation, as in Singapore.

All of the above, however, is essentially static in approach, trying to answer the question: what are the poor like? Attempts to answer the dynamic question, what happens to the poor?, are more difficult to find. Of course, at a micro level, it is more difficult and expensive to do good longitudinal work, and at the national level, the base material is usually cross-sectional studies. Comparison of a number of these over time will allow statements to be made about changes in distribution and general patterns, for example, of expenditure, but these do not normally allow the formation of dynamic theories. Theories of migration do often have a dynamic aspect, in particular those of the neoclassical economic school which see the process as one of equalisation between the rural and urban sector, but at most these impinge on the process of urban poverty by giving a rather dubious methodology for quantifying the size of the problem over time.

One approach which potentially has some bearing on describing dynamically some aspects of urban poverty is the model devised by Turner to describe the demand for housing in cities, in particular by migrants in spontaneous settlements.[17] He identifies three basic characteristics of housing, location, tenure

and amenity, and describes the housing demand of
three types of urban population: the very low-income
"bridgeheader"; the low-income "consolidator" and the
middle-income "status seeker". The "bridgeheader",
usually a recent migrant, is in a very insecure
position and often still trying to get an entry to
the urban system. Location will be the strategic
factor here, in order to improve the chances of
getting a job and minimise the costs of so doing.
This is the typical occupant of an inner-city slum,
probably renting either a room in a building or a
delapidated shack in a squatter settlement. The
"consolidator" has lived in the city longer, is more
likely to have a regular job and a higher income.
With greater security, he has a wider possible choice
of housing and is more likely to build his own in the
urban periphery, i.e. tenure is the dominant demand.
As his income improves, he improves the house and
gradually develops into a middle-income status
seeker. This is a life cycle type of theory of
housing and it has several interesting features. It
implies that all slum and squatter settlements are
not alike. Outlying settlements are likely to be
better off than inner city ones, and also to have a
wide variety of housing standards according to the
owner's income. In these cases, it may be that the
only necessary government action would be to
regularise the land tenure situation, so as to allow
the formal provision of services.

   Turner bases his model on his experiences in Latin
America. Individual Asian case studies show patterns
of settlement that do not conform in some important
aspects to this. For example, implicit in Turner's
picture is a certain level of mobility among squatter
settlements. Yet a study of four shanty towns in
Dhaka showed 71 per cent of the occupants to have
been resident in the settlements for much the same
time that they had been in the city, though only 31
per cent of them were born in Dhaka. Of that 71 per
cent, 91 per cent had lived in Dhaka for over six
years.[18] Obviously some movement did take place,
and Dhaka is only one example, but there are dangers
in assuming that this theory gives a representational
picture for Asia. Possibly the overall level of
economic growth in some of the large Asian
metropolises is insufficient to allow these patterns
to appear and it is impossible for sufficient of the

poor to increase their income over time to exhibit what may very possibly be latent characteristics.

The variety of experience of urbanisation in Asia and the Middle East is very great. Egypt and the Indian subcontinent both have large and very old cities which have grown over a long period of time and where growth is now due much more to natural increase than migration. The poor are then clearly by no means all migrants. Hong Kong and Singapore are basically city states with little internal migration to influence policy and no rural poverty to pull down urban income levels. Other countries such as the Republic of Korea and the Islamic Republic of Iran have experienced fairly rapid urbanisation. These present different problems in terms of the growth of both adequate employment opportunities and urban infrastructure. It is unlikely that any detailed theory will be universally applicable. The degree of generalisation necessary for universality may lead, at worst to tautology, and at best to a broad base on which specific characteristics have to be built to give a useful description.

Government attitudes towards urban poverty

Although it is difficult to make any very specific statements about urban poverty which have policy implications outside a national context, it is much easier to analyse government policies towards the poor and bring out specific issues and principles. This is even more the case when the question of government provision of basic needs services is concerned. In many ways, the narrower the issue the easier it is to define the constraints and outline the possibilities. However, before going into detail, it is useful to place the discussion in the context of general government attitudes towards the urban poor.

Attitudes are slowly changing but it is fair to say that, until recently, for many governments, national and not just municipal, the poor were simply an obstacle in the way of achieving their vision of a modern city. The following chapter in fact describes turning points in the approaches of many Asian governments towards slum eradication and squatter relocation. As has been mentioned before, the urban poor are often very visible. They tend to live together in inner city slums and squatter settlements. They try to minimise transport costs, so they are likely to squat on any vacant land which is near commercial or industrial centres. If this is privately owned land, it can be seen as threatening property rights. If it is state-owned land, then it hinders the planned development of the area. The urban poor do not conform to commercial, residential and industrial zoning. At the very least they are a blot on the urban landscape. In addition, they are often seen as a source of political unrest. The fact that they live closely congregated, and from the outside appear to have common interests is perceived to be threatening, though most evidence indicates that the urban poor are too concerned with the logistics of day-to-day survival to be anything other than politically apathetic.[19]

Negative official attitudes towards the urban poor have existed side by side with overall policies of implementing universal health care and education and a commitment to providing basic needs and social services. Other macro-level policies have, of course, had the effect of stimulating rural-urban migration and clearly urban employers welcome more competition in the labour market. Nevertheless the urban poor are often seen as a nuisance.

This perception of the poor as an aberration, and what is more an unpleasant and ominous aberration, has led to some very negative government policies. In parts of Manila, in particular on the airport road, walls have been built to conceal the presence of squatter settlements from the visitor. More seriously, McGee gives a vivid account of the actions of the Jakarta authorities in declaring Jakarta closed to migrants and limiting the activities of street vendors and becak drivers (a form of low-income transport).[20] Also in the early 1970s was the enforced eviction of some of the squatters from the Tondo region of Manila to sites outside the city which were inadequately prepared and where there were few employment opportunities.[21] Even the relatively enlightened housing policies of Hong Kong can be dated to a series of bad fires in 1953 which left 53,000 squatter inhabitants homeless.[22]

The approach to urban poverty has modified somewhat. There is now more emphasis on sites and services programmes and slum and squatter upgrading, rather than clearance programmes. This is partly in response to the cost of resettlement programmes and their relative failure, partly to the emphasis being placed on the appropriate technology approach and its implications, not just for physical infrastructure but also for the provision of education and medical services. This approach has been increasingly important in development circles and in particular in international agencies such as the World Bank, who provide much of the finance for setting up and expanding basic needs services.

Government provision of basic needs services
    The basic needs services which are being considered in this volume are water, sanitation, housing, transport, education and medical services. Although some governments provide food subsidies in some form or another (e.g. food stamps in Sri Lanka, subsidised rice in Kerala), this is not examined here, because some of the issues involved are rather different. Food subsidy programmes have a tendency to become involved with issues over agricultural pricing and increased dependence on food imports, though the political rationale for providing them is often very similar to that for government providing housing.
    In general terms, all the services considered here are provided by government because of the existence of some type of externality, i.e. not all the benefits and costs accrue to the individual who supplies or demands the commodity or service. However, the government can undertake these services which are beneficial in situations where it would be difficult for a private firm to make them financially viable. This is true to some extent, at least potentially, for all the services under consideration here, though other factors also influence government provision.
    Piped water and sewerage provision are what might be called natural monopolies, in so far as it would be impractical to allow a number of different pipe systems to exist and compete commercially with one another. The externality argument also applies, in terms of the effect on urban cleanliness and the effect on the spread of disease. Some element of natural monopoly does exist with transport when it takes the form of rail transport, but this is not the principal argument for government provision of transport. Rather, the rationale takes one of two forms: either it is claimed that significant economies of scale exist in the transport sector, so that it makes sense for any particular mode of public

transport to be run as a monopoly, and if the state did not do this a private company might exploit the consumer; or it is argued that certain routes have insufficient custom to make them profitable on a private basis, but that the state feels a social obligation to provide transport for those who live in those areas. This latter argument is more applicable to rural than urban areas and in fact a state monopoly may actually deprive people in illegal peripheral squatter settlements of transport because of unwillingness to consider them as legitimate clients, whereas the private sector has, or would have, no such scruples. As far as the former reasoning is concerned, as the chapter on transport in this volume points out, in many cases there is evidence that the state sector is, if anything, less efficient at providing transport than the private sector. It is not clear, on the whole, that the state should necessarily see the provision of urban transport as one of its functions, except in so far as it facilitates traffic management and control. It should be noted, however, that substantial private ownership of means of transport, such as bicycles, may reduce considerably the possibility for profitable private transport systems and in these circumstances there may be a very strong case for a state-run public transport system, as has happened in developed countries.

With the provision of medical and education services, the situation is more clear cut. Both have aspects of externalities and of social welfare. The state benefits from a literate and healthy work force, both through potentially greater output and also through the effect on other state programmes of social management, such as family planning programmes. Both literacy and health are also seen as basic rights, but rights which the poor would be unable to afford if they had to pay the full cost of provision, therefore social welfare reasons become important.

Housing programmes also are largely undertaken to promote social welfare, though one of the principal side effects, the facilitation of controlled urban development, may be very significant in determining the size and nature of housing programmes. An examination of housing programmes, however, brings out the fact that the provision of housing for the urban poor has rather different characteristics from

the other services. In all the other cases, the
concern is with extending services which already
exist and benefit the more affluent section of the
urban population so that they reach the poor. Housing
is concerned with providing a commodity to the poor,
which is provided by the private sector to the higher
income groups.

This broad outline does not address the question
of what the overall level of investment in these
areas should be. Traditional economic methods, such
as examining incremental capital output ratios, or
undertaking some form of cost-benefit analysis at the
project level frequently run into measurement
problems. It is difficult to quantify many of the
much-stressed social effects and such studies as are
undertaken are usually done ex-post and are not an
element in decision making.[23] Opinion amongst
economists is rather diverse over the role of social
overhead capital investment, and certainly does not
lead to easily applicable criteria.

Burton and Lee,[24] discussing appropriate rates
of investment in water supply infrastructure, examine
four ways of trying to answer the basic question
posed by lovers of appropriate investment criteria:
experienced judgement and rules of thumb; strict
financial criteria, in that only projects which are
self-financing should be undertaken; popular demand,
that is that only projects should be undertaken for
which there is a felt need in the community; and
minimal standards, i.e. projects should be undertaken
so that a certain minimal provision of services is
acquired by the whole community. Burton and Lee
suggest that initially a minimal standards approach
should be undertaken and that further expansion
should be on the basis of financial criteria. This
point will be taken up again when the design of
delivery for services is discussed, but the path of
investment they suggest could be followed for most of
the services under discussion here though it is
unlikely that many countries would expect education
or medical services to be financially self-supporting.

One factor which should be taken into account when
discussing appropriate levels of investment in basic
needs services is the interaction among the different
services. It is difficult to quantify the importance
of this but there are much greater benefits in, for
example, investing in water supply and sewerage
systems simultaneously than in doing so separately.

Education should add to the benefits of all the other systems and the provision of medical services and public health services are reinforcing. In many countries, the definition of housing services subsumes those of water supply and sewage. Thus, it may be more important to look at levels of investment in all the appropriate basic needs services together than to examine them individually.

Not only is it difficult to identify clear guidelines as to what governments ought to do in terms of aggregate expenditure on basic needs services, but also it is difficult to get reasonable data on what they actually do. Some agencies which provide services are national, some are run by local government and in some cases public expenditure takes the form of subsidy to the private sector. There is wide variation in the level of government expenditure on any one service. Table 3 shows the level of public expenditure on housing in a number of countries. The figures reflect, not only the relative importance given by governments to providing housing, but also the size of the public sector. If governments were following the type of policy outlined above, i.e. of first providing a minimal standard of service, then concentrating on financially viable expansion, one would expect a higher proportional expenditure on housing in low-income countries. The figures here show exactly the opposite, that it is the highest income countries which have the highest proportional public expenditure on housing. This probably reflects a feeling of what countries think they can afford. The political pressures on government, too, are different at a higher income level. However, the question is not simply one of the overall amount of expenditure and investment, but also of how that amount is distributed.

There are three fundamental decisions to be made when designing the delivery of basic needs services, in terms of their structure. (1) Should the implementation be carried out by the public sector, the private sector or a mixture? (2) Should the programme be self-financing or subsidised? (3) Should the level of the service to be delivered be determined by effective demand or some definition of need? These three decisions are not independent; in particular the latter two are very closely related. It is unlikely that the most appropriate type of programme would be exactly the same for all the

Table 3:   Public expenditure on housing in selected
            developing countries in various years

| Country | Year | Housing as percentage of: | |
		Total public expenditure	GNP
Algeria	1970	0.7	0.2
Hong Kong	1971	6.1	0.9
Ireland	1970-71	5.4	2.0
Republic of Korea	1970	0.2	n.a.
Peru	1971	0.5	0.1
Sri Lanka	1969-70	1.1	0.3
Venezuela	1970	6.6	1.5

n.a. = not available

Source: O.F. Grimes, Jr., op. cit.

services considered. Therefore it is useful to look
at these questions in more detail in relation to the
individual services.

Both education and medical services are provided
both publicly and privately in most Asian countries.
The demand for private education comes, in general,
from the better off sections of the population, to a
large degree because the private sector is seen as
providing a better, more specialised or more socially
appropriate education. It seems reasonably clear here
that from the state's point of view public provision
of education is the preferred course for reaching the
urban poor, rather than an expansion of the private
sector with subsidies for poor children, if for no
other reason than the inherently political nature of
the education process. This would also seem to be the
case with medical services. Here the private
provision of medical services is not always confined
to the more affluent. Traditional medicine is paid
for by the poor because it is preferred, or because
there are costs, of time and/or of transport, in
taking advantage of the public system. The approach
to this, however, would seem to lie in determining

the appropriate location, number and style of centres
of the public health system, rather than a subsidy of
the private.

Public transport (in the sense of for the public
rather than provided by the public sector) is rather
more complex. Where traffic congestion is a problem,
as it is in most large Asian cities, the existence of
a number of competing bus systems may add to it, as
may the smaller informal transport systems, such as
jeepneys and becaks. However, they equally provide a
cheap system and a flexible one. Private provision
within careful state regulation may be the best
option, though in some cases this has led to
excessively strict regulation of the informal sector
and reduced income earning opportunities for the
urban poor.

Water supply, sewerage and sanitation are, as
mentioned above, natural monopolies and therefore are
best undertaken by the public sector. Where the
public sector has failed to provide these facilities,
the private sector has moved in. Water sellers
provide an inferior service, in terms of low
availability, at higher cost. Where sanitation
systems are not water based, and depend on physical
movement of waste, the private sector may provide a
rather irregular collection system. Etherton[25]
quotes an extremely graphic description of the
unpleasant side effects of the private sewage
disposal system in Kabul. The issue here is one of
the level of provision of services, not of public
versus private.

This leaves the most complex case of all, housing.
Although transport is both public and private, the
arguments against private provision of transport are
on the basis of the resulting organisation, or lack
of it, not on the basis of the public sector
providing a service which the private sector does
not, at least not in urban areas. In housing, the
public sector generally steps in because of a failure
of the private sector at the bottom end of the urban
income distribution. At the lowest extremes, income
is simply inadequate to purchase a minimum form of
shelter, but this is by no means the whole picture.
Land tenure systems and land prices are also
important, as are building regulations. The erection
of sometimes quite elaborate structures in squatter
settlements, and certainly the variation in quality
indicate that there is a suppressed demand for

housing resulting in this, often illegal, construction. The nature of financial markets in many developing countries also has an impact. An insecure climate in capital markets may well lead to increased speculation in land, thus raising prices. Similarly insufficiently developed credit systems for the low-income population may inhibit their ability to move out of an overcrowded rental market.

Variations on public, and public plus private, action have been tried in housing programmes. At one extreme are the Hong Kong and Singapore examples of large-scale provision of public housing, at the other are the types of site and service projects which establish building plots with roads and water and sewage facilities and leave the occupants to build their own houses round this, in accordance with certain minimum building regulations. Slum upgrading programmes also leave much up to the individual houseowner. They usually concentrate on providing services and regularising tenure, with perhaps some facilities to encourage improvements by the houseowners. The best path to take is not clear-cut but it is worth noting, that with the exception of Hong Kong and Singapore, programmes have, in general, succeeded in reaching only middle income groups. This is partly because of the relatively small size of most housing programmes relative to the demand for housing. Even where there is reasonably careful targetting towards the lower income groups, rights to access may be bought by the relatively better off, or the housing may subsequently change hands.

The other two issues, whether the programme should be self-financing or subsidised, or what level of need or demand it should try to satisfy, are closely related through the pricing decision. A programme which has to be self-financing may require a level of pricing which rules out the ability of the poor to pay for a needs level of supply.

There are two major reasons for programmes to be self-financing. One is the overall shortage of resources that characterises most developing countries. Self-financing prevents an oversupply of a service relative to what a country can afford. In the absence of an effective pricing mechanism to regulate the demand for the commodity or service, some form of rationing has to evolve, either formally, as is the case for waiting lists for housing programmes or entrance requirements for higher education, or

informally, as when the flow of water in the system
becomes irregular because of excessive use, or waste
through leakage. These rationing mechanisms can be
very inegalitarian and lend themselves to abuse.
Also, an emphasis on self-financing is more likely to
encourage the development of an adequate
administrative system for collecting payment and
monitoring flows through the programme. The second
reason is that self-financing programmes tend to be
stronger in terms of their ability to withstand
changes in the political and economic climate.

Against this is the whole issue of whether pricing
at self-financing levels prevents the poor from
benefiting from these services. There are undoubtedly
areas where this would be the case, for example, in
education and medical services. There are other areas
where effective pricing might actually improve supply
to the poor. If water were priced on an upward
sliding scale, this might reduce middle class
consumption and wastage and increase the flow of
water to poorer areas, until such time as the system
could be extended to meet the needs of all areas.
Equally, cross-subsidisation within housing
programmes could allow greater access to the poor
while maintaining a financially viable scheme.

There is nothing inherently wrong with subsidies
as a means of increasing the access of the poor.
Problems arise when subsidies are attached to
commodities and services which are in short supply,
and to which a broad section of the population has
access either by design or in practice. In this
situation, the bulk of subsidy often ends up accruing
to middle income groups, either because they consume
relatively more of the commodity, or because by their
consumption they deprive lower-income groups of
consumption.

It is difficult to determine how much charging for
a commodity exactly deprives the poor of its use.
Looking at household expenditure patterns does give
some idea, however, of those areas of expenditure for
which it is likely to be most important. Table 4
shows how expenditure changes from the lowest income
or expenditure class to the highest in percentage
terms for six countries. (Any variation in government
subsidies for specific commodities might give a bias
to these figures but its extent will be minor.) With
the exception of expenditures on medical services in
Pakistan, the trends shown are very consistent.

Table 4: Urban household consumption expenditure by expenditure or income[7] class, various countries, various years in percentages

Country	Food and drink	Rent, fuel and other housing	Medical and health	Education	Transport and communications	Other
Egypt[1] (1974-75)						
lowest expenditure class	67.1	19.6	1.7	0.1	0.4	11.1
highest expenditure class	42.9	10.6	2.1	2.9	9.7	31.8
Islamic Republic of Iran[1] (1974-75)						
lowest expenditure class	47.3	22.3	2.6	0.6	1.7	25.5
highest expenditure class	16.8	19.3	9.5	1.2	14.0	39.2
Republic of Korea[1] (1975)						
lowest expenditure class	57.3	13.4	2.9	4.3	4.0	18.1
highest expenditure class	40.7	7.8	5.1	7.3	5.0	34.1
Pakistan (1971-72)						
lowest income class	50.9	21.3	2.6	1.2	0.8	23.2
highest income class	27.3	18.3	1.6	2.8	19.9	30.1
Singapore (1972-73)						
lowest expenditure class	56.9	18.2	1.1	1.7	6.2	15.9
highest expenditure class	32.4	11.6	2.8	4.2	15.3	33.7

1 expenditure classes   2 income classes

Source: International Labour Organisation: Household income and expenditure statistics, 1968-76.

Relative expenditure on health, education and transport and communications rises substantially with income, and it is in these areas that subsidies are likely to have the biggest impact, in terms of increasing consumption of the poor, though these are also the areas where middle income demand is likely to be strongest. That is not to say that there is no impact on housing. Although relative expenditure falls, absolute expenditure rises. These figures reflect the fact that housing is a more basic need than the other categories.

Expenditure figures also give some guidance as to what the poor can afford to pay for certain categories of consumption. Projects whose success is dependent on changing this are unlikely to achieve their aims, so a more fruitful approach may be to try for a substantial improvement on what the poor can purchase for these amounts. It is this, in conjunction with the degree of subsidy which can be afforded, can be suitably administered and is politically feasible, which will ultimately determine the level of services the poor receive.

In some cases this will be equivalent to a minimum level of basic needs approach. But it should be noted that for many of these services it is difficult to define a minimum adequate standard in absolute terms. Even in the case of food, where there is physiological evidence on average requirements for health, there is debate on the implications of individual variation and adaptability for appropriate food consumption policies. With water, sanitation, housing, etc. there is bound to be a high degree of country specificity in setting minimum standards.

Evidence on the restriction of access to public services of the poor because of low income is presented in a study of the distribution of benefits from public expenditure in Malaysia.[26] This shows, for example, that of those who could be connected to the existing urban water supply system 14 per cent are not, principally for cost reasons. Twenty-two per cent do not have the option, as the system does not extend to them. However, perhaps the most important result of this study concerns education, which is almost completely free as far as payments for attendance are concerned within the state system. Out-of-pocket costs, for transport, uniform, exercise books, etc., can take up to 18 per cent of the income of the lowest income groups. This is a substantial barrier to participation and is reflected in higher drop-out rates at all stages of the education system. In comparison with an equity norm, of equal educational expenditure per child, this drop-out rate results in state expenditure on the lowest quintile households being $111 less than the average, and high income households $139 more. This is for the country as a whole and the discrepancy is probably less for the urban sector on its own, but it illustrates an important point; there are often costs involved to households in participating in services other than the nominal price and these costs are likely to be much more important to poor households.

In addition to the above factors the question of the acceptability of the proposed services to the poor must not be forgotten. A programme can be logistically efficient and pass all the appropriate tests of economic viability, yet if the poor do not wish to participate in it, it will be a failure. It must be seen to be relevant to their needs and to be culturally acceptable. This is true of all the services discussed here, but the sensitivity of recipients to programme design will depend on the perceived importance of the area in which the programme operates and the other options open to the poor. It is therefore probably most important in the areas of education and medical services and possibly sanitation.

In summary, the success of provision of urban services to the poor is highly dependent on the way the relevant programmes are designed. Pricing is important both in positive and negative ways. Positively it can help make the programme viable, and can also be used in a discriminatory fashion to try to restrict the access of the non-poor. Negatively it can restrict the access of the poor themselves, especially if hidden costs are not taken into account. Where squatter settlements are concerned, the question of legality has to be faced and regularised in some way to prevent the exclusion of the inhabitants from government provided services. The relative importance of these issues and appropriate ways around them will vary from country to country, as will the level of provision of services feasible.

What evidence is there on the importance of these services in improving the long-term position of the urban poor? Most of them have either a direct or an

indirect effect on the level of human capital
embodied in the poor. Is this sufficient to improve
their position and give them an upward impetus? In
general, those countries which have higher levels of
GNP and higher growth rates also have more
comprehensive provision of services for the poor. Can
one attribute part of the relative prosperity to the
concern for provision of public services, or is this
a chicken-and-egg question? Unfortunately the answer
seems to be the latter. Although provision of basic
needs services can improve the quality of life in the
short term, it does not necessarily lead to the
creation of a more dynamic economy where the
employment opportunities for the poor, necessary to
consolidate that improvement, are also expanding.
This does not mean that these services should not be
provided, but it places extreme importance on the
ability to devise a system of provision which can be
built up gradually, within both the country's and the
poor's ability to pay, in a much more egalitarian
fashion than is at present the case in most countries.

Notes

    1. World Bank: World development report
(Washington, DC, 1979).
    2. O.F. Grimes. Jr.: Housing for low-income
families - economics and policy in the developing
world, World Bank Research Publication (Baltimore,
Maryland, John Hopkins University Press, 1976).
    3. W. Scott: Concepts and measurements on poverty
(Geneva, United Nations Research Institute for Social
Development, 1981).
    4. M. Lipton: Why poor people stay poor, (London,
Temple Smith, 1977).
    5. idem.
    6. Grimes, op. cit.
    7. D.J. Dwyer: People and housing in third world
cities: Perspectives on the problems of spontaneous
settlements (London, Longman, 1975).
    8. International Labour Organisation: Household
income and expenditure statistics, 1968-76 (Geneva,
1979).
    9. Dwyer, op. cit.
    10. A. Wegelin: Urban low-income housing and
development (Leiden, Boston, Martinus Nijhoff Social
Sciences Division, 1978).

11. World Bank: Indonesia: employment and income distribution in Indonesia (Washington, DC, 1980).

12. World Bank: Aspects of poverty in the Philippines: A review and assessment, Vol. II (Washington, DC, 1980).

13. Wegelin, op. cit.

14. G.F. Papanek: "The poor of Jakarta", in Economic Development and Cultural Change (Chicago) Vol. 24, No. 1, 1975.

15. T.G. McGee: "Hawkers and hookers: making out in the third world city. Some Southeast Asian examples", in Manpower and Unemployment Research (Center for Developing Area Studies, McGill University, Montreal) Vol. 9, No. 1, 1976.

16. U. Wikan: Life among the poor in Cairo (London, Tavistock Publications, 1980).

17. J. Turner: "Housing priorities, settlement patterns and urban development in modernising countries", in Journal of the American Institute of Planners (American Planning Institute, Columbus, Ohio) Vol. 34, 1968, No. 1.

18. K. Ashraf Huque: Limits of self-help housing: Case studies of four shanty towns in Dacca, Working Report (Stockholm, Institute of Technology, Department of Building Function Analysis, 1981).

19. J. Nelson: "The urban poor: disruption or political integration in third world cities", in World Politics (Princetown University Press) Vol. 22, 1970, No. 2.

20. McGee, op. cit.

21. Grimes, op. cit.

22. Dwyer, op. cit.

23. Wegelin, op. cit.

24. I. Burton and T.R. Lee: "Water supply and economic development: The scale and timing of investment", in L. Jakobson and V. Prakash (eds.): Metropolitan growth: Public policy for South and Southeast Asia (New York, John Wiley and Sons, 1974).

25. D. Etherton: Water and sanitation in slums and shanty towns, Report for the Urban Sector, Programme Division (New York, United Nations Children's Fund, 1980).

26. J. Meerman: Public expenditure in Malaysia: Who benefits and why, World Bank Research Publication (London, Oxford University Press, 1979).

3 URBAN LOW-INCOME HOUSING IN SOUTH-EAST ASIA

by S. Yeh

Introduction

This chapter, on housing, discusses perhaps the most crucial variable in the approach this volume takes towards the provision of basic needs for the urban poor. The chapter concentrates on problems of shelter and the difficulties involved in finding and providing it. Shelter, of course, is generally accompanied by such other basic needs facilities as water and sanitation. However, the approach of this volume is to take these various items separately. Nevertheless the discussion in this chapter bears these ancillary features explicitly in mind. The chapter ascribes priority to the role of national and municipal authorities not so much in directly providing housing as in creating the conditions for its development. The chapter first discusses the major variables which combine to explain housing conditions in any country and shows how housing demand and supply interact to define the urban housing problem. Next, it briefly reviews and evaluates urban low-income housing policies and programmes in five South-east Asian countries and Hong Kong in order to illustrate those policies and administrative inputs critically associated with the effective provision of housing as a package of services for the urban poor.

Determinants of housing conditions

"Housing" is as complex as the societies it serves. Nevertheless, four variables together define the housing situation in any city; these are income, city size, rate of urban growth and policy. Per capita income and its distribution, together with the price of housing, establish the amount of housing that families can afford. Cities with relatively high per capita income, heavily concentrated among upper-income groups may still have a difficult housing problem, as in Hong Kong. A country or city

with a more even income distribution may deal with
its housing problem more equitably, as may have
happened in China.

City size affects accessibility to employment, to
commercial and social services and to other urban
facilities. Accessibility is reflected in land
prices. In large and relatively old cities, land with
ready access to urban facilities is generally scarce
and highly priced. This scarcity can be aggravated
when large quantities of centrally located public and
private land are not intensively used. Land tends to
be less expensive on the fringe of large cities,
often because infrastructure provision has failed to
keep pace with urban expansion and such areas are not
functionally integrated with other parts of the city.
Inadequate transport on the urban fringe makes access
to employment and urban services costly and time
consuming. In contrast, provincial centres and
smaller cities generally have lower land prices.
Therefore, the characteristics of a national urban
system, i.e. the number of principal cities and their
size, can significantly affect housing provision.

The rate of urban growth intensifies the housing
problems created by city size. Many cities in
developing countries have grown faster in the last 30
years than ever before and their rate of growth is
expected to accelerate. Urban planning and
infrastructure development have usually lagged behind
city growth, resulting in vast areas of unserviced
urban sprawl. Public transport has also usually
failed to keep pace; private car ownership has
expanded causing traffic congestion and pollution.
The urban population of South-east Asia has grown
rapidly. While the total population growth rate for
1950-70 was about 2.6 per cent, the urban population
growth rate for the region was some 5 per cent. Urban
population will have doubled between 1970 and 1985.

Primary cities such as Bangkok, Kuala Lumpur,
Jakarta and Manila have grown fastest and have
experienced the gravest problems. These, more than
other cities, have had to absorb new households with
dependent children and low-skilled, job-seeking
migrants. Their basic urban services are usually
severely strained and reach only a portion of the
population. City land is scarce and sometimes made
scarcer by uncontrolled speculation. On the periphery
of these cities, more land is available but it is
rarely functionally integrated with the inner city.

Their large size, high rates of urban growth and low and unevenly distributed incomes cause the spread of the slum and squatter population. The slum and squatter population has been estimated to be at least one-third of the population of Kuala Lumpur and Manila and one-fourth in Bangkok and Jakarta. In Colombo, it may be more than half of the city population.

Beyond these three variables, housing conditions vary greatly among cities with a similar income, size and growth rate because of different policies and programmes. Not only the resource potential but also the means of mobilising and applying resources are crucial for housing. South-east Asia shows examples of both past success and failure in housing policy. Poor policies make housing conditions worse. Some housing policies have been unconscious, partial, uncoordinated and negative. They were unconscious in that decision-makers were unaware of the true nature of the housing problem and of the policy's overall implications; partial because many governments did not use the policy instruments at their disposal effectively; uncoordinated because some housing policies were formulated apart from other urban development plans; and negative because much public investment and intervention was aimed at slowing or stopping urban growth rather than at increasing and improving housing supply for the poor.

When viewed in the narrow sense of shelter, housing has tended to be built without regard for the services it and its dwellers need. Yet housing is really a package of services: land, public facilities, access to employment and to other social services, as well as the dwelling structure itself. Effective responses to housing problems have considered affordability and employment needs combined with realistic standards of construction.

However, many governments have promoted unrealistically high housing standards for the poor so that default in payment is common. Housing for the poor is sometimes raided by the middle-income population who become the ultimate beneficiaries of subsidies. Slum demolition and squatter removal without appropriate alternative accommodation has merely destroyed housing stock and eliminated jobs. Besides inappropriate standards, other common faults in housing policy and administration include western-style zoning and building codes, which tend

to restrict mixed land use and thereby employment
creation, and providing high-cost, subsidised housing
which few among the poor can afford. These policies
share a piecemeal approach to housing rather than
treating it, land-use regulations, public services,
transport and employment, as a whole.

Urban housing demand and supply
    The need for housing reflects the desire to enjoy
the services provided by the physical components of
its lot and dwelling structure. The most important
attributes are access, space, tenure, on-site
services and shelter; these combine to define housing.
    "Access" refers to contact with employment and
income-generating opportunities, with off-site
services such as health and education and with the
community. Space constrains the size of the dwelling
structure and determines agricultural, commercial and
recreational activities as well as privacy. Tenure
has two dimensions; security of tenure, i.e.
protection from being forced to move involuntarily
which encourages low-income households to maintain
and improve their shelter and ownership rights,
including such benefits as the ability to let out all
or part of the lot or house, the right to carry out
commercial activities and to benefit from any
increase in property value. Security of tenure and
ownership rights and thus the value of property, can
be altered extensively by public action, including
expropriation or conferral of title, expulsion from
squatted land, zoning restrictions on commercial
activities and taxation of rents or capital gains.
    On-site services, such as water and energy supply,
waste disposal, drainage and security from fires and
crime convey direct benefits over and above the costs
borne by the user. These benefits and costs vary with
the service, the scale at which it is provided and
the pricing policies of the supplier. Finally, the
shelter provides protection from the elements,
privacy, conveniences, domestic living space and
aesthetic pleasure. It may also provide an
opportunity to earn an income by renting.
    Housing preferences vary according to climate,
income, household size and composition, as well as
price. Locational preferences tend to differ with
income levels. A pattern, originally postulated for
Latin America, is generally applicable to South-east
Asia:

The poorest are mainly interested in location.
Being near job markets saves on transportation
costs... The only amenity they need is space for
sleeping. The next group... is interested in
security of tenure. This group is willing to trade
location for security of tenure. A temporary job
loss or other economic misfortune does not mean
displacement of residence as well. They are also
more interested in space than amenity and are
willing to pay for it. Finally the richest income
group is more interested in amenity, having a
stable income and subsistence essentials.
Electricity, plumbing, well-designed houses and
recreation then become important and will be
demanded by this group.[1]

Of course, the precise ranking of the attributes
varies. However, two important lessons emerge. First,
within their budget, the urban poor generally give
high priority to access, space and some security of
tenure and service amenities, but are less interested
in high quality shelter and services. The last two,
however, have often been emphasised in traditional
public housing policies which ignored access and
affordability. Secondly, an economically efficient
housing policy should consider the preferences of the
poor by providing maximum flexibility in access, lot
size or floor space, tenure, services and shelter
structure.

Many agents interact in the provision of housing,
including not only shelter construction but also
subdivision, the provision of on-site as well as
off-site services and security of tenure. The
suppliers may be private developers, owners,
squatters and other service providers as well as
urban government, public utilities and housing
agencies. In most cities both the public and private
sectors provide housing for all income groups.

For the poor raw land is typically subdivided by
developers, squatters, or absentee land owners;
occasionally by local government or public housing
agencies. On-site services to low-income housing are
frequently provided by owner occupiers, squatters,
absentee owners or renters. Low-income shelters are
generally constructed by landlords, where tenements
are concerned, and by owner occupiers or squatters,
who normally improve their dwellings in stages.
Renters rarely make significant improvements to their
housing and public housing agencies have also rarely

contributed to large-scale low-income housing. The government generally provides security of tenure, determining whether squatters and illegal subdivisions on public and private land are given secure free- or lease-hold tenure.

Since squatters and occupiers of illegal subdivisions are a major proportion of the urban population of developing countries, especially the large cities, two points are important. First these people contribute importantly to shelter construction and the provision of on-site services. Secondly, whatever their responsibilities, urban governments and public utilities are little involved in such shelter construction.

Three constraints limit the supply of new housing. When cities expand rapidly raw land may be available on the urban fringe but subdivision there is often impeded by municipal ordinances which prevent a quick response to the demand for urban land. Land conversion can be slow because of zoning regulations, land registration requirements and land transfer taxes. Lengthy expropriation proceedings to acquire land for services are also common. City size presents the second constraint. The cost of public services may increase because of natural resource constraints, e.g. on water supply, or because the city is expanding into mountainous or swampy areas that are more difficult to service. The cost of transport also tends to increase with city size. This problem is sometimes compounded by high service standards and by subsidies, which undermine the financial viability of public utilities and limit their expansion.

Thirdly, the construction and improvement of shelter may be constrained. The supply of material inputs for construction is usually quite inelastic in the short run. During construction booms in all major South-east Asian cities in the 1960s and early 1970s material prices increased rapidly and limited the expansion of low-income self-constructed housing. Mortgage markets are generally very weak and require high down payments and quick repayment; mortgage funds are in any case usually restricted to higher income groups. High standards and subsidies limit the expansion of public housing. Furthermore the wholesale destruction of slum or squatter areas without providing alternative accommodation obviously destroys considerable amounts of housing.

Given the increasing need for housing arising from overall urbanisation and the constraints on low-income housing supply, the latter is naturally insufficient. Consequently, real housing prices have increased substantially leading to greater overcrowding, a lower quality of shelter, poorer services and worse access than had supply adjusted more rapidly.

Supply can be significantly influenced by government action. Experience in South-east Asia and elsewhere repeatedly demonstrates that public action on investment, pricing and regulation may be wrong. High cost supplies may be provided to a few beneficiaries where lower cost supplies could have helped the poor. Increases in private supply may be impeded through regulations and taxes. Equity and efficiency may both be increased by better policies. Such policies may involve both removing constraints on housing supply and providing public incentives for increased housing stock, or direct construction. The next section briefly reviews actual policies in South-east Asia and Hong Kong, assesses their relative effectiveness and draws lessons for the improvement of urban low-income housing policies.

Survey of policies and programmes
Hong Kong
Since 1964, Hong Kong's solution to the housing problems of its more than 5 million population has been the provision of conventional public housing. In recent years the creation of new towns to integrate housing, social services and employment has been emphasised. From the beginning housing policy included squatter relocation since practically all Hong Kong's squatters lived on the hills where improvements were very costly or technically difficult. Hong Kong's housing record has been comparatively good in terms of meeting need; the government built 336,000 units by 1972 and nearly 413,000 units by 1979. Since 1972 many large and essentially self-sufficient new towns have been completed or are under construction; these will provide the bulk of new public housing in the future. In 1973 all housing agencies were streamlined into one single housing authority. Since then the delivery of low-income housing has become more and more a component of overall planned urbanisation, mostly through planning new towns. To meet foreseeable

need current low-income housing targets call for at
least 43,000 new units a year, including 30,000 from
the private sector. This target may well strain the
government's already over-extended capacity.

In 1972, the government decided to gradually
provide adequate self-contained dwellings for all
"needy" households, i.e. families inadequately
housed, those affected by development clearance and
those created by natural population growth. This gave
a target of public housing for 1.5 million persons
within ten years. The contribution of the private
sector or the need for temporary housing and sharing
during the period of housing shortage were hardly
considered. In other words, the housing standards,
and hence targets, implied by the policy were too
high and unrealistic. These limitations
notwithstanding, the 1972 exercise provided a needed
framework.

In 1975, a housing reappraisal study established
that some 244,000 flats could be produced in the
public sector and 120,000 units in the private
sector, leaving a likely deficit of 127,000 units by
1984. However, the study concentrated on
affordability and overlooked housing needs arising
from development clearance. It also ignored the need
to tolerate the large amount of non-permanent
squatter housing, which Hong Kong still has. While
the 1975 study grossly underestimated the possible
contribution of private developers, it did
demonstrate the need to maintain the large public
housing programme.

Hong Kong has identified land areas for housing
and other urban use so as to concentrate private
redevelopment in some inner city districts and public
housing on the urban periphery. For public housing,
however, the most economical step is now the
accelerated development of the five new towns
expected to reach full capacity in the late 1980s.
Overall, about 70 per cent of their residents will be
in public housing.

New town development is complex and requires
considerable administrative and technical inputs
besides political support and adequate finance. The
efficiency of such inputs depends largely on the
expertise of the civil service as well as on a sound
organisation to co-ordinate at least 20 government
bodies and different agents in the private sector.
Programming Hong Kong's new towns comprises a number

of "packages", such as land and services for housing, industry, social facilities and other uses. In turn, the elements in each package must come on stream by certain dates and this requires both sequential and parallel action. There is no need to give a detailed account of programming and monitoring here; but the larger the project, the more critical are the administrative and technical requirements for planning and implementation. Such skills do not exist in most developing countries.

In exactly two decades Hong Kong's housing policy has matured from total neglect to meeting most of the demand for low-income housing. Policy is effective and administration is efficient in that housing provided largely meets the test of affordability both in purchase and rental, and supply takes access into account through new town development and a reasonably good mass transit system. The present housing policy is couched in a long-term perspective and is integrated into the overall context of urban development strategy.

However, the outlook for the future cannot be overly optimistic. Demand has been substantially affected by legal and illegal immigration from China. This reached nearly 300,000 persons during 1978-80 and most of these constituted an additional need for government housing. Land for housing must compete with other uses, such as industry, social facilities, infrastructure and transport. Finally, there are limits to the capacity of the construction industry arising from competition for skilled labour, for materials and contractors.

Indonesia

In Indonesia's First Five-Year Plan (1969-74), major emphasis was placed on the agricultural sector and rural development. Urban housing was given no priority; no construction was provided for in the plan, which only called for some research and development projects including prototype design and the study of land-use patterns. However, the very rapid growth of Jakarta and the consequent deterioration in housing conditions exerted pressure on the local government of the "Special Capital Region of Jakarta" (DKI) to inaugurate the Kampung Improvement Programme (KIP) and upgrade physical infrastructure in some kampungs. A "kampung" in Indonesia is a predominantly residential area, often a previous village engulfed by urban expansion. These "urban villages", which include both low- and middle-income households, have generally inadequate physical infrastructure and social services. However, a great many of them were and are socially cohesive communities. The term "kampung" is not synonymous with a squatter settlement because in Indonesia the occupancy of land confers considerable right of possession.

The KIP is an attempt to meet the minimum infrastructure needs of large numbers of the urban poor at low cost. The DKI realised that it could not provide all the resources necessary to rebuild the kampungs and concentrated instead on improving the physical infrastructure which the people found most difficult, if not impossible, to organise and construct themselves. The KIP involved no direct investment in housing per se; it provided paved roads and footpaths, drainage ditches, communal water taps, latrines, garbage bins and social services, such as schools and health clinics. The DKI hoped that kampung residents would be encouraged to improve their own dwellings in line with environmental improvements. Work was planned and implemented to minimise disruption and the relocation of households. During 1969-1974 DKI upgraded 2,400 ha. or 20 per cent of its 1969 urbanised area. The programme directly benefitted 1.2 million residents, estimated at 40 per cent of the kampung population in 1974. On average the first 5 years cost US$6,500 per ha. and US$13 per capita. In all, 98 kampungs were improved.

The Second Five Year Plan (1975-79) foresaw substantial provision of housing and municipal services. A National Housing Authority was established in 1974 to formulate broad policies, which the National Urban Development Authority was set up to implement. The target for low-cost housing for this period was 315,000 units for low- and middle-income groups while the KIP was to be greatly accelerated throughout Indonesia. Without understanding the complex requirements for large-scale housing projects and without previous experience, the target for low-cost housing was largely based on calculations of "need", giving little attention to implementation capacity. Difficulties in land acquisition, housing legislation and finance quickly developed and the target was never met.

On the other hand, the KIP was substantially expanded during 1974-79, partly due to World Bank participation. The programme's standards and components increased moderately and its pace of activity significantly. Primary schools and garbage trucks were added to the list of KIP components. Standards for water supply and sanitation were raised. The most important change was speeding up the programme; 1,890 ha. were upgraded during 1974-76, directly benefitting nearly 900,000 people. Because of higher standards, the cost went up as well, to US$40 per capita.

In 1976 a second World Bank loan continued the KIP in both Jakarta and Surabaya, Indonesia's next largest city. The three-year period, 1976-79, saw a further increase in scope and standards. The rate of improving 1,000 ha. per year was maintained and more effort was made to introduce a social component into the programme, including training community health workers to staff the physical facilities. Community involvement in planning also improved. During 1979 a third World Bank loan was negotiated for the KIP to extend to the newer remaining kampungs and to improve the water supply and sanitation in the oldest kampungs in Jakarta. Assistance for KIP is also being extended to four other cities in the country.

Under the present Third Five-Year Plan (1979-84), there are three different programmes for urban Indonesia. First, the KIP is being further expanded. With yet a fourth World Bank loan, the intended scope of the programme covers 200 cities and involves some 15,000 ha. of urban kampung areas which constitute some 50 per cent of the existing urban kampung area. The second programme is for 120,000 low-cost housing units for low- and middle-income groups, with minimum standards set at a $15m^2$ core house on a $200m^2$ lot. This target will probably not be met for much the same reasons as before, although it is below that of 1969-74. The third housing programme provides higher income groups with long-term loans at market rates to purchase privately built new homes.

Indonesia is the first major developing country to mount a substantial on-site upgrading programme which may be large enough to soon catch up with the backlog and with current growth. Eighty per cent of the kampungs of Jakarta have been improved and the KIP is being rapidly expanded to many other cities. Even though standards are low and the dwelling units are not improved, there is nevertheless considerable equity in the distribution of benefits. Investment so far has generally been within the range the government can afford. Programme planning and implementation has been relatively efficient partly because of a simple design approach, a high degree of discipline with respect to the timing and budget cycle and "command planning" from the top downwards.

The planning, implementation and maintenance of the KIP has so far been without the community participation generally considered desirable in slum improvement projects. The few attempts that DKI made to provide supplies and to encourage kampung residents to provide a large labour input were not successful, despite the Indonesian tradition of gotong royong (community mutual self-help). One explanation is that under the KIP, land is not transferred, very few dwelling structures are affected by relocation while the servicing cost is not recovered directly from the beneficiaries. As a result residents have little incentive to become deeply involved in time-consuming discussions with government planners and to contribute labour. Thus the level of participation desired should probably be closely related to the degree to which the household's assets and expenditures are involved.

The KIP is essentially the responsibility of local governments, including funding. Given its low level of investment, financing is generally not a problem for large cities. As the KIP expands to many medium and small cities, municipal governments will be less able to finance it from their own budgets and will seek support from the central government. Similarly, medium and small cities usually do not have sufficient administrative and technical expertise to undertake the required feasibility studies, project design, tendering, implementation, supervision and monitoring, not to mention community development work. Again, the central government is expected to increase its technical assistance to local governments as the scope of KIP expands.

Two other problems affect the financing of the KIP. Firstly, no real attempt has been made to settle the old problem of unclear titles to land ownership so no urban land registration system exists. Secondly, there has been only inadequate reform of the urban property tax, which is partly based on land registration and is the main form of recovering the cost of the KIP. Until these problems are solved, government subsidies will substantially increase as the KIP expands, which may lead to funding problems as well as impeding efforts for income redistribution. Both of these issues significantly affect other urban projects, including the assembly of land for low-income housing.

Finally, the KIP alone is not the solution to Indonesia's urban housing problem. It increases neither the amount of housing stock nor its quality. To accommodate new migrant households and to cater for natural population growth, the probably more difficult challenge is to provide serviced sites for the poor to build their own homes (the site and service approach) as well as direct low-income housing construction on an increasingly large scale.

Malaysia

The Malaysian public housing programme began in 1946, but attracted no serious attention until the late 1960s. Output increased steadily from 13,000 units completed during the Second Plan (1971-75) to approximately 40,000 during the Third Plan (1976-80). While output thus more than tripled, the number of units completed in both plan periods fell far short of targets. The target for the 1976-80 plan was 110,320 units, of which only 36 per cent was built. It also became clear that target setting in the plans did not involve a realistic approach to the amount the poor could afford. The government admitted in the Third Malaysian Plan (1976-80) that up to 70 per cent of the urban public could not afford the cheapest house constructed by the public sector. Thus most that was built went to the middle-income group, together with the subsidies granted. The Mid-term Review of the Third Malaysian Plan, also stated that the main shortfall in the housing sector was in low-cost housing, reflecting inadequate building capacity and delay in obtaining suitable land and providing complementary infrastructure.

In the current Fourth Plan (1981-85) targets are 176,000 low-cost public housing units and 90,000 private sector low-cost housing units. Other improvements include a much larger revolving fund for each state to finance land acquisition, site preparation and infrastructure development; a liaison committee in each state responsible for implementation and requiring the private sector to make between 30 to 50 per cent of its housing in low-cost condominiums. Research and training will also be expanded. However, evidence so far suggests that the ambitious targets will not be met by 1985.

The Malaysian housing policy and programmes have been unable to meet the needs of the rapidly growing urban low-income population, despite some improvement in the volume of output over the years. A number of factors explain the relatively low output and why low-cost housing is still beyond the reach of many of the poor.

The first point is administrative fragmentation, which often leads to operational confusion. Public housing is the responsibility of the state governments and the municipalities. With the exception of Kuala Lumpur, land ownership is with the states which have to provide the land for low-income housing. The federal government gives broad policies and guidelines and provides the states with favourable housing loans. It also provides infrastructure, services and maintenance free to the state or municipal governments, as well as architectural and engineering services. This two-tier (sometimes three-tier) system has not helped planning and implementation. Given the substantial power of the states to control land, the responsibilities of the state and municipal governments in planning and implementation and the number of federal ministries involved in housing, co-ordination is difficult and time-consuming. The present administrative system involves dealings at each of the two or three tiers while functions and linkages are often not clear. It is also not always recognised in Malaysia (and elsewhere) that a political line system operates alongside the administrative system. Agents within this political system can exert strong positive or negative influence on the functions and performance of the administration. Political support for public housing from decision-makers in the central government, sultans (heads of state) and mayors is crucial in land acquisition and in implementation. In the past, many state governments appeared to display little real political commitment to public housing. Thus political commitment by the central government is not enough; it must also continuously generate political support for its housing policies at the lower levels.

Government-built housing has been too expensive for the urban poor in many countries, including Malaysia, the Philippines and Thailand. Certainly low-cost housing is not necessarily low-income housing; "low-cost" usually means housing priced below the prevailing market level while "low-income" means housing the poor can afford. Given the importance of affordability, governments have to attempt further cost reductions in both public and private housing. Clearly this is difficult but governments have a role to play.

In Malaysia land purchase and preparation amount to a fairly reasonable 30 per cent of total cost per unit. However, land prices have been rising and the rather weak speculation tax has had little effect on reducing prices. State governments already hold a good deal of land around the urban areas but are generally reluctant to release it for low-cost public housing, wanting to keep it for more economically productive uses. In this sense, state governments are themselves reluctant speculators. Land costs, especially for private sector housing are also boosted by the administrative delay in conversion, subdivision and the distribution of titles. Land is usually held for about six years while these items are sorted out and during that period is subject to a holding charge, which is passed on to the final consumer. Such delays provide an additional reason for speculation. Federal, state and municipal governments could reduce costs by acquiring and assembling land for low-cost housing projects. However, even this would also depend on streamlining administrative procedures. Costs could be further reduced through the use of alienation powers and perhaps by subsidised selling or leasing prices. Cost reductions could then be substantial if accompanied by subsidised land preparation and infrastructure provision.

The need to reform building and planning legislation in order to reduce costs is also accepted. However, reforms have been slow. Most building standards and regulations date from the 1930s and reflect the "middle class" values of the British colonial administration. One example is the road and drainage reserve requirement which, together with recreational space, constitute up to 60 per cent of the prepared building land, leaving fewer house plots for the developer to derive a profit. Moreover,

some standards within housing units such as minimum
room size may be excessive, while cheaper materials
could be used and communal plumbing or sanitary
facilities installed.

Another important issue in Malaysia is the
proliferation of slums and squatter settlements.
Until the mid-1970s, the government was against
squatting; it was blamed for a breakdown of law and
order and was called an impediment to urban economic
and social development and a source of ill health.
This was reflected in slum eradication with
relocation to public housing, although this was never
practised on a large scale. In 1972 Kuala Lumpur had
evicted some 6,000 squatter families or 28,000
people, of whom 34 per cent were relocated to public
housing. Nevertheless, because of immigration
(perhaps 1,000 persons a day) there were as many
squatters in 1973 as in the year before.

The Third Plan (1976-80) enunciated a housing
strategy of "aided self help" which was taken to mean
on-site slum improvement and sites and services
provided by the local government of Kuala Lumpur for
squatters. The Fourth Plan (1981-85) restated this.
However, at least at the broad policy level, the
government is considering the merits of slum
improvement in addition to public housing, while not
totally abandoning clearance. The squatter areas
which qualify for on-site upgrading seem to be those
whose land is not immediately needed for other
purposes and where alternative housing cannot be
provided. Since 1974 the Kuala Lumpur municipality
has carried out basic infrastructure improvements
(roads, drainage, street lighting and water stand
pipes) in over 60 squatter areas with minimum
investment. No attempt was made to rationalise land
tenure which suggests that these improved communities
are not completely recognised as permanent fixtures.
Most of the upgraded settlements are predominantly
Malay. Meanwhile, the clearance of other squatter
settlements in Kuala Lumpur for redevelopment has
continued slowly. The sites and service approach has
hardly been implemented, partly because of the lack
of suitable land; only one small sites and service
scheme exists.

The housing conditions of the urban poor in
Malaysia have deteriorated in recent years. The size
of large cities has increased rapidly, while
government output of low-cost housing, although it

has increased, has met the rising need neither in volume nor in terms of affordability. Given increasing political pressure to solve the urban housing problem, the government needs a more effective policy mix, comprising cost reduction in public housing, on-site improvement, sites and service and increased private sector participation.

The Philippines

Although the provision of public housing in the Philippines dates back to the 1930s national development plans only began to address the housing sector in 1970 when the severity of the urban housing problem became visible. As elsewhere the initial policy response was conventional public housing and the clearance of slum and squatter settlements. These housing construction programmes have been largely unsuccessful. Until the mid-1970s, output was limited and some directly benefitted the middle-income group. The location of public housing was frequently based on land availability rather than suitability for access to employment and social services. High cost, due partly to high standards, resulted in a high degree of default in rental payments. Meanwhile squatter settlements were often cleared without providing other accommodation. The large-scale sites and service project in Sapang Palay of 1972, meant to resettle Manila squatters, failed because it was located too far from the central city, too poorly serviced, and was totally without jobs and social services in its neighbourhood. Consequently, most of those relocated to Sapang Palay soon moved back to Manila and squatted again. Meanwhile the population of metropolitan Manila and other large cities was expanding rapidly. The natural population growth rate for metropolitan Manila averaged 3 per cent per year, the city population grew at 6 per cent per year and the slum and squatter population at 12 per cent per year. Housing conditions deteriorated as the share of the squatter population increased.

Housing policy, programmes and administration in the Philippines changed substantially in the 1970s. In 1975 the National Housing Authority (NHA) was created to integrate the existing seven official agencies directly responsible for housing and resettlement and streamlined or integrated another 13 government departments or agencies indirectly involved. The budgetary resources of many agencies, which had not been systematic and continuous, were improved.

A major development in 1974 was the Tondo Redevelopment Project which marked a drastic change in policy from slum eradication to slum improvement. Tondo was a large and old squatter settlement on public land in the heart of Manila. With a population of 180,000 it had low levels of urban services and generally poor living conditions. The Tondo Project, with World Bank assistance, aimed to upgrade the social and economic as well as physical living conditions of the community through on-site improvement coupled with a nearby sites and services project to accommodate the population overflow caused by the development schemes. A successful project was hoped to have a demonstration effect and be reproduced not only in metropolitan Manila but elsewhere. Since 1975, the NHA has started more than 20 slum improvement projects inside and outside metropolitan Manila, mostly with World Bank support.

Improvement standards for Tondo are much higher than for the KIP in Indonesia. Implementation involves long discussions and negotiations with community representatives, block by block, over levels of services to be provided and on alternative layouts. Improvements included land tenure for structure owners, the provision of roads, footpaths, drainage, piped water supply to each house and individual sewerage connections, schools, clinics, playgrounds, loans for building materials to improve dwelling structures and assistance to small-scale businesses. The cost of services and land were to be recovered through mortgage payments and user charges for water, and these terms were discussed and agreed with the community. The mortgage payment for development and land costs amounts to US$13 per month, which over 80 per cent of Tondo households can afford. Occupants who are not owners of structures, usually the poorest 20 per cent, would benefit from improved services but have to remain tenants.

Three site-planning options developed for each block were discussed with residents. No scheme involved relocating houses outside the community but plans ranged from a minimum disturbance of existing structures to the movement of houses into a grid pattern. Most residents chose the last approach and by self-help moved their wood-frame houses to new plots. Some houses in fact required 50 people to lift them. The high degree of community participation slowed the process of upgrading and thus delayed the benefits of upgrading to other areas. It also involved families in additional expenditure, averaging about US$100 each.

By 1982 the Tondo Project was largely completed and successful. The community is clean and attractive and secure land tenure has encouraged most households to put enormous efforts into improving their structures. The fear that owners would sell out to higher income groups was false. Loans for building materials have been repaid. The residents' ability to call on personal savings was greatly under-estimated, which suggests that income should not be the sole criterion to assess what people can afford. A weak feature is the assistance to small-scale enterprises; this has hardly developed because of inexperience with such a programme and because of local banks' requirements for collateral.

Tondo demonstrated that the poor are willing and able to mobilise considerable assets to improve their environment and individual plots provided that their own priorities for land tenure and services are respected and that they are brought in as serious partners in making the plans. The larger question now is the extent and speed at which the Tondo project can be reproduced. In metropolitan Manila alone, some 200 such settlements (out of over 300) have been earmarked for improvement.

Land tenure is usually critical in expanding slum improvement projects in the Philippines (and elsewhere). It was not a problem in Tondo since the land belonged to the government, which practically gave it away at some US 15 cents per m^2. This greatly reduced the total cost of improvement to the residents but it also created expectations in other squatter colonies which may not be met. A very large share of squatter settlements in Manila and beyond is on private land, expropriation is time-consuming and the normal land cost is too high for most of the residents. The government cannot subsidise land costs substantially and the squatters cannot afford it. But if tenure is not secure major improvements in infrastructure may benefit the private landowner more than the residents.

Land acquisition is also important because in many upgrading projects some families must leave in order to provide land for infrastructure. Thus, a sites and services scheme should ideally be located nearby. In reality, such land is often not available and expropriation is not feasible. When population density is very high (as it usually is) and land is not available to rehouse some families, then providing certain types of infrastructure can be difficult and standards may have to be reduced. In a larger context, the government should be undertaking large-scale land assembly for sites and service projects in order to accommodate new migrants and thus to reduce new squatter settlements or overcrowding in existing ones. Unlike slum improvement, sites and service projects do create new housing stock. However, the NHA has done very little in this direction because of the unavailability of suitable public land and the high cost of expropriation.

Improvement programmes may also become over-politicised. Some mayors see such projects as opportunities to expand their mass base; this is desirable in moderation. A project can, however, be exploited to favour the mayors' supporters in selecting sites for improvement, award of home lots and construction contracts. The concept of slum improvement needs to be safeguarded by intensive indoctrination of local government leaders to achieve a more or less uniform level of participation.

In 1978 the Ministry of Human Settlements was created, which took over some of the functions of the NHA. Since then there has been further decentralisation of administrative organisation for housing; in 1982 there were more than ten central government departments or agencies directly or indirectly concerned with housing and related activities, plus a number of local governments. This fragmentation, although often necessary, may well have worsened co-ordination and increased the project cycle, thus raising costs. The NHA now assumes main responsibility for slum improvement and sites and services while the Ministry concentrates on providing low- and middle-income housing. This is usually low-rise apartments using some indigenous and cheaper building materials which the poor cannot usually afford.

While housing policy and programmes in the Philippines have improved significantly since 1970, the urban housing problem is still immense. Growth of the urban poor population, including a large percentage of squatters, has been outpacing the number of beneficiaries of slum improvement and other programmes. During the eight years it took to improve Tondo, with 180,000 people, the slum and squatter population in metropolitan Manila may well have increased by one and a half million. It is doubtful whether the government can rapidly generate sufficient housing supply to catch up with demand in the foreseeable future, given heavy reliance on World Bank loans so far and the country's overall slow economic growth.

Singapore
    In the 1950s Singapore had one of the worse slum and squatter problems in South-east Asia. Substantial increases in public housing construction and subsequent urban renewal did not begin until 1960 when the present government took power and assumed direct responsibility for providing homes for lower and subsequently middle-income groups. Within 20 years, the Singapore Housing and Development Board (HDB) has generated over 400,000 units, providing shelter for well over 70 per cent of the population of approximately 2.6 million people. In the 1980s the government intends to build another 290,000 units and by 1990 some 80 per cent of the population is expected to be living in public housing estates. The level of home ownership of public housing has been rapidly increasing; in 1982 at least 70 per cent of public housing residents owned their homes. Since the early 1970s Singapore has built several large new towns which provide not only housing but also social amenities and employment within the housing estates. Many more new towns are either planned or under construction. The largest so far has a population of over 200,000.
    Public housing, together with effective urban renewal and resettlement has been used to help shape the overall pattern of urban growth. Locations have been carefully chosen to correspond to a longer-term city development plan. Therefore, public housing has integrated physical, social and economic planning at the same time, linking territorially bound activities associated with work, school, shopping, recreation and residence and producing functional neighbourhoods with relatively strong social networks. In short, the success of public housing in Singapore must be seen in its ability to integrate housing and the immediate

living environment into the overall management of
urbanisation of the city-state.
    In housing the meaning of "success" changes with
time. The success of Singapore is not just that
quantitative housing output has been matched to
various levels of demand. While physical living
conditions have steadily improved over the last two
decades, repeated sample household surveys since 1968
have indicated a consistently high level of
satisfaction with a host of components of the living
environment. This covered housing, its location,
social environment, services and shopping as well as
satisfaction with a variety of changes that took
place after relocation to public housing.[2]
    Several HDB measures help explain the nature of
this success. First, the size of flats (apartments)
has been gradually increased in line with higher
expectations and incomes. Secondly, people can own
their own homes by using their balance in the Central
Provident Fund. Thirdly, the HDB gradually reduced
the eligibility ceiling in terms of household size
from 5 to 2 persons (even certain single people are
eligible if they share) which also served as an
incentive for family planning. Meanwhile, income
ceilings have been raised several times not only to
take inflation into account but also to extend
housing to more of the middle-income population as
supply increased. Fourthly, the effectiveness of
public housing is dependent on urban renewal and
resettlement, and vice versa. By blending both social
and economic objectives in urban renewal, i.e.
redeveloping cleared sites for both housing and
commercial or industrial use, serious dislocation
effects have largely been avoided and significant
cross-subsidies achieved. Public housing provides the
basis to resettle both households and shops; all are
paid compensation and offered alternative
accommodation which is usually accepted. Land
acquisition, as part of urban renewal and public
housing, affects all income groups and all types of
structures. Thus, there are public housing estates
located not only on former slum and squatter areas
but also in middle-income areas as well. Over the
years more than three-fourths of the households under
clearance have opted for public housing and remained
in it. Survey results show that satisfaction with the
housing change is high and resettled households are
as satisfied as those who moved in voluntarily. More

than 75 per cent of the public housing residents in Singapore moved in on their own accord.

Political commitment has been demonstrated in several ways. Housing policies usually receive fast clearance by the prime minister and cabinet. The HDB has been a monolithic organisation from the beginning, with wide powers to undertake almost all phases of planning and implementation, except infrastructure. It has direct responsibility for land assembly, planning and design, the supervision of construction, estates management, urban renewal and resettlement. This centralisation of functions has worked efficiently for Singapore, although urban renewal was detached from HDB with the establishment of the Urban Renewal Authority in 1977 which, like HDB, comes under the Ministry for National Development.

Other administrative inputs include large-scale advance land assembly. Singapore is probably the only country in the region with an effective land banking system which acquires land for housing three to five years in advance of construction. On a still broader scale, HDB's overall advance planning sees ten years ahead. HDB also plays an active role in the supply of building materials by establishing quarries, brickworks and piling plants to supplement local production. In the allocation of flats, the "first come, first served" policy has worked well because the system is administratively simple and easily understood by the public. A recent emphasis is on community development to strengthen the social fabric of the public housing estates through a system of residents' committees. Finally, the contracting system for public housing has been improved and the entire construction industry is being upgraded to benefit both the public and private sectors.

Despite its accomplishments public housing in Singapore still faces a challenge in the 1980s. Since the government has assumed direct responsibility to meet the housing needs of approximately 85-90 per cent of the population, the demand for this decade could well reach 300,000 units, due to high fertility in the 1950s and 1960s and to the splitting up of multi-family households. Recent inflation in construction costs together with a labour shortage have delayed thousands of public housing units. The current waiting list to buy or rent public housing is still some 100,000. However, since Singapore has no problem of rural-urban migration, in the long run the government should be able to meet demand as it occurs. By the end of the century, the HDB is expected to have provided adequate housing for all those who desire it, except the very high-income group and the very poor, estimated together at about 5 per cent of the population.

Thailand
    Although Thailand started its public housing programme in 1950, output was minimal for the following two decades; there was no housing policy until 1973 with the overthrow of the military government and the formation of the National Housing Authority (NHA). Before 1972, only 17,000 public housing units were completed, but from 1974 to 1980 about 40,000 were built. The NHA contributed about 16 per cent of this; the rest were mainly living quarters provided by other government agencies for their own staff.
    The NHA first proposed a target of 120,000 units of urban public housing throughout the country over a five-year period (1976-80). This was to be financed by guaranteed loans which the government would repay at ten per cent each year; the NHA would pass on a portion of the capital as subsidies and retain the part it recovered as a revolving fund. Standards were not questioned, thus making the programme very expensive. Feasibility studies were not properly conducted and NHA's implementation capacity was overestimated. In addition, political support for large-scale public housing was fragmented at best. Not unexpectedly, the programme was stopped after two years.
    A typical example of public housing built around that time is the Din Daeng project in Bangkok. This consisted of 39 walk-up blocks each of five or six storeys, with either 56 or 80 units in each block. The $50m^2$ units comprise one large room with separate kitchen, toilet and a small porch. The units were intended for households with a monthly income of less than US$130. Most of the original occupants were resettled squatters with irregular incomes. Din Daeng itself is in the outer suburbs of Bangkok, far from the major sources of employment. No commercial activities are allowed in the estate except in a few expensive licensed areas thus removing an important source of supplementary income. Rents are heavily subsidised at US$6 per month (water, electricity and

rubbish disposal extra). Nevertheless the regular payments impose severe pressure on many families already burdened with commuting expenses. The great majority of the original occupants have since sold their residential rights for sums up to US$500 to middle-income people for whom Din Daeng offers acceptable and relatively cheap accommodation.

After terminating the first housing programme, one year was spent on policy discussions, a soul-searching time for the NHA staff. Lower standard, incremental housing solutions were debated at length, various subsidy options were explored, and there was increasing awareness of the requirements of administrative and technical capacity to implement large-scale housing. It was finally decided that the lowest income groups should receive a subsidy for the cost of infrastructure, but not for the housing plot or the initial shelter (core house). The subsidy would be graduated inversely to income. It was also decided that if the government required the NHA to build flats for rent, this programme would have to be fully subsidised since cost recovery is slow, if at all possible. Slum improvement projects would be included in the housing programme, a departure from the previous public housing approach.

In mid-1978 a NHA-sponsored housing policy and programme was reviewed by the prime minister, who rejected some basic NHA concepts and proposed slum clearance, while the previous government had approved a limited slum upgrading programme. Subsequent lobbying finally led to slum improvement becoming part of housing policy again.

Towards the end of 1978, the government approved a four-year programme (1979–82) which was a compromise package of 50,000 housing units. This included 5,000 rental apartments fully subsidised by the government, 20,000 units of incremental housing (core house) and slum improvement projects affecting 26,000 families. The total subsidy would be limited to US$75 million while about US$35 million of borrowed funds would be fully recovered from the beneficiaries.

Approximately 7,000 or 30 per cent of the new units would be built in the regional cities, the first public housing outside Bangkok. Housing starts per annum (not including slum upgrading) were lowered to about 5,000 as compared with the previous programme's 24,000, which had proved to be unrealistic. The reduced level of government funding made this target low. Meanwhile, a small pilot sites and service project was set up with overwhelming response. While most of the targets were not met by the end of the plan period, valuable lessons of sound planning and implementation were learned by the NHA staff.

Thailand's housing programme for 1982–86 includes a target of 10,000 public housing units per year for those who wish to buy but no subsidised rental housing. Instead the slum improvement component includes some 30,000 units in 21 slums, less than ten per cent of Bangkok's slums and squatter settlements. Slum improvement will be initially government financed. The NHA will be called upon to develop turn-key housing projects for other government agencies as well as commercial projects to offset some of its own loss-making undertakings. These include the maintenance of rental housing where the NHA has not been permitted to increase rents.

The NHA's initial and limited experience in slum improvement has suggested some basic difficulties. The first is land acquisition in order to regularise the residents' land tenure. There is little problem with public land but the acquisition of private land has proved very difficult and time consuming. The second problem is a lack of understanding and co-operation from the affected squatter population. Because of past eviction policy and because of inadequate community education, some slum residents tend to be suspicious of government activities if not at times hostile.

The NHA was established and the first housing programme formulated over ten years ago. Costly lessons have been learned about the multiple inputs necessary for a sound public housing programme and the importance of political support. The relatively small output achieved means that housing conditions of the poor have probably deteriorated further and hence present a greater challenge for the years to come. Political support will continue to be a crucial issue, especially for the recently initiated slum improvement programme.

Implementation: Lessons of experience
 The policy framework
    To understand why governments give such different emphasis to urban low-income housing, it is necessary to view housing policy in the overall development

context. There are two distinct types of housing
policy, the policies towards housing, primarily at
the macro level and the more familiar policies on
housing generally at the micro level. To a large
extent policies on housing are shaped by policies
towards housing which are characterised by four
stages in decision-making.[3]

At the most general level there is a broad
political philosophy of each government, from central
planning to free market orientation with all shades
in between. Within this broad context, policies
towards housing are also determined by attitudes
towards urbanisation, which reflect varying degrees
of urban bias (positive or negative). For a number of
years Indonesia and Malaysia had a marked negative
urban bias in their development strategies. Indonesia
has a control system of issuing permits to migrants
to Jakarta; and until recently, Malaysia gave greater
priority to rural rather than urban development to
improve the economic position of the Malays. An
extreme example of negative urban bias was the near
total de-population of Phnom Penh. On the other hand,
the development philosophy of the Philippines and
Thailand may be described as pro-urban, although some
shift has now taken place. Hong Kong and Singapore
have no rural areas to speak of.

Macro policies are further affected by the
relative balance given to economic and social
objectives. Positive attitudes toward urban growth do
not necessarily lead to positive policies for the
urban poor; the planned suburbs of Makati in
metropolitan Manila and Petaling Jaya in Kuala Lumpur
are overwhelmingly middle- and upper-class
residential districts. The amount of low-income
housing in the new towns of Hong Kong and Singapore
is very much an exception to the rule. In urban
areas, the desire for a better balance between
economic and social development during the last
decade has stressed the need to orient urban growth
towards the poor. While the gap between theory and
practice is often great this does illustrate the
broad changes necessary at the macro-level before
micro-level policies can be effective.

Finally, the provision of better housing is only
part of the task of improving the life of the urban
poor. Effective social development also requires
expenditure on education and health facilities and
the expansion of employment. Housing is only one of

many worthwhile areas of investment for social development. However, policy makers too often regard housing improvement as an end in itself rather than as a component of a larger package. To a large extent, the relative size of public investment in low-cost housing corresponds to a government's perception of its role. In China, the government assumes total responsibility for improving the housing conditions of the urban poor. For the countries under discussion, there has been a wide range of policy response as a result of different development philosophies, attitudes towards urbanisation, general development goals and social development priorities.

Given the country's emphasis on agriculture, Indonesia's attitude to housing was indifferent until the mid-1970s. Housing programmes are still too restricted to meet the real needs of many of the urban poor. Migration controls are in force to prevent any increase in the demand for urban housing. Its innovative element is the KIP, originally initiated by the local government in Jakarta and subsequently adopted by the central government. Even so, its level of investment is low and it creates no new housing stock.

In Malaysia official housing output is small and beyond the reach of a high percentage of the poor, partly because of unrealistically high, western standards in planning and design. Nor has squatter eradication been accompanied by the provision of suitable alternative accommodation. In view of the recent emphasis on the reduction of urban poverty, the political motivation for low-income housing is stronger now although programme scope and implementation can be made more effective.

Although public resource allocation in the Philippines has consistently shown a pro-urban (especially pro-Manila) bias, little concern for the housing needs of the poor was shown until the mid-1970s. Earlier housing programmes had a small output and involved squatter eviction without a sound resettlement strategy. Present housing policy has shown a marked change in the inclusion of slum improvement and the sites and service approach, which are innovative. However, some have questioned whether these projects are designed more to win approval and votes or to impress overseas visitors than to meet the needs of the poor. The validity of such criticisms will be seen in the scale of expansion of such programmes and the relative allocation of public resources in the near future.

Like the Philippines, Thailand's political philosophy is essentially market-oriented, pro-urban (especially pro-Bangkok), with much greater emphasis on economic than on social development. Housing policy of successive governments has involved very limited allocation of public resources. This put severe constraints on the construction of public housing, which again had high standards and was beyond the reach of the poor. Appropriate alternative accommodation was not provided along with slum clearance.

Singapore's development philosophy is a blend of socialism and capitalism but from 1960 the present government has maintained that social development, including housing, is both an integral part of development and has links to economic growth and political stability. This philosophy is manifested in the continuous flow of substantial public resources to public housing which, together with sound planning and implementation, have resulted in a fairly successful housing policy. Success is defined in terms of scale (75 per cent of the population) and meeting effective demand at an acceptable cost. Hong Kong, on the other hand, initially viewed public housing from a more economic perspective: the release of land for development and tight control over metropolitan expansion. However, the social or welfare objective of public housing became more prominent in time and it is also seen as a path towards political stability. Like Singapore, public housing in Hong Kong has reached an impressive scale (50 per cent of the population) and the dwelling units are truly low-cost. The innovative part of the housing policies of Hong Kong and Singapore lies in the integration of physical and socio-economic planning in large estates and new towns with a well-defined low-income population, something which other countries in the region have not been able to do despite a positive attitude towards urban growth.

Micro-policies on housing are affected by wide-ranging considerations in the same way as macro-policies. Factors influencing policies for and on housing and their evaluation are likely to be unique for each country, although some broad features are common. The provision of low-income housing is not a separate segment of development but part of overall political economy. In addition, the urban poor are themselves very heterogeneous. Therefore, a single universal remedy to overcome the low-income housing shortage is not only difficult to formulate but also of dubious value. However, most governments in the Third World agree on the need for improved policies and programmes to meet the basic needs of the urban poor and in this sense maximum possible investment in low-cost housing must be emphasised. Besides the issue of investment, which sets the broad limits of each government's housing programme, many other factors affect its planning and implementation. Based on the experience of the countries under discussion, the following elements are crucial.

Public housing
    That public housing has failed to solve the low-income housing problem of many countries does not mean that public housing per se has no place. There will always be a segment of a country's low-income population which can benefit from well formulated and executed public housing. The experience of Singapore and Hong Kong suggests some positive lessons. What warrants attention is not the high-rise, high-density approach, which is appropriate for the comparatively high-income island cities with a "closed" territory; rather, it is the other less visible but more important planning and implementation requirements that a successful public housing programme should meet.
    Singapore and Hong Kong both placed housing policy into an effective overall policy framework for urban growth. Housing is thus regarded as an instrument for shaping the city and enhancing urban productivity as well as for improving the living conditions of the poor. The two cities both effectively mix general public policies with housing policies, producing shelter as part of a package of urban services.
    Both cities consider that housing costs should represent a low proportion of household income, that production should be at a scale to meet effective demand, and that standards should be in line with income levels, i.e. they seek affordability, equity, and flexibility. Given the heterogeneity of the poor there may be considerable variation in housing demand in terms of affordability and desirability. To meet

the different needs, both Singapore and Hong Kong have been able to produce a comprehensive range of dwelling units for rent and purchase, at a steadily increasing volume that at least promises to meet effective demand. While the cheapest public housing unit is still expensive for the poorest of the poor in both cities, their housing programmes have benefitted a very large percentage of low-income rather than the middle-income population. There is also flexibility in housing programmes; as incomes have risen, adjustments in housing standards have been made to include larger units with better facilities as well as making more units available for sale.

Singapore and Hong Kong have demonstrated the importance of planning for the total residential environment and not merely the dwelling unit. Moreover, both cities have integrated housing with efforts to provide jobs. In Singapore, "flatted factories" for small-scale industry have been built in the housing estates and leased factory space has been provided to large-scale labour-intensive industries. Creating employment in the public housing estates of both cities is a deliberate policy to diversify the economy and to reduce commuting time and expense and inner city congestion. In Hong Kong, this policy was adopted as part of resettlement schemes. Early public housing followed the relocation of existing flatted factories which served as squatter workshops. Later, new industrial sites were located near housing developments.

The two city states have been able to combine zoning measures with land development, housing construction, and the provision of land for industry. Singapore in particular has used town planning legislation and practice very effectively to rezone areas and manipulate density controls, ensuring ample land for public housing. Some countries fail to realise that zoning is a potentially valuable instrument of urban and housing policy. It can protect an aesthetically pleasing urban environment, group commercial and other activities efficiently and segregate incompatible activities. Inappropriate zoning may exclude the poor from residence near the job-providing industrial, commercial and high-income residential areas. Properly used, zoning can help to ensure a supply of land in an expanding city and to provide the public purse with a share in any gains.

Good policies must also be complemented by considerable administrative know-how which takes time to establish and is the result of recruitment, training and experience. At least in Singapore, the efficiency of the HDB reflects the upgrading of the entire civil service. Perhaps such countries as Indonesia with little experience in public housing should first take a learning-by-doing approach and not aim at large volumes of construction too early. Although large-scale projects may achieve economy of scale, large-scale failures are extremely expensive both economically and socially.

Urban renewal
      In large cities of the developing world population density in and around the central commercial areas is high. Without new, low-cost housing near the city centre, slums invariably offer the cheapest private accommodation for both low- and middle-income groups. People in the inner city slums are the focus of any urban renewal programme and they comprise a very heterogeneous population. While most slum households undoubtedly need better housing, they are usually reluctant to break their established economic and social ties in order to relocate to a peripheral estate or a new town. In these circumstances it is best to allow some of the slum population to be rehoused within the renewal districts themselves.
      The objectives of urban renewal can be social, economic or both. The social objective would be to improve the living conditions of the residents through clearance and rehousing most if not all of the affected population on or near the renewal site. The purely economic objective would be to enhance the site value through commercial redevelopment, rehousing the affected population elsewhere with compensation. In practice, few cities in South-east Asia can undertake effective urban renewal; the problems of coping with general housing shortages sufficiently discourage any further reduction in housing stock by slum clearance. Few governments, if any, would face the political consequences of wholesale dislocation of the inner city population for commercial redevelopment. Urban renewal is therefore limited to the relatively high-income cities of Singapore and Hong Kong.
      Urban renewal in Singapore is complemented by sound public housing and resettlement. After land

acquisition and clearance a part of the site is used for public housing and the rest for private sector projects. Revenue from the latter provides a cross-subsidy for public housing. Not all structures on the renewal sites are demolished; rebuilding is only one of three elements in urban renewal. The other two, although minor in Singapore, are conservation and rehabilitation. Finally, there is a social cost: the community structures that disappear cannot be resurrected and evaluation has shown that a small percentage of the resettled households and shops had still not fared well some years after relocation.

Slum improvement

In many cities where public housing is too expensive there is another option, on-site upgrading of slums and squatter settlements, complemented by a sites-and-service programme. A slum improvement programme can involve upgrading dwelling units but it usually consists of inserting basic infrastructure and social services. The main aims of upgrading are to reduce the costs of improved housing for the residents and to avoid the relocation which disrupts access to employment and social services and cuts ties within the community structure. Slum improvement accepts that the importance of location, security of land tenure and urban services far outweigh the desirability of "standard" space requirements, building materials or indoor toilets. In this respect, community participation in planning for improvement is essential and its labour input will help lower costs. Furthermore housing for the poor should be seen as incremental rather than as a one-shot, instant development, since the poor cannot invest large sums on their dwelling unit and their environment all at once. With better land tenure and improved infrastructure many squatter residents can be expected to gradually improve their dwelling unit on their own.

Very often squatter improvement programmes cannot be undertaken without complementary sites and service projects to absorb families unavoidably displaced. These schemes usually involve developing vacant land on the urban periphery and adding infrastructure. Lots are then sold or leased and the new residents either build the dwelling structure themselves or contract them out. Government subsidies may extend to building materials or to cash loans. This approach enables the separation of the land, utilities and shelter components within housing provision, thus giving considerable operational flexibility. The function of sites and services programmes goes beyond the accommodation of population overflow from upgrading; they can also absorb rural migrants, who would otherwise increase the density of existing slums or develop new squatter areas.

Slum improvement programmes have complexities not encountered in public housing. One major obstacle is precisely the shortage of serviced land near the upgraded site to accommodate population overflow. Thus either improvement standards must fall or some of the population must be relocated far away. When the improvement programme is large and includes many sites, the pressure on the government to prepare complementary sites and service projects can also be great. In metropolitan Manila, some squatter areas were not selected for upgrading because of the shortage of suitable land for complementary sites and service projects.

Another issue is that of land tenure. The severity of the problem varies from country to country, city to city, and site to site. One reason why the Kampung Improvement Programme in Indonesia expanded so rapidly was because land tenure was not an issue. In Thailand, legal structures make land expropriation extremely lengthy and complex, taking at least five years and often over ten, a serious impediment to all public projects including slum improvement. The extent of political commitment is also important since the sites selected for upgrading or sites and service projects may belong to other government agencies unwilling to part with them. Where an inner city landlord is a private person or agency, residents simply cannot afford to buy their lot unless the government provides a substantial subsidy. Given the hundreds of slums and squatter areas in Bangkok and Manila alone, the governments can probably not generate sufficient financial resources to improve them all.

In principle, slum improvement projects should involve a well-organised and participating community that mobilises its own goods and services. Such a community would ideally be friendly, satisfied and proud of its community with its own associations to tackle social problems and with broad-based indigenous leadership. However, slums and squatter communities selected for upgrading do not necessarily come with this cohesion. It is difficult to measure community structure; however, it varies substantially according to the size, age, location and ethnicity of the community.[4]

The most celebrated example of community involvement in slum improvement in South-east Asia was Tondo. Tondo had produced a well-organised "Zone One Tondo Organisation" (ZOTO) which fought the government for years before the area was considered for upgrading in 1973. Unlike the co-operative approach of community development, stressing requests to government, ZOTO continued with a conflict confrontation negotiation approach, stressing demands to the government. Open hostility between ZOTO and the administration led the latter always to give preference in discussion to barangay leaders who were closely integrated into the local government system. While ZOTO attempted to organise other squatter communities into a bigger political force to deal with the government on housing issues, in all subsequent improvement projects the government has negotiated only with barangay leaders.

The existence of ZOTO in Tondo is atypical of slums and squatter settlements in Manila and in the Philippines; unwarranted generalisation from one example should be avoided. In any event, the government has the responsibility for community development in any upgrading project and should involve the residents. Indonesian experience suggests that the intensity of participation desired should perhaps be closely related to the degree to which a household's assets and expenditure are involved. To create a community organisation from nothing, to involve the community in orderly planning and to solicit a labour input in implementation and infrastructure maintenance is difficult and time consuming. The "unlocking" of popular energies among the poor has not always materialised as expected. Such energies and resources have tended to be focused on short-run and emotionally charged activities that constitute one-time, do-or-die efforts. It has been difficult to encourage community participation in large-scale, planned and institutionalised activities such as the construction of core housing or digging ditches for sewerage and water systems.[5]

The difficulty may be enhanced by fear, suspicion and hostility due to past eviction policies.

Upgrading slums and squatter settlements alone cannot solve low-income housing problems. Not all such areas can be upgraded for a variety of technical and land-use considerations. A criticism of Jakarta's Kampung Improvement Programme is that it has taken place on a large scale without an overall city development plan and will make overall planning more difficult later. Bangkok has an intermediate position whereby some slums are designated temporary residential areas scheduled for minimum improvement without the guarantee of land tenure. Indeed, some slum clearance and resettlement will be necessary in all large cities for infrastructure development alone. Secondly, slum improvement hardly increases new housing stock. In Bangkok, Jakarta and Manila, there is no evidence that governments are acquiring land on a large scale for complementary sites and service programmes. Finally, the governments involved in slum improvement may not be willing and able to generate the resources to meet the very substantial existing demand.

The private sector
    At present the private sector is widely assumed to make a negligible contribution to housing the urban poor since profits are greater in commercial and industrial projects and in middle- to high-income housing. However, commercial builders are involved in low-cost housing construction in several ways. Firstly, the private sector usually undertakes the actual construction of government-financed low-cost housing. Secondly, low-cost commercial housing can be found in squatter settlements, since not all squatter housing is self-built. While not systematically documented, a sizeable portion of squatter housing seems to be either partially or wholly built by small units within the squatter settlements.

    In addition to these "specialist" types of production, there is also low-cost housing on the open market. There are usually some small firms in any city prepared to accept low profit margins, but their collective output is limited at best. This leaves large-scale developers whose products are generally far beyond the reach of the poor but who nevertheless may play a more active role. There has been little direct investigation of the potential of the private sector for low-cost housing and its structure in individual cities is inadequately known. No doubt its potential role varies. However, it would be desirable to explore the possibility of private and public sector co-operative schemes. Large-scale developers might be able to provide low-cost housing in quantity while the government could ensure that benefits reach the identified target group.

Some governments rushed into joint ventures with private contractors without careful study and without retaining control. An earlier scheme proposed by the National Housing Authority of the Philippines failed because the private developer was required to produce the land and the government part of the financing; the reverse would have been more appropriate.

In Malaysia, to make use of the private sector will require several changes in policy and programmes. The present attempt to reduce costs through changes in building and planning regulations or through the introduction of more sophisticated techniques is unlikely to work. More attention must be given to the supply of land, materials and credit if costs are to fall substantially. Furthermore, to reach even the upper part of the low-income group, the private sector needs some government subsidy which could best come through providing inexpensive and prepared sites. But serviced land suitable for housing is precisely what most governments do not have and this lack will be a continuing major obstacle for low-cost housing, with or without the private sector participation.

Conclusions

The 1970s saw improved policy, administration and performance in all the countries under review. Singapore and Hong Kong, by providing housing through new towns, demonstrated their ability both to solve the housing problem eventually and to achieve other social and economic objectives. Expanding slum improvement programmes in Indonesia, and to a lesser extent in the Philippines, has benefitted an increasing proportion of their low-income population. The political commitment at least to experiment with slum upgrading in Malaysia and Thailand shows a better understanding of the nature of the housing problem and of effective demand. On the other hand, painful and costly lessons have been learned in Indonesia, Malaysia, the Philippines and Thailand that providing public housing on a sufficiently large scale requires a much more complex host of inputs than was anticipated.

It is unrealistic for the large South-east Asian countries to expect to solve their housing problems this decade. Given the rate of urban population growth, the rapid increase in slum and squatter areas in large cities and the substantial backlog in infrastructure and housing, in addition to the changes that would be necessary in political thinking, in legislation, administration and resource allocation, a comprehensive solution requires decades rather than years. Some governments would do well to generate sufficient supply to meet city population growth, let alone to correct existing deficits.

Although sites-and-services and slum upgrading programmes are, in principle, equitable and cheaper than alternative strategies, they may be administratively challenging and by no means inexpensive. Most upgrading projects in Indonesia and the Philippines have been financed by the World Bank and other international agencies; their continued expansion cannot, and perhaps should not, depend too much on such loans. Without a very sizeable increase in domestic funding and a rapid development of land banks, these countries can probably only begin a few projects at any time. Learning by doing takes time, but it is urgent to build up rapidly the capacity to plan and implement large-scale programmes.

An effective housing policy requires not only a sound strategy but also good administration. Most countries would not seem to have given enough attention to developing institutions with the capacity to design and implement urban development plans and housing programmes. Good housing administration requires a legislative base which some countries have also neglected. In Malaysia, for example, housing legislation goes back to colonial days when laws aimed to ensure high housing standards for Europeans. Consequently, zoning laws, subdivision procedures and building codes are all real constraints on housing and increase costs. Legislation also defines the housing finance system; it establishes finance institutions and their authority, it affects land tenure, mortgageability, title registration and other legal considerations. A challenge in any slum improvement policy is to introduce legislation appropriate to the residents' requirements, such as for housing improvement loans, not obtainable from conventional sources. Given all the country variations discussed, no standard set of housing strategies can be formulated. Each country must review its own options. Similarly, housing standards depend on the financial and other resources available, especially those available to the poor. Housing standards should be improved for the whole urban population and not just for certain segments. However, three characteristics are desirable in all housing policies and programmes. They should be flexible to cope successfully with changing social, political and economic circumstances; they should be comprehensive and draw on all possible sources of low-cost housing, whether conventional or not. Finally, they should be scaled to meet the specific requirements of the poor, within their financial capabilities and employing local resources. Unquestioning attempts to emulate the apparent success of other and wealthier countries should be particularly avoided.

Any positive policy towards low-income housing may encourage further rural-urban migration and city growth. But the alternative, to try to slow the migration flow and to eliminate low-income housing which fails to meet some city standard, is probably futile. The urban bias shown in the development philosophy of many governments, whether through food pricing policies or public investment in infrastructure and social services, has accentuated rural-urban inequality and encouraged migration. Therefore, urbanisation is likely to continue. In practice, most national and urban governments are under pressure to accept the large and growing proportion of the urban poor and to help them find shelter suitable to their immediate needs which they can afford. Thus, for most governments, a sound housing policy must accept that much slum and squatter housing represents a positive response by the poor to the lack of low-income housing.

Notes

1. R. Mohan: "Urban land policy, income distribution and the urban poor", in C. Frank Jr. and R. Webb (eds.): Income distribution and growth in

less developed countries (Washington, DC, The Brookings Institute, 1977).

2. S. Yeh and Tan Soo Lee: "Satisfaction with living conditions", in S. Yeh (ed.): Public housing in Singapore: A multidisciplinary study (Singapore, University of Singapore Press, 1975).

3. D. Drakakis-Smith: "Low cost housing provision in the Third World: Some theoretical and practical alternatives", in H.S. Murrison and J.P. Lea (eds.): Housing in third world countries (London, Macmillan Press, 1979).

4. For a more detailed discussion see S. Yeh: "On characteristics of urban low-income settlements and improvement strategies: An Asian perspective", in United Nations Centre for Human Settlements (ed.): The residential circumstances of the urban poor in developing countries (New York, Praeger, 1981).

5. A. Laquian: "Whither site and services?", in Science (Washington, DC, American Association for the Advancement of Science), June 1976.

4 BUILDING CODES AND REGULATIONS IN LOW INCOME SETTLEMENTS

by D.B. Cook

Introduction

This short chapter on building codes and regulations expands on one item mentioned in the previous chapter, namely legal impediments to producing housing which is cheap but still an improvement over existing slums and squatter settlements. Of course, slums and squatter settlements themselves generally pay no attention to building codes and regulations. Old tenements would often require immense investment to be brought up to scratch while most squatter settlements are anyway illegal. But it is precisely during the next step of upgrading and legalising settlements that building codes may play a discouraging role.

By the end of the century urban populations will be huge and inescapably most urban dwellers will be poor. Will slums, squalor and disease necessarily be the order of the day? Probably yes, if present trends continue. Codes and regulations designed to prevent precisely this have unfortunately influenced the present situation and will worsen it if they remain unchanged. It is ironic that codes, which have the laudable aim of preserving those standards which are perceived as "appropriate", have been partly responsible for the present and unsatisfactory low income urban settlements.

Building codes and standards are a by-product of later 19th century European health acts. Their stimulus was the widespread plagues and diseases of the day. Building codes, specifying minimum basic requirements for the siting, size and construction of residential buildings supported the health acts. Subsequently by-laws under town planning legislation extended building control. These European building codes, followed by similar regulations in the United States, were designed for the urbanisation which followed the industrial revolution. But, the rate of urbanisation in Europe and the eastern United States

in the late 19th century was slow compared to the
developing world today. Many developing countries have either inherited or
adopted the codes of industrial countries. These
largely achieved their objectives when, up to 1939,
urban growth was low. After 1950 however the
situation changed, towns and cities grew so fast that
time and again building regulations were ignored or
regarded by most people as inappropriate or
irrelevant: people built despite the regulations.
Official recognition of this has been slow and it is
only now being realised that building codes based on
developed country models are irrelevant to all but
the upper income areas, modern commercial structures
and government complexes. They are inapplicable to
the vast majority living in hinterland villages,
urban slums and squatter settlements.

The built environment
    The built environment has always been a response
to social and economic issues. Where 60 per cent or
more of new urban building will be extra-legal and
largely built by the poor, it is not enough for
governments to try to control development or, as so
often happens, ignore low income settlements.
Building control of low income development in
developing countries is almost impossible to achieve
and it may be better for governments not to attempt
it. The same applies to land use and zoning
regulations. Where jobs are scarce and poverty
endemic, employment often takes place in the home.
Low income settlements should not be zoned as purely
residential. Buildings, rooms and compounds
frequently have a multipurpose use: better to
recognise this than to pretend it is not so. For the
poor, legislation on building and planning control is
yet another threat contributing to their
uncertainties and marginal existence.
    Not all structures built outside the formal and
legal sector are badly built. In parts of North
Africa and in other higher income developing
countries, substantial buildings are frequently
privately erected but, because formal planning and
building permission was not obtained, they frequently
remain formally unrecognised. As a result,
infrastructure and municipal services are not
provided and the catalogue of urban deficiencies
lengthens. Makeshift building plus a lack of

infrastructure produces a degraded environment and
encourages decision-makers to dream of unaffordable
solutions and to think of slum clearance. Thus the
problem is frequently seen as the removal of
unsanitary and unsightly buildings rather than the
plight of people desperate for shelter.
The built environment of low income communities is
naturally affected by patterns of land and structure
ownership. Squatters build without legal entitlement
on public and private land, though in the latter case
they occasionally pay a ground rent to the landlord.
The absence of ownership rights however does not
prevent plots and dwellings from being sold, leased
or sublet although such transactions have no judicial
protection. Structures in illegal settlements tend to
remain built of temporary or cheap materials pending
official "recognition", but once governments
legitimatise such settlements by providing services
or by granting leasehold or other title, squatters
invariably respond by upgrading the quality of their
housing. The buildings however usually remain,
officially illegal because they fail to conform to
building codes and regulations.

Social and economic aspects
    During the 1960s and 1970s governments, anxious to
"do something" about housing problems, sometimes
turned to large-scale industrialised building
packages as a solution. Unfortunately time and again
the hope that industrially produced mass housing
modules would ease the housing shortage has been
proved to be a myth. Industrialised building systems
are also capital intensive and their
inappropriateness in developing countries has been
well documented by I.D. Terner and J.F.C. Turner.[1]
The enormous future demand for shelter and
infrastructure, however, particularly in low income
settlements, could provide a large market for locally
developed building materials. Codes and regulations
allowing such materials, and appropriate affordable
infrastructure, will encourage construction
investment. This in turn should ease balance of
payments problems since many materials which conform
to traditional building codes are manufactured by the
formal sector and often imported. In 1975 more than
half of the total expenditure of US$5 thousand
million on building materials in Africa was for
imports.[2]

There are often considerable indirect foreign exchange costs associated with building materials. A good example is the concrete block, which consists of crushed stone, sand and cement. As currently manufactured energy prices largely determine the cost of a concrete block and its rapid increase in cost in recent years reflects this. Rock is usually quarried, crushed and transported by imported equipment, cement is manufactured capital-intensively and fired by coal, gas or oil, concrete is mixed in imported machines and trucks transport the blocks to the sites. Codes do not always permit such alternatives as mud and wattle, adobe, rammed earth or other traditional materials. However, much information is developing on the use of agricultural wastes in low cost construction, brickmaking, hand compressed soil/cement blocks, hand-made sulphur bonded roofing sheets, etc. Local building research stations would be advised to test these products, assess their response to the local climate and if found appropriate, recommend waivers or "deemed to satisfy status" in respect of building codes.

Environmental health and fire aspects

There is little specific evidence that improved housing leads to improved health and even less evidence to indicate the nature of minimum housing standards to achieve any such improvements.[3] However, without improved shelter (and other socio-economic improvements) "good" health cannot be achieved. The difficulty in linking health to shelter lies in all the other social and economic factors associated with substandard shelter, e.g. overcrowding, poverty, malnutrition, etc. Probably, subject to reaching certain levels of other social and economic factors, a securely sheltered and employed family provides the best possible environment for the healthy development of children and this includes much more than the absence of disease. Housing is a desirable component of social and economic progress but the role of physical standards in improving socio-economic well-being has not been precisely established. But regulations which push people into building forms of shelter they cannot afford can be detrimental to health by reducing other necessary expenditure.

A government desire to follow their own building codes and house citizens in "acceptable" low cost housing has spawned its own problems. Rising land prices and construction costs have led to very small units being built often five to six storeys high. Such units cannot be expanded, they do not support multipurpose use, it is not easy to keep animals, young children are too confined and, where toilets and kitchens are shared, there is little privacy. They may also need to be heavily subsidised.

Building standards in developing countries may in fact serve more as an instrument of social stratification than as a means of meeting the shelter needs of the population. They differentiate and enforce with the power of law, between those who can afford a minimum legal house and those who cannot. Any legal dwelling is placed beyond the reach of the poor, they are forced to live in unserviced, illegal settlements on marginal land and are almost guaranteed the associated ill health. However, as noted, shelter standards themselves have perhaps no explicit bearing on health status. What is as or more important is the provision of water, both for drinking and other purposes, and waste disposal. These are discussed in other chapters.

Politicians rarely defend housing or development schemes built in an incremental way or with indigenous or traditional materials. Official pronouncements usually stress the aim of providing "decent and dignified" housing for all. The reasons for this are usually based on perception and not analysis. At the local level, civic leaders and officials are often part of an elite which sees speculative opportunities in building rental housing for all income groups: shortages and constraints in the shelter market work to their advantage.

Legal, financial and administrative aspects

Codes or by-laws are regulations enacted by a lesser authority than the national legislature. They frequently flow from acts passed by that body, e.g. public health, housing or town planning acts which require local authorities to adopt building and town planning codes and by-laws. Model codes are usually drafted nationally, with local authorities given the option of accepting the model or changing and adapting it to local situations, subject to

ratification by a parent ministry. Current building
codes tend to be conservative, negative and static.
They restrict the freedom for innovative design and
restrain the timely entry of new and appropriate
materials to the market. Experience has shown them to
be difficult and cumbersome to change.

Building by-laws spawned under public health
legislation have often proved the most difficult to
change. Public health officials while acknowledging
the need to move with the times and adapt to emerging
technologies have difficulty in approving revisions
to legal statutes. There are many misgivings in
granting official approval to a development or
situation thought to incorporate even the smallest
health risk. While understandable, this approach is
unrealistic; many people cannot afford the solutions
conforming to traditional health controls. What
health benefit is there in producing small islands of
legal conformity surrounded by a sea of squalor?

Administratively, building by-laws usually require
the owner to seek approval for his plans and
proposals before building. This invariably involves
filling in forms and the submission of plans (often
in triplicate with one print on linen or other
approved material). Approval to proceed is given by a
legislative body after scrutiny and recommendation by
officials. The process of approval can be
time-consuming and requires comments from officials
ranging from building and public health officials to
traffic engineers and fire officers. Once approval is
given inspectors must still visit the building to
ensure accordance with the approved drawings.

These procedures are not relevant to rapidly
growing low income communities. Staff are
insufficient to "police" the process nor are they
mobile enough to cope. Their background and training
does not equip them to analyse and judge proposals
which conform to the spirit of the regulations; as a
result they stand behind the "letter of the law" in
some instances and turn a "blind eye" to what is
happening elsewhere. Where public salaries are low
building inspectors are under a strong temptation to
exploit others or to be corrupted.

Legislation by itself will not produce ideal
settlements. In fact, the so-called by-law
development which determined the nature of the
housing units in much of northern England has left an
unfortunate legacy, and its current equivalent in

developing countries, the public sector 4-storey walk-up unit, will leave a similar legacy. These problems result from stereotyped interpretation of some of the technical aspects of codes which cover, for example, plot sizes and ratios, street widths, building lines, water supply, sanitation and plumbing, electrical installations, room sizes and heights, materials and construction standards, lighting and ventilation. All these subjects are relevant, but it must be asked whether quality standards, technical specifications and regulations which we have seen have not always proved to be appropriate to the formal sector, can take into account non-conventional and informal construction activities using salvaged materials and simple tools. Instead of adapting codes to respond to the reality of informal sector building there is a trend in the public sector in developing countries to reduce plot and room sizes, cut down on western style finishes and to provide multi-family sanitary and ablution facilities. This tends to be part of the "standards" issue, and to break away from such policies, new and radical thinking is required.

Need for building regulations
The foregoing discussion has tried to demonstrate that building codes based on European models are by and large irrelevant in developing countries; arguments have been advanced that standards enshrined in building codes are a constraint to the development of low income settlements. It is appropriate therefore to ask whether building control legislation is needed at all?

Building regulations in Europe hardly existed in their current form until the late 19th century. This was tolerable when the rate of urbanisation was low and some control was exercised by landlords. In principle, at least, the situation in developing countries was similar and up to 1939, even in cities, the problems posed by low income communities were not great and leaders were generally able to ignore them. Today the large numbers of urban dwellers require some form of government policy response and guidance to avoid unserviced development, or exploitation by the few impinging on the lives of others. Some building control regulations are needed, but which, and how can they be administered?

The declared aim of building regulations is to protect the health, safety and well-being of the community. Building regulations should ensure that buildings serve the needs of their users and not put them to unacceptable health, fire or structural risks. Regulations should also be applicable to all families in the community they intend to serve. Some countries, e.g. Kenya, have enacted adoptive building by-laws, known as Grade II by-laws, which apply to designated areas and are designed to reduce "acceptable" standards to a level lower income groups can afford. These Grade II building by-laws were designed for peri-urban areas which became part of the municipality after boundary changes. But the Grade II code is not being administered in the manner expected. The flexibility it offers is not being used and areas designated in this way risk having a stigma attached to them: it is felt that such regulations apply only to second class citizens.

Any discussion of the scope and range of building regulations must refer to standards. Legislators frequently claim that changing building control legislation means lowering standards or letting profiteers "get away" with unsatisfactory buildings: they argue that the end result will be a proliferation of slums. Cities, however, should not be seen as collections of elaborate architecture, or as city planners' theories perpetuated in stone; it is essential, in order to respond to the urban challenge, that they be viewed as instruments for providing all their inhabitants with a more productive life.

Official housing standards, often in the form of rigid specifications, set the minimum quality theoretically acceptable to government agencies. These standards reveal the perceptions, values and professional judgements of those who set them, and, in the end, administrators' preconceptions dictate what is acceptable. A solution to this conundrum is to define what is expected in terms of the performance of the building or element and offer a wide range of possibilities which satisfy the basic performance requirement. A statement like "an external wall shall resist the penetration of rain, support the roof or floor (and any other likely live or use loadings) and offer an acceptable degree of insulation to heat and/or cold", establishes what is expected of an outside wall. A designer can then

propose any construction that satisfies the
specification; the builder's degrees of freedom are
increased, he can use his imagination and skill to
meet the requirements with the resources he has
available. Such a specification is known as a
"performance type specification" and, when backed by
examples which are "deemed to satisfy", the
specification becomes a flexible building regulation.
There is no question of high or low standards: if the
building element satisfies the basic requirements it
conforms to the standard.

The Shankland Cox Partnership[4] stress that
controls should be kept to the absolute minimum
consistent with reasonable levels of hygiene, with
safety in respect of fire, hurricanes, earthquakes,
etc. and with the avoidance of unnecessary conflicts
between neighbours. They cite an example from Port
Moresby in Papua New Guinea where after five years,
365 lots were still vacant, on a Sites and Services
Scheme providing 749 lots:

The principal reason for this was probably lack of
conveniently sited employment opportunities.
However two other interrelated factors probably
discouraged applicants. These were that the
minimum standards were too high and difficult for
people to attain, while there was not at that time
sufficient input from Public Authorities to help
people comply. In this instance, the regulations
covered matters such as height of building and its
location on site, maximum ground cover and minimum
size of house, location of pit latrines, minimum
room dimensions (plan and height), window areas,
staircase pitch, wall and roof construction,
minimum strength of wall frames, etc.: probably
most important in its deterrent effect was the
requirement that plans and specifications should
be drawn up and submitted to the Building Board
for approval.

They go on to conclude:

This lesson has, of course, now been learnt and
revised minimum standards are being considered
which would deal only with site coverage,
set-backs, the building of adequate properly sited
pit latrines, and the construction of
non-inflammable roofs. The contribution made by
the experience of pioneers such as the housing
authorities in Papua New Guinea is of enormous
value. With variations reflecting special local

conditions, it is our view that these second thoughts represent the right approach to the degree and complexity of controls appropriate in site and services or similar projects.

It is not easy to frame legal instruments to ensure public health and safety and yet not place difficulties in the way of those who seek to create some kind of shelter with minimum resources. However, the following points may help:

Recommendations

A. Building codes and regulations should recognise the step by step building methods utilised by the informal sector and be redrafted in the form of performance specifications supported by "deemed to satisfy" clauses.

B. District offices should be established in appropriate areas and staffed by appropriately trained development advisers.

The system of individuals formally applying for a building permit before starting to build is hardly relevant in low income districts. It is much better to decentralise building control offices and turn the inspection staff into an outreach service. The building inspection staff instead of negatively telling people what they cannot do, would become advisers, counselling on how to build, in a manner which is deemed to satisfy the building regulations.

C. Extensive programmes covering education, training and information needs should be instituted, appropriate to the building needs of low income households.

Ignorance of the objectives and requirements of codes and regulations contributes greatly to non-compliance. This can be overcome by publicity and by improving the training schedules of technical training establishments. Such schedules should train students in the use of appropriate technologies which can respond to the "deemed to satisfy" clauses.

D. Priority should be given to the establishment of research programmes in the building field and the subsequent application of research findings.

Many institutions throughout the world are developing new materials and technologies through research and pilot programmes, aimed at improving the delivery and construction of cheaper shelter units. It is necessary to assess whether such new materials and techniques are relevant to the climatic and socio-economic condition of a particular country and they should be reviewed by the local building research institute.

E. Type plans, specifications and material schedules should be available at nominal cost to assist individuals interested in building. These should be made available after an economic, social, technical and financial review of the needs and type of structures being built by low income families. Plans should incorporate the findings of the building research station and allow for the use of new materials as they become recognised and "deemed to satisfy".

Notes

1. I.D. Terner and J.F.C. Turner: Industrial housing: The opportunity and the problem in developing areas, Ideas and Methods Series, No. 66, Department of Housing and Urban Development (Washington, DC, Office of International Affairs, 1972).

2. The seminar of experts on building codes and regulations in developing countries; Tallberg, Sweden, March 17-24, 1980.

3. Co-operative Housing Foundation: Housing and health, study prepared for the Office of Housing, (Washington, DC, United States Agency for International Development, Nov. 1981).

4. Shankland Cox Partnership: Third World housing (London, Building Research Establishment, 1977).

5 HEALTH CARE AND THE URBAN POOR

by G.J. Ebrahim

Introduction

This chapter reviews urban health care policies in the context of the overall urban environment with its specific disease problems and the child care difficulties of working parents. The chapter argues that reproducing western-type medical systems in the urban areas of the developing world is inappropriate both because it may lead to the neglect of environmental improvement (especially the control of infection) and because it gives no scope for community participation. Health care, of course, is strongly linked to such other features of basic needs satisfaction as adequate shelter, water supply and sanitation; nevertheless it has its own contribution to make because, above all, it deals with persons individually.

Growth of large urban conurbations is a relatively recent phenomenon in human history. Before 1850 no nation was fully urbanised and at the beginning of this century there was only one, namely the United Kingdom. Today most industrial nations of Western Europe and North America as well as Japan are in effect urbanised societies and there is remarkable urban growth occurring in many less developed countries. On present trends by the year 2000 over half the people of the world may be residing in cities with populations of 100,000 or more.

Because of the rapidity of urbanisation, sociological studies of the urban community are relatively few. Several fundamental questions need answers. How will a species that has evolved during hundreds of millenia in small communities and rural settlements adapt to existence in huge, dense agglomerations? The background to man's religious and cultural heritage is overwhelmingly rural. Besides cultural adaptation there are also problems of physical conditioning. The change has been too rapid for the process of natural selection to occur, and

93

the adaptive process between man and cities mainly consists of physical alterations in the cities. The more complex the technology for adapting to city life, the larger have the cities grown, and the more elaborate have become the techniques needed to adjust them to man.[1] In this process of continuing change those who have the political power to control techniques do well and the weak get pushed to the wall.

During the growth of many of the cities in the Western industrial world there was a phase of high morbidity and mortality amongst their populations compared to the countryside. The townsfolk were more exposed to disease because of living together in close proximity, because of unhygienic surroundings, because trade and travel brought disease from elsewhere (e.g. cholera in London), because the cities provided the opportunity for the multiplication of pests and vectors (e.g. the rats which brought the black death) and through polluted food and drink. It is only since the beginning of the present century, and in some cases the post-war period, that death rates in Western industrial cities have dropped to their present levels.

Measuring health and welfare

The cities of the developing world will be called upon to absorb around 70 per cent of the projected population increase of Asia, Africa and Latin America and the welfare of the urban poor will be of particular concern to health planners. The health status of the population of many developing countries today is no better than that of nineteenth-century Europe and the quality of life in some rural and urban groups is even worse. Vital statistics, however useful, may not project a full measure of the quality of life and welfare and instead the Physical Quality of Life Index (PQLI) has been suggested as a more adequate measure by the Overseas Development Council.[2] This is a composite index of three key measures: infant mortality, life expectancy at age 1, and literacy. Infant mortality reflects the quality of the environment, e.g. nutrition, availability of clean water, housing, home conditions and the state of development of maternal and child health services. The second measure relates to more general environmental conditions including nutrition and the control of communicable diseases. Literacy reflects

the educational status of society as a whole,
particularly that of women.

On the basis of the PQLI, developing countries
vary from as low an index as 14 (Mali) to 82 (Sri
Lanka) in comparison with the United States, 95. Very
few studies have been carried out amongst the urban
poor but the indications are that the PQLI in
squatter settlements is very low. Several studies
indicate that even though immigration into the cities
is largely in search of jobs, most of the poor end up
in informal self-employment, odd-jobs of one kind or
another, casual labour or dealing in contraband. Many
of the major cities of the developing world report
infant mortality rates of between 75 and 90 per
thousand births, but amongst the urban poor these
rates are far higher. In the bustees of New Delhi the
overall child mortality rate (0-5 years) is 221 per
1,000 children, but reaches twice that number amongst
certain castes. In the city of Manila, the infant
mortality rate is three times higher in the slums
than the rest of the city. The rates for tuberculosis
per 100,000 population were nine times higher and
diarrhoea twice as common as in the rest of the city.
Twice as many people were found to be anaemic and
three times as many were suffering from malnutrition
as in the rest of the city.[3]

Frequent stagnation in the growth of rural output
combined with higher levels of landlessness and
greater social and economic stratification have
resulted in dispossessed families moving to the
cities in search of their livelihood. By now several
generations have been born and have grown up in
circumstances of urban poverty. A recent United
Nations study has shown that natural increase is
responsible for an average of 61 per cent of urban
population growth in developing countries compared to
only 39 per cent from rural migration.[4] But in
spite of living in the city for a considerable number
of years the urban poor lack the necessary knowledge
and skills to perform effectively in a modern
environment. Moreover, the existing social and
commercial systems often operate against them,
leading to their exclusion from service and welfare
programmes. A vast majority live a precarious
existence. In Lima's Cono Sur shanty town 54 per cent
of the population have to depend on their own
initiative to earn their living. Naturally, their
nutritional status is poor and virtually 60 per cent

are malnourished and cannot meet even 80 per cent of their caloric requirements. Only 7 per cent of families have running water in their homes, 72 per cent obtain water from standpipes or public fountains and the rest rely on private water trucks. In the absence of services, 195 tons of solid waste have to be disposed of daily, commonly by tipping at the periphery of the inhabited area, thus creating vast piles of refuse and litter and a proliferation of insects, rodents and scavenging dogs.[5] The home environment is equally poor with low rates of female literacy and little stimulation or education of children at home. The stage is well set for creating the inter-generational transmission of disadvantage. This description is typical of slums elsewhere and provides a measure of the precariousness of the lives of the people who live in them.

Common health problems of the urban poor
in the developing world
    The presence of a large number of susceptible human hosts living in overcrowded circumstances in the septic fringes of the cities creates an ideal situation for epidemics of infective illness and for reservoirs of infective illness to build up. In the slums of industrial London in the nineteenth-century a common illness and cause of prolonged debility leading to pauperism was the pyrexia of typhus. (Such outbreaks have not yet been described largely on account of the very few and episodic contacts between the urban poor and the formal health services.) But the stage is set by severe overcrowding, poor personal hygiene because of the lack of washing facilities and the susceptibility of the host. On the other hand, epidemics of dengue haemorrhagic fever and increased transmission of filariasis have occurred. These vector-borne diseases have been associated with the need of each individual household to store water in iron drums or large earthenware containers leading to the breeding of the mosquito A.aegypti in areas such as that shown in figure 1. At the same time the accumulation of waste water in pools and puddles around the settlements favours the breeding of another species of the mosquito, C.fatigans, the vector that transmits filariasis.[6] Old scourges like tuberculosis and leprosy continue to be a problem together with nutritional disorders and sexually-transmitted diseases. New dangers are

Figure 1

Raised squatter housing in Bangkok

likely to arise. In the overcrowded settlements where several thousand live cheek by jowl there is the ever present danger of meningococcal meningitis. In many of the squatter areas of Latin America the incidence of leishmaniasis has been rising, and several cases of rabies are being reported each year on account of both the large number of stray dogs scavenging in the garbage heaps and the ubiquitous litter around the settlements.

In one study of a large slum in Bombay, half the families surveyed reported some major illness during the previous year. The most common complaint was diarrhoea and other gastro-intestinal disorders (19 per cent) and one in ten reported tuberculosis.[7]

Environmental contamination was measured in one study
of Jakarta with cultures from a river running through
a residential area, from open drains, roadside
puddles, riverside wells and ice lollies sold to
school children in the street.[8] A large number of
micro-organisms were found including enteric
pathogens, like Salmonella typhii, Shigella flexner
and Escherichia coli. High bacterial counts, in the
range of 3.1×10^4 to 3.6×10^7 per ml., indicate
the degree of environmental contamination. In some
specimens the river water contained a density of
bacterial population of the same order as the gut
flora. Such heavy environmental contamination leads
to microbial contamination of the gut and
oropharyngeal secretions, as reported in several
studies, and is responsible for a high incidence of
diarrhoeal disease.

The heavy build-up of a susceptible population
with poor hygiene and a contaminated environment has
largely been responsible for the recent cholera
epidemics that swept through parts of Asia, Africa
and Latin America (figure 2). As a result, cholera
has become endemic in some countries like the
Philippines, Bangladesh, India and Indonesia. Another
recent epidemic illness was dengue haemorrhagic fever
- a virus disease transmitted by a mosquito vector
(as noted above). Conditions are ideal for outbreaks
of a variety of communicable diseases. All that is
needed is the introduction of an infective agent, a
vector or an intermediate host. Thus there is an
urgent need to improve the living conditions and the
quality of the physical environment together with
facilities for basic health care in order to avoid
epidemics of transmissible illness.

High prevalence rates of preventable infections in
children like measles, whooping cough and polio
reflect the very low levels of health facilities for
the urban poor. Both measles and whooping cough are
highly infectious and spread rapidly in communities
where overcrowding in the home is such that a family
of six shares a small living and sleeping space,
separated by a flimsy partition made out of a mat or
plywood from similar families next door.[9] Adequate
coverage with immunisation is a priority in such
overcrowded communities. Failure to provide such
elementary health care is an example of the antipathy
with which city health planners view the urban poor.

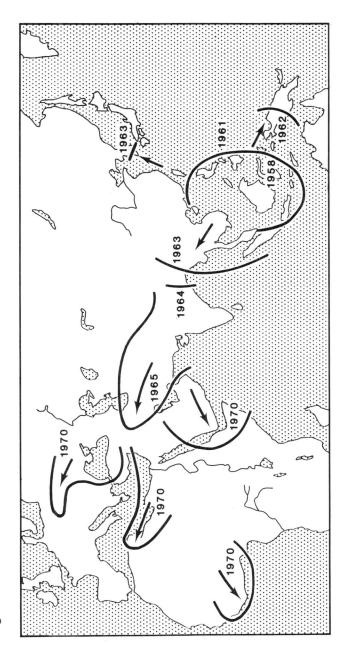

Figure 2   The spread of cholera

Malnutrition, the most pervasive symptom
of urban poverty

Even though a large proportion of the urban poor
or their parents or grandparents left their rural
homes because they could not support themselves and
their families, the city has changed their lot very
little. Between 40 and 60 per cent of the children
under the age of 5 in the bustees of Delhi show
evidence of malnutrition.[10] More than 90 per cent
of the squatter families cannot afford a balanced
diet in spite of spending more than 80 per cent of
their earnings on food. When more than two-thirds of
income goes on food, there is little room for being
selective. Satisfaction of hunger is the prime need.
This leaves little for fuel, rent, clothing and other
necessities such as the education of children.
Economic necessity requires all adults including the
women to seek work. Seventy per cent of the women
workers in the bustees of Delhi said that their
earnings go almost entirely towards the purchase of
food for the family. When both parents go out to work
there are no facilities for the care of children and
it is a rare employer who would allow the worker to
bring along a child. Forty per cent of the women in
the bustees of Delhi said they left their children at
home by themselves. Infant and child feeding becomes
more difficult under such circumstances and the young
infant is usually left in the care of an older
sibling who offers feeds from a bottle or leftovers
from the previous day.

In a study of families of 100 malnourished
children in Jamaica it was found that family income
for 98 per cent of the children was so low that to
bottle feed a baby adequately would take up half of
it, not counting the price of the bottle, the
utensils and the fuel for sterilisation.[11] For most
countries it can be said that the poor are seduced
into spending disproportionately on powdered milk,
canned baby foods and similar items at the expense of
more needed and readily available common foods.[12]
The presence of large numbers of illiterate people is
looked upon as a large untapped market by the baby
food industry. All the varieties of seductive
persuasion that the imagination of the advertising
industry can provide have been let loose, resulting
in a marked decline in traditional infant feeding
practices.[13] Attempts by governments and civic
groups to control the advertising and intensive

promotion of baby foods have been thwarted by the
manufacturers, who point to the sanctity of free
trade.

   In the meantime infant feeding practices have
changed to an incredible extent amongst the urban
poor. Condensed milk, barley water,[14] and aerated
soft drinks[15] are used instead of breast milk or of
even some other form of milk and traditional weaning
foods. The result has been a rising incidence of
blinding malnutrition (xerophthalmia) and marasmus
(figure 3). It is believed that every year some

Figure 3

Marasnus and bottle feeding

250,000 children go blind on account of
xerophthalmia, chiefly in South-east Asia. A large
proportion of these children are urban. In the harsh
environment of poverty the blind child has very poor
chances of survival. Studies have shown that between
30 and 40 per cent die within six months of discharge
from hospital. With regard to marasmus the average
age at the onset of this severe form of malnutrition
has dropped from 18 months to 8 months during the
past two decades. The United Nations Children's Fund

estimates that 1 million infant deaths occur annually largely on account of the decline in breast feeding. Considering that the brain is the most rapidly growing organ of the body in the first years of life and that the effect of environmental deprivation is most critical on a rapidly growing organ, intellectual stunting is one of the most dreaded sequelae of marasmus.[16] When we take into account the large number of infants affected by marasmus in the slums and shanty towns there is a danger of creating a permanent under-class of second rate citizens who will lack the mental capabilities to enter occupations requiring learning and skills.

The rise in "commerciogenic" malnutrition is largely because the only nutritional or consumer information the urban poor receive is commercial advertising. In the move to the city the urban poor have lost most of the traditions and customs which encouraged sharing of food resources, however meagre. The complex network of reciprocal obligations between farmers and the landless helps through the ritual sharing of food after harvest and during festivities. In the crowded city there is not even land to grow vegetables or fruits. Even though the latter may not satisfy hunger, they are important sources of nutrients. A handful of amaranth leaves (a form of spinach), three tomatoes or a slice of pawpaw can provide the daily requirements of vitamin A for a young child. In the chaotic existence of the crowded squatter areas there is no place to call one's own and no possibility of gardening. The urban life-style imposes an urban economy on migrants. Everything must be budgeted for in terms both of time and money and then purchased in small quantities daily since there is no storage space for food and fuel in the overcrowded shack. The prices paid for small purchases in the local shops are usually higher than those paid by more affluent citizens for bulk purchases in the supermarkets. The urban poor tend to rely on ready-made or easy-to-prepare foods. Thus bakery bread is preferred to tortillas, and hot-dogs to a traditional meal. Such foods are more expensive and less nutritious. Moreover, in the city there is a wide variety of such unaccustomed foods on sale and it is difficult for the urban poor to choose wisely unless helped to do so.

All the large cities of the developing world are suffering from an acute shortage of water. As

discussed in another chapter in this study all the
schemes for bringing in more water to the cities
suffer from basic in-built inequities so that the
more vocal and politically effective elite sector is
preferred and the needs of the urban poor are
overlooked. As that chapter notes, metropolitan water
development projects are mainly responsive to the
needs of the modern urban and commercial sectors and
millions of families in the squatter areas are left
to buy water by the tin or pail at several times the
price paid by the rich. Water drainage suffers from
the same biases so that squatter settlements tend to
have a pervasive smell caused by stagnant water with
decomposing household waste. Flooding during heavy
rains often carries this highly polluted water into
homes in the low lying parts of the settlements. Part
of the sense of exclusion so common amongst squatter
families is because they lack facilities for washing.
They know that their dirty clothing and malodorous
bodies set them apart from other social groups,
something experienced especially by school children
and youths. Every day is a struggle to obtain the
basic human needs of shelter, food and water. Life is
thus lived on the margin excluded from full
participation in commercial and civic life.
Continuous stress and ostracism breed alienation,
especially where conspicuous consumption lives
alongside destitution.

Appropriate health care for squatter settlements
- what do the urban poor need?
    Until recently town and housing planners appeared
convinced that slums bred the well-known pathologies
associated with poverty and they attempted to tear
down slums and scatter the inhabitants all over the
city. But it soon became clear that the so-called
urban renewal only moved slum dwellers to other
slums. For decades slum dwellers in country after
country had been saying that they needed more jobs,
better wages, more low-cost housing and the basic
necessities of life, and not just slum clearance. It
was not until they began to oppose urban renewal and
then to rebel and riot that the town planners began
to take notice of them.
    The urban planner largely plans for himself and
his peers. He also plans bearing in mind the
requirements of the politicians and the business and
civic leaders who sit on planning committees. For

them and for the planners the ideal city is the one which is good for business and for ownership of property. The urban planner is also planning on the basis of his class culture which is far removed from the culture of poverty.

Planners and bureaucrats often forget that the urban poor suffer not only from economic problems but also from the social and cultural breakdowns which come with being poor. Alcoholism, family strife, vice and violence are part of life of the urban poor. These pathologies are the by-products of the culture of poverty and are ways of adapting to poverty. City planners are more concerned with downtown residential areas, roads, parks and shopping areas which will bring out shoppers in large numbers and attract business. The culture of poverty concerns them only very fleetingly.

So much of medical pathology arises out of social pathology that it would be futile to address the problem of health care without considering the social, economic and physical environment. For example, income-generating activities, adequate and well-enforced minimum wage, job training programmes for youth, facilities for the care of unmarried mothers, abandoned families, the old and the handicapped are all part of the programme for integrated health care.

This is particularly true for maternal and child health services where the main preoccupation in squatter areas is to devise ways and means of ensuring the health of the family, providing support and counselling during periods of stress, and helping to hold the family together at times of family crisis. The lack of such supportive networks has resulted in one problem of growing concern in many large cities - the abandonment of women and children. Severing the extended family and similar social institutions initiated by the move to the city, lack of friends, unemployment, poverty and destitution leading to despair and frustration are the combined factors which cause family break-up. It is almost always the male head of the household who leaves home first, abandoning the wife to be the sole supporter of her children. With little or no education, and with a full day's housework load already on her hands, and in despair, it is hardly surprising that the woman is forced to fend for herself. Children drift away or get pushed out and there is a vicious

build-up of social pathology. The United Nations
Children's Fund estimates that there may be up to 40
million abandoned children in Latin America and the
Caribbean.[17] Perhaps abandonment of women and
children has not yet become a major problem in the
squatter settlements in Africa and Asia because of
strong cultural traditions. But as several
generations are born in the environment of the
squatter settlements and grow up knowing nothing
better than what the culture of poverty brings, the
trend is likely to increase.

Assuming that adequate health care can be
organised for the urban poor in all countries, how
can a health service with its roots in a
fee-for-service tradition become a force capable of
holding together families which are buffeted by
strong economic forces in an exploiting city? Surely
the traditional nature of health services must change
to face this new challenge, and the training of
health workers must be modified to promote the
required attitudes within the service. Far too many
of the world's medical schools prepare doctors not to
promote family health but to cure diseases and to do
so by the application of increasingly expensive
medical technology. The present format of medical
curricula and training prepares doctors to deal with
the less common clinical conditions rather than with
common health problems. It trains them for looking at
disease episodes rather than at the whole individual
within the family and his interaction with society.
Many systems of medical care and the insurance
systems that help them are oriented towards
in-patient hospital care rather than home care and
self care.

Urban health services - experience in industrial
countries
     Many cities in Europe faced similar challenges
during their periods of rapid growth and in part
their experience may be relevant to the problems of
the growing cities of the developing world. For
example, in the United Kingdom almost 92 per cent of
the country's population is now urban and this
century's major developments in public health have
taken place against a predominantly urban background.
The best starting point to examine the present
National Health Service (NHS) in the United Kingdom
is the Royal Commission on the Poor Laws and Relief

of Distress appointed in 1909. It condemned the existing Poor Law institutions, where two-thirds of the sick were being cared for in mixed workhouses, as a public scandal. These infirmaries were understaffed, lacked elementary facilities, and had effectively become penal institutions instead of places of care. Many free hospitals in developing countries today cannot be very different. Between them the majority and minority reports of the Commission raised all the issues which continued to be debated until 1948, for example:

- should a health service be comprehensive, providing care for all types of illness and disability as well as prevention, or should some, like psychiatric illness, be excluded?
- should the services be available to all or only to identifiable groups, e.g. those under a certain income limit?
- should the service be free on demand and financed by some form of insurance and/or taxation, or should it depend on charges for services?
- how should the physicians, dentists, nurses and other professionals be paid?
- how should the service be administered both locally and centrally?
- what part, if any, should professional or academic bodies play in its administration?

Lloyd George campaigned for National Health Insurance to attack poverty through cash payments during sickness-induced absence from work parallel to old age pensions. The National Health Insurance Bill of 1911 contributed greatly to the relief of poverty among manual workers during sickness and provided minimal care, although not to dependants. The Maternal and Child Welfare Act (1918) made antenatal and young child care statutory services for local authorities to provide. The National Health Service as it exists now is centred on a single universal social security scheme which provides insurance against the interruption of earnings because of sickness, maternity, disability, old age, unemployment or injury. A comprehensive health service is provided free to all (figure 4).

From the very beginning the NHS was criticised for not meeting expectations. Environmental services, housing, nutrition and most preventive health measures have always been outside its scope. Some prevention, however, for communicable diseases like tuberculosis, polio, sexually-transmitted diseases and control through immunisation were applied through the NHS with remarkable success. The most striking characteristics of the service have been:

(i) its comprehensiveness, embodying health and allied services;

(ii) its availability for all. Together with a social insurance system, such a health system provides an effective safeguard against destitution;

(iii) a growing concern to make the services equally accessible in all geographical areas and to all social groups.

Many Western European countries have undergone similar experiences on their way to the Welfare State. In fact, most of the major concepts in public health that came out of the industrial West during the period 1900-75 were based on their experience in looking after the health of urban populations. The present state of public health in cities like London, Paris and Amsterdam is largely the result of a struggle by the town to rid itself of squalor and disease and to provide jobs, homes, schools and medical care. As a result, large concentrations of population are able to live and work together with little detriment to health. Among the main contributions to this progress have been:

(a) A reduction of destitution and a consequent improvement in nutrition and in the provision of other material needs including housing. The central problem of public health at the beginning of this century was poverty. Medicine alone can do little to prevent disease and disability unless the poor are first raised out of poverty by social and economic measures. Social security schemes have largely enhanced the impact of health services.

(b) The development of adequate surveillance services for vulnerable groups e.g. maternal and child health services, school health services, health visiting and district nurse services, general practitioner services and so on. The bedrock of better infant and child care has always been the health visitor service, which provided a personal approach to the education of mothers in the home.

(c) The provision of adequate curative services.

(d) Compulsory primary education, which enabled the population to understand the health education provided. It also had the sound advantage of taking

Figure 4

Infant mortality and social legislation in
England and Wales

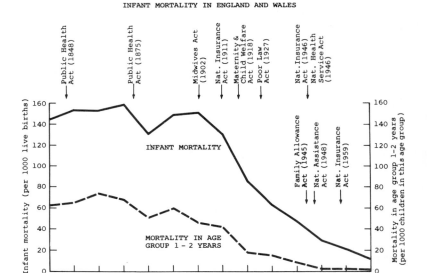

INFANT MORTALITY IN ENGLAND AND WALES

children out of factories or workshops and into
schools.

(e) Absorption of social concepts into medical
education so that medical technology came to be the
handmaiden of medical need and not vice versa.

These experiences project health care in a new
light. Health services have become part of the
process of social engineering intended to safeguard
the weak and to protect them from the strong social
and economic currents characteristic of urbanisation.

Concepts into practice – the problems

Parallel to the above a remarkable growth in
medical technology has also occurred, especially for
intensive care of the acutely ill. Large hospitals
have been built for this technology and for the new
specialist teaching programmes that disseminate it.

Health planners and professionals in developing countries have tended to lean towards the growing areas of intensive care and technology so that today 80 per cent or more of the health budgets of many developing countries is spent on hospital medicine. The recurrent expenditure of large teaching hospitals can equal the total health budget of the province or even the nation. Consequently new resources must be found to improve health services for the rural areas and the urban poor. Even with greater funds hospitals and peripheral services will probably still make competing demands. The future role of the hospital in supporting community services, as a staging post for community health activities and in monitoring changes in disease patterns within the community will need to be carefully worked out. Small, efficient and flexible units are likely to be more effective than the prestigious glass and concrete ivory towers which have sprung up all over the developing world in the last two decades. Thus the debate on the future role of hospitals will centre around two main issues, firstly, smaller units as against large hospitals and secondly, training health workers to fulfil new roles, e.g. more training in practical epidemiology, managerial techniques, behavioural and social sciences and skills in communication with the semi-or totally illiterate.

In particular there is a need to improve coverage with maternal and child health services, to shift the emphasis of such services from the diagnosis of rare conditions to surveillance and counselling and to providing support to families during periods of stress and crisis. Once adequate coverage is established, with the regular surveillance of vulnerable groups as its goal, then selection of those "at risk" according to established criteria is the next improvement. Such selection would ensure closer surveillance and more help for those in need and would make a more rational use of scarce resources. The principle to follow would be "appropriate surveillance and care for all but more for those in need". This approach will also solve the preventive versus curative debate. With adequate (i.e. more than 80 per cent) coverage, early diagnosis and treatment is a good form of preventive care; within a system of adequate coverage, the identification of those at risk and their close supervision is good curative medicine. Thus with proper coverage and with rational use of the "at-risk" concept, the curative versus preventive debate merges into one form of comprehensive care.

Concepts into practice - examples
Hong Kong
    The town of Kwun Tong is a new town east of Hong Kong's airport. Close to 700,000 people living in overcrowded industrial and dirty surroundings manufacture a fifth of Hong Kong's products. A voluntary agency hospital with 580 beds serves the community. The hospital planning team, aware that hospitals are not normally designed to influence the health of the surrounding community, decided from the outset to help the community raise its health level. The following four-pronged programme was evolved:[18]
    (a) A system of health centres, each in the heart of a housing estate with several thousand families living within a hundred yards. The health centres provide basic health and dental services and serve as staging posts for community health activities.
    (b) A community nursing service to provide home nursing care for early discharge patients from hospital and for long-term illnesses. This service has effectively added 250 convalescent and long-term beds to the hospital bed strength. Besides home nursing, the community nurses are trained to provide exercise therapy, family health education, social welfare counselling as well as in turn to train the volunteer health workers. The community nursing service has increased the outreach of the hospital into housing estates, squatter huts, houseboats anchored in the harbour and into every conceivable human habitat.
    (c) A variety of health maintenance programmes have begun:
    (1) infant health maintenance through monthly weighing and clinical check-up clinics, physical and psychomotor screening, counselling and easy access to curative services if needed;
    (2) school-child health maintenance through health screening, curative and dental services and health education;
    (3) an adult programme which provides annual screening including laboratory tests and X-rays with special emphasis on reduction of excess weight, smoking, alcoholism, psychological stress and so on;

(4) a geriatric health maintenance programme which
provides clubs for old people, medical screening and
screening for problems of old age.
Community health workers with a background of
training in social work are attached to each
programme. They stimulate people to accept more
responsibility for their own health and encourage
neighbourhood health committees, drama clubs,
children's organisations, promotional activities like
health weeks and the training of community health
volunteers.
(d) The hospital forges links with the community
through its training programme. Each student nurse is
assigned a family which she visits regularly
throughout her three years of training. The
observations and records of the students provide a
useful feedback for the trainers and programme
organisers.

Manila
Metropolitan Manila is organised in small
community units of about 100 families each called
barangays, with one primary health care unit for
about every six barangays. Regular dialogue between
the health personnel at the PHCU and the barangay
residents was encouraged in order to foster community
involvement and participation. Four key health
programmes were implemented at the PHCU: (a) maternal
care and family planning; (b) child care and
nutrition; (c) control and treatment of infectious
diseases; (d) environmental sanitation.
Health education and information campaigns have
encouraged people to utilise their local health
services. At the same time hospitals were encouraged
to link up with their catchment area through
appropriate service departments and through
reorganised staff training. Such developments are
likely elsewhere in the Philippines and will create
new roles and responsibilities for hospitals. Besides
their traditional role of providing patient care and
training health personnel, hospitals will need to
emphasise research in epidemiologic and social
aspects of disease patterns and health care in their
neighbourhood. Such research is helping to change
training programmes. Improved management of health
services, especially in the barangays, is helping to
prevent the by-passing of local facilities.[19]

Hyderabad, India[20]

In the slums of old Hyderabad about 60,000 people live in circumstances of near destitution, another 225,000 live a marginal existence and the remainder belong to the low middle class. Seventy per cent of the families have lived in the city since birth. Of these, 42 per cent have always been living in the same locality. Sixty-two per cent of the women are illiterate and up to 44 per cent of the families have more than eight members. Thirty-three per cent of the families are without basic services like water, latrines, drainage and washing facilities.

The main thrust of the Hyderabad Slum Project is towards social and environmental improvement together with economic development. The objective is to provide for people's immediate needs and to work towards long term changes through people participation. The main activities generated by the development project are:

1. environmental sanitation: provision of water and other physical improvements, e.g. repair of roads, street lighting, etc.;
2. family health activities like (a) immunisation (b) first aid and family health education (c) cookery classes to obtain the best buy in nutrition (d) health surveillance of mothers and children (e) eye care (f) family planning;
3. feeding programme;
4. recreational and cultural activities and youth clubs;
5. educational activities such as (a) play groups and primary schools (b) night schools (c) vocational training in sewing classes, typing and shorthand classes, training in photography, radio repairs, car repairs, air conditioner and refrigerator servicing and so on (d) study tours (e) cultural activities like community festivals, variety shows, libraries and reading rooms, etc.;
6. income-generating activities like dressmaking and other co-operatives, facilities for bank loans, etc.;
7. construction of community halls and housing improvement.

The Hyderabad Slum Project has demonstrated the importance of certain basic linkages in the upliftment of squatter communities:

(i) the integration of health with the improvement of the physical environment through adequate water

supply, drainage, paved lanes, garbage and waste
disposal and improved housing;
(ii) linking slum communities with aid agencies
and non-governmental organisations by forming local
developmental committees, youth clubs, women's
organisations and other social groups;
(iii) linking income generating and other business
activities in the slums with financial, commercial
and industrial institutions in the formal urban
sector.

Mexico City
The new town of Netzahualcoyoti houses between 1.8
and 2 million people. It grew up on the site of an
old salt lake and the land is largely unsuitable for
agriculture. Lack of a proper system of garbage
collection together with the common practice of open
air defaecation causes large scale pollution,
especially during seasonal dust storms. Approximately
30 per cent of adult men are unemployed; being a
dormitory area, there is very little local
employment. For the same reason during the daytime
the inhabitants are mainly women and childrer
   In 1974 the only health facilities in the area
were a 259-bedded hospital and one health centre.
Since then seven more health centres have been
constructed. In the early stages the doctors working
in the health centres were mainly hospital residents
from medical specialities and lacked the skills and
approaches for delivering primary care. However, a
one-year programme of in-service training now has the
doctors working in the mornings and attending classes
in the afternoons. Each health centre has a
geographical catchment area of between 100,000 and
400,000 people. Since 1979 smaller catchment areas of
about 3,000 people (micro units) have also been
defined. For each micro unit a community health
worker - prodiap - has been trained.
   In 1980 the national programme for marginal
populations in large cities was launched, and in
Netzahualcoyoti 13 sub-centres were constructed. Each
sub-centre is responsible for ten micro regions
(30,000). The sub-centre has one physician, one
nursing assistant and a number of prodiaps.
   The provision of health care to the marginal
population is thus conceptually organised into three
levels of care:

(a) The first level of health care comprises three basic activities at the level of the micro unit: self-care in the home, health surveillance of mothers and children, first aid and primary care. It is felt that 85 per cent of health problems can be dealt with at this level, for which 70 per cent of the budget is earmarked. Community leaders, teachers, priests, together with the prodiaps, are the main sources of this level of health care and advice.

(b) The second level of care is provided by specialists at the health centre who deal with referred medical and surgical problems. Twelve per cent of health problems may require this type of care.

(c) The third level of care is provided in hospitals. Approximately three per cent of health problems need this type of intensive health care.

The seven cities study of basic care for urban populations in South America[21]

In recent years several city authorities in South America have initiated programmes of basic health care for disadvantaged groups. Projects have been funded by the United Nations Children's Fund or by similar funding agencies. Most programmes operate through the local municipal departments although one or two are part of the university departments of community health and serve as field practice areas for medical and other students.

Though each project has tended to develop its own programme, a number of common approaches can be identified as follows:

(a) The integrated approach with a varying mix of health and non-health activities is preferred. Environmental improvements, provision of water and sanitation, literacy especially for women, stimulation and adequate nutrition for the growing child, income-generating activities together with preventive and curative health services form the core of the activities generated by the projects.

(b) Community organisation and involvement in the planning and implementation of programmes is one of the main objectives of all the projects. This objective has been achieved with varying degrees of success in different projects, largely on account of resistance from the local power groups, the skills of the local workers in creating community awareness and in bringing about organisation, as well as the

ability of the community to participate wholeheartedly in the activities being promoted.
(c) All the projects lean heavily on auxiliaries and local promoters as the front-line workers.
(d) Several projects have rightly selected the home as the main focus of the preventive and promotional work carried out through regular home visits by the health promoters.
(e) A supportive network of health posts, subcentres and base hospitals has been built to provide the necessary backup for the work being carried out in the home and the community.
(f) A system of identifying individuals and families at risk'has been initiated so as to provide more concentrated care where needed.

The experience of these projects tends to emphasise the urgent need to link up the urban poor communities with the health sector on the one hand and the commercial and industrial sector on the other. For both of these objectives to be achieved, the need for community organisation and the formation of local caretaker committees is paramount. Such committees and groups help in creating awareness through local dialogue and generate a concensus amongst the beneficiaries and the providers of care to give direction to the programme.

Concepts into practice - measuring the impact

These case studies are examples of the variety of approaches being developed in different countries under differing socio-economic circumstances and political climates. Unlike models of integrated health care for rural areas,[22] no well demarcated approaches have emerged. The trend is perhaps towards linking hospital services with community health action (e.g. Hong Kong, Manila and Mexico). Only a few cities (e.g. Hyderabad) have developed an integrated approach where environmental improvement, education and income-generation are combined with a health component. These case studies, however, indicate a major positive shift in the thinking of urban planners and health officials. Instead of considering squatters as eyesores calling for removal, or at best as a transitional phenomenon, they are being treated as victims and sufferers from a major social problem. Their contribution to the city's economic and commercial activity is being recognised and their welfare and full inclusion into the city's social and commercial life is receiving attention.

How do these slowly emerging health programmes in squatter areas affect the health of the population? How important indeed are health services to the people's health? These questions are being increasingly asked in all countries, developed and developing alike. Since many health activities in the developing world are modelled on the health experiences of the previous European world powers, it is helpful to consider mortality trends in the latter. The United Kingdom National Health Service (NHS) has been a major academic attraction and a desirable social goal for both commonwealth and non-commonwealth countries. And yet the NHS has failed to reduce mortality and ill-health amongst the lower social classes to the same extent as in the upper classes (table 5).

The data in table 5 indicate the difficulty in providing health care to the working class groups who largely occupy inner city areas. It has been estimated that if the mortality rates of occupational class I had applied to classes IV and V in the United Kingdom during 1970-72, 74,000 lives of people aged under 75 would not have been lost. This calculation includes nearly 10,000 children and 32,000 men aged 15 to 64.[23] Thus, despite more than 30 years of a National Health Service committed to offering equal care for all, there continues to remain a marked gradient in standards of health between the social classes. The growth of social policies since 1870 has no doubt helped to ameliorate some of the worst effects of poverty. The urban poor in London and Glasgow, as also in other cities, suffer less overcrowding; they have adequate clothes; better and adequate food and enjoy better opportunities for the education of their children. But the disparities between the social classes remain and are evident in their most brutal form in the health and mortality experience of the working class.

Several studies in the United Kingdom have indicated the relatively poor primary care in London, Glasgow and other industrial towns.[24] Social problems like poor housing, large numbers of elderly persons living alone, high population mobility, ethnic minorities, single-parent families, children in care, unemployment, psychiatric problems and so on are more prevalent in inner cities. The variation,

Table 5: Neo-natal mortality rates per 1,000 legitimate live births by father's social class, England and Wales, 1911-1970/72

Father's social class	1911[a]	1921[a]	1930-32[a]	1939[a]	1949-50[a]	1970-72[b]	Per cent decrease from 1911
			Neo-natal deaths				
I Professionals	26.8	23.4	21.7	18.9	13.5	17.4	35.1
II Intermediate	34.8	28.3	27.3	23.4	16.0	19.8	43.1
III Skilled workers		33.7	29.4	25.4	17.8	21.2	46.5
IV Partly skilled workers	39.6	36.7	31.9	27.7	19.9	25.7	35.1
V Unskilled workers	42.5	36.9	32.5	30.1	21.9	35.17	17.25
Per cent excess V/I	58.6	57.7	49.8	59.3	62.2	101	

Source: (a) J.N. Morris and J.A. Hendy: The Lancet (London, 1955), p. 554; (b) Office of Population Censuses and Surveys: Occupational mortality, The Registrar General's Decennial Supplement for England and Wales, 1970-72 (Her Majesty's Stationery Office, London, 1978), P. 157.

for example, between the best areas in outer London to the worst in inner London could be five times or more. Inevitably the areas with the worst problems in inner London have the least suitable primary care services available to them.

The above discussion illustrates the difficulty of overcoming the effect of inadequate material resources and low income through conventional health services aided by social security, however desirable the two are. Part of the difficulty lies in the organisation of health systems and medical education. In spite of increasing historical evidence on the impact of the environment on health, the mechanistic view has prevailed of likening the human body to a machine and disease to malfunctioning which can be corrected by therapeutics or surgery. In this view the "fault" for a disease lies with the individual and, by implication, the socio-political and economic environment is absolved from responsibility. Once the cause of problems of ill-health is perceived as lying with the individual then the nature of intervention will be individually oriented, e.g., health education or curative and diagnostic medicine. Consequently the main thrust of professional bodies and government policies is usually to encourage those health programmes aimed at changes in the individual rather than changes in the economic or political environment. Failure to control the promotion of cigarettes, baby foods or alcoholic drink is a prime example of such an attitude.

All the signs indicate that the developing countries are moving in the same direction and are likely to develop patterns of health care which bring in little value for money. This can be avoided if community participation is itself the main objective of health planning. There will understandably be many obstacles to overcome. There is the deep-rooted conviction that the élite specialist knows best. The urban poor are themselves often not interested because of their alienation and exclusion from the mainstream of urban life. National planners resist the idea of such participation because they fear countless delays, arguments, even at times confrontation and subversion. Nations with socialist ideologies and governmental processes have found it easier to involve communities in planning their own health programmes, e.g. the United Republic of Tanzania, Ethiopia, Cuba and China. Those with political ideologies to the extreme right have largely opted for token participation. Thus, depending on the political ideology and the maturity of the democratic processes in the nation concerned, the following modes of people participation can be identified.[25]

1. A "solid citizen" group appointed from amongst the squatters by outside authorities.
2. Appointed local leaders in the government bureaucracy.

(These two modes make use of the community development approach. Social workers organise community councils to channel the flow of services and materials from the larger society into the squatter community. Income generation activities, the creation of credit facilities and training programmes are planned as part of self-help. People are only minimally involved in decision-making. Instead, programmes planned by outside agencies are legitimised and implemented by local appointed leaders.)

3. Planners come to consult and discuss programmes with the people before implementation.
4. Planners consult with people from the beginning of plan formulation.

(In these modes people get a share in decision-making at the stage at which plans are discussed with them. Depending upon the incorporation of people's views into the final plans, the participation may vary from token to full. However, planners still control the process.)

5. People have representatives, varying from one or two to a clear majority, on the planning board.

(This is true grass-root planning with significant participation by the people and a major share in decision-making.)

Conclusion

The above description of hyper-urbanisation considers the importance of health as part of the main issue of providing basic needs for squatter settlements. The experience of some of the major industrial cities of the developed world provides useful leads to explore. Environmental improvement is considered far more rewarding than the provision of conventional curative services. Within such a framework improvement of nutrition and control of infection are stressed as the main objectives, especially for vulnerable groups like pregnant and lactating women and for children. The organisation of health facilities and other resources is considered through a number of case studies of urban connurbations of the developing world. The importance of community participation in the improvement of their environment is stressed. An integrated approach is finally described where income generation activities, training and education programmes, welfare and social services together with community organisation help to strengthen the impact of health services and make health care more meaningful.

Notes

1. K. Davis: Introduction in: Cities, their origin, growth and human impact: Readings from the Scientific American (San Francisco, W.H. Freeman and Co., 1973).

2. J.P. Grant: World Health Forum, Vol. 2, No. 3, 1981, pp. 373-384.

3. S. Basta: "Nutrition and health in low income urban areas of the Third World", in Ecology of Food and Nutrition, Vol. 6, 1977, pp. 115.

4. Department of International Economic and Social Affairs: Patterns of urban and rural population growth, Population Studies No. 68 (New York, United Nations, 1980).

5. M.Y Mores: Situacion socio-economica y nutricional de las familias de ingresos minimos en Lima Metropolitana (Lima, Grados, 1980).

6. G.J. Ebrahim: "Primary care and the urban poor", in Journal of Tropical Paediatrics (London) 1983 (in press).

7. A.R. Desai and S.D. Pillai: A profile of an Indian slum (Bombay, Bombay University Press, 1972).

8. M. Gracey, D.E. Stone, Sutoto and Sutejo: "Environmental pollution and diarrhoeal disease in Jakarta, Indonesia", in Journal of Tropical Paediatrics (London) Vol. 22, 1976, pp. 18-23.

9. A.M. Singh: "Women and the family: coping with poverty in the Bastis of Delhi", in A. D'Souza (ed.): The Indian city: Poverty, ecology and urban development (New Delhi, Manohar, 1978); and Sidney M. Canter Associates: The Tamil Nadu nutrition study, Vol. 1 (Haverford, 1973).

10. Ibid.

11. E.F.P. Jelliffe: "The impact of the food industry on the nutritional status of infants and pre-school children in developing countries", in Priorities in child nutrition in developing countries, Vol. II (Harvard, Harvard University School of Public Health, 1975), p. 265.

12. A. Berg: "Industry's struggle with world malnutrition", in Harvard Business Review, Vol. 50, 1972, pp. 135.

13. M. Muller: The baby killer (London, War on Want, 1975), and A. Chetley: The baby killer scandal (London, War on Want, 1979).

14. M. Schweiger and W.A.M. Cutting: "Barley water babies - a commerciogenic condition", in Journal of Tropical Paediatrics (London) Vol. 24, 1978, pp. 89-91.

15. F.M. Lappa and J. Collins: Food first (Boston, Houghton Mifflin Co., 1977), p. 307.

16. J. Dobbing: "The later development of the brain and its vulnerability", in J.A. Davis and J. Dobbing (eds.): Scientific foundations of paediatrics, 2nd ed. (London, Wm. Heinemann Medical Books Ltd., 1981), p. 744.

17. P. Tacon: My child minus one (United Nations Children's Fund, 1981) (mimeo).

18. E.H. Paterson: "An urban community health project", in British Medical Journal (London) Vol. I, 1980, pp. 29-31.

19. G.G. Carreon: "The role of the hospital in promoting and providing primary health care", in World Hospitals (London) Vol. 17, 1981, pp. 9-12.

20. W.J. Cousins: "Urban community development in Hyderabad", in A. de Souza (ed.), op. cit.

21. United Nations Children's Fund: Urban examples for basic services development in cities (New York, Mar. 1983).

22. P.H. Coombs (ed.): Meeting the basic needs of the rural poor (New York and Oxford, Pergamon Press, 1980).

23. P. Townsend and N. Davidson: Inequalities in health (Harmondsworth, Middlesex, Penguin Books, 1982).

24. London Health Planning Consortium: Primary health care in inner London, Report of a Study Group (May 1981) (mimeo).

25. M.R. Hollnsteiner: "People power: community participation in the planning of human settlements", in Assignment Children (UNICEF, Paris) Vol. 40, 1977, pp. 11-47.

6 WATER SUPPLY ISSUES

by J. Kirke and J. Arthur

Introduction

Water and the air we breathe are the two most fundamental needs of mankind. A regular supply of potable water is essential for survival, and quantities in excess of the minimum amount to support life bestow a variety of health benefits and improvements to living standards.

This chapter reviews the means which many if not most major cities in developing countries use to provide water to their citizens. By and large these means, large-scale water supply and distribution systems, are profoundly inappropriate to the task at hand and increasingly benefit established areas of permanent and middle-class housing. Water authorities seek to meet financial targets and consider customers not needs.

Assessing need

The United Nations designated the 1980s the International Drinking Water Supply and Sanitation Decade, ostensibly with the objective of providing clean drinking water and sanitation facilities for everyone by the year 1990. Whether or not this goal is achieved in full, the decade offers the possibility of a considerable improvement in the quality of life. The provision of reliable, safe and convenient sources of potable water will not only reduce mortality and morbidity but will also release those now engaged in collecting water for more useful tasks. The greatest concern must naturally be with the rapidly expanding urban areas of developing countries.[1] Within these cities the poor suffer most from inadequate water supply as they have neither the means to provide facilities themselves nor the information to minimise the effects of their insanitary conditions.[2] This chapter therefore

123

addresses itself primarily to urban water supply issues, particularly as they affect the urban poor.

Where the existing supply is poor, improvements in water supply should offer some benefit to health, depending on the types of disease prevalent in the area. The major infectious diseases whose incidence can be reduced by water supply improvements are as follows:[3]

(a) water-borne diseases: infectious diseases spread through water supply systems, often via the faecal-oral route;

(b) water-washed diseases: diseases caused by a lack of personal hygiene, also often faecal-oral;

(c) water-based diseases: diseases transmitted through an aquatic inverterbrate animal;

(d) water-related diseases: diseases spread by insects that depend on water.

The first two are particularly affected by improvements in water supply and there are often conflicts between the requirements for water quality (affecting water-borne disease) and water quantity (affecting water-washed disease). Any choice between improved quality and increased quantity should be based on the greater prevalence of water-borne or water-washed diseases.

To reap the full benefits of investments in the improvement of water supply these should be linked to improvements in associated engineering infrastructure, such as drainage, solid waste disposal, and, particularly, sanitation and wastewater disposal. Where sanitation methods reflect low water usage (e.g. the use of pit latrines without water seals) the availability of significantly increased quantities of water (from a domestic water connection or even from an adjacent public standpipe) may cause problems. Methods of removing wastewater from the home and the implications of increased water usage for excreta disposal must be considered concurrently with any proposals for new or better water supply. In the Philippines cities of Iloilo and Bacolod (see below) many individual household water connections have been made in areas of high density middle to low income housing without any corresponding provision or improvement of drainage or excreta disposal facilities. Consequently, these flat and low-lying areas suffer from polluted surface water and sullage, with inadequate and blocked open-earth drains and permanently flooded pit latrines. At best this is a nuisance, at worst an immediate hazard to health and hygiene.

The provision of water for new and expanding urban areas has generally led to the construction and operation of centralised extraction, treatment and distribution systems. However, it may sometimes be better to consider a number of smaller sources, such as local deep wells, either with or without associated distribution systems.

Standards for water supply are usually fixed in both quantitative and qualitative terms. Although widely used these standards vary considerably. The most widely used qualitative standards are those of the World Health Organisation,[4] based on a variety of chemical, physical and biological indicators. Although these standards should generally be met for piped drinking water, some specific requirements (e.g. a minimum level 1 E. Coli per 100 ml) may be far too strict for universal application. Some other standards have no bearing on health and may be relaxed. Decisions whether a raw water source requires some form of treatment must reflect the water needs of the community. In general, water should not contain chemical or biological matter which could affect its safety or acceptability to the end users or which might tend to cause technical problems such as pipe encrustation.

The quantity of water required will depend on location, culture, socio-economic status and local political aspirations. Usually all this will be dictated by the consumers' ability to pay for the supply proposed. If water has to be carried long distances, or purchased from itinerant water-vendors, consumption may fall to about 5 litres per capita per day (lcd), the minimum necessary to sustain life.[5] Levels of consumption will increase when water is drawn from shallow wells (5-30 lcd), from public standpipes or neighbours (10-50 lcd), from a single on-plot tap (20-150 lcd) or from multiple household taps (30-300 lcd).[6] Under most circumstances 30-40 lcd is enough for a reasonable level of personal and community health. Where water is scarce and expensive, or where urban supply is geared towards low income families, and thus single tap households, consumption is seldom less than 60 lcd or more than 100 lcd.

It is not possible to specify either widely applicable minimum standards for quantity and quality or maximum levels of service above which no health benefits can be identified or proved which would justify further improvements in supply. However, neither personal hygiene nor public health requires water for domestic consumption to exceed 100 litres per capita per day.[7] At this level the full health benefits of a reliable water supply can be enjoyed and a water-borne sewerage system can be operated, if feasible and affordable. Domestic consumption above this level probably contributes little to further health or to a better environment and would only be utilised by middle-and upper-income families.

Despite all this higher design figures are often assumed, and in the four specific examples considered below, current and proposed average total production and domestic consumption are as in table 6.

Levels of urban per capita water consumption vary greatly throughout the world both in developed and developing countries. Average consumption figures for a number of cities in the United Kingdom are as in table 7.

Water consumption in urban areas of some developing countries is given in table 8.

A number of factors help in assessing the likely future demand for drinking water. Firstly, it will seldom be economically feasible to provide sufficient water to satisfy more privileged urban dwellers and the primary objective should be to meet the basic water needs of the whole community. Secondly, in a poor society where drinking water has traditionally been scarce and valuable, increases in consumption are likely to be gradual. Provided new supplies are realistically priced unlimited and indiscriminate use is very unlikely and consumption levels will remain reasonably low. Thirdly, a household's capacity to consume water is limited by its plot size and "wet area" (i.e. kitchen and toilet space). The latter is often less than 3 square metres per family and in such households consumption simply cannot exceed 100 lcd. For a family of five to consume over 150 lcd it would need quite large shower and kitchen space and modern, cistern flush toilets.

Supply systems

Centralised supply systems are common in almost all urban areas. Water is extracted from either surface water sources (rivers, lakes, reservoirs and springs) or underground sources (wells and infiltration galleries). Extracted water is usually

Table 6: Current and proposed water production for four cities in developing countries

City	Design year[1]	Pop.('000) Forecast	Pop.('000) Actual	Total water production (lcd) Actual	Proposed	Water production for domestic consumption only Actual	Proposed
Cairo	1976		6 724	307		179	
	2000	16 000			517		383
Manila	1979		5 800	228		137	
	1987	9 185			357		194
Iloilo	1980		244	120		100	
	2000	400			216		160
Bacolod	1980		266	166		130	
	1990		360	180		140	

Source: Internal reports.

Table 7: Water production in selected cities of the United Kingdom

City	Year	Pop. ('000)	Total water production (lcd)	Water production for domestic consumption only (lcd)
London	1979	5 540	346	286
Manchester	1979	1 500	337	217
Birmingham	1979	1 197	269	–
Bristol	1979	982	315	–
Edinburgh	1979	755	343	–
Southampton	1979	564	326	245

Source: Water authorities of the above areas.

treated, although high quality underground sources may need no treatment, and distributed to the main parts of the city by a primary network of underground pipes and to sub-areas and groups of houses by secondary and tertiary mains. The pipe network is designed to distribute water to the service areas in sufficient quantity and with sufficient pressure to provide an adequate service to the consumer, while maintaining sufficient system pressure for water from hydrants to be used for fire fighting. The distribution system itself is like a tree; the primary distribution network is the trunk and main branches, the smaller branches the secondary distribution pipes and the smallest branches the tertiary system. Operational advantages and additional flexibility may sometimes be provided by a closed loop of primary distribution pipe or a "ring main" with secondary and tertiary mains branching off. Pipe sizes also fall progressively from the largest diameter delivery main (from the treatment works to the city) down to the smallest tertiary mains, which may be only 25 millimetres in diameter.

Individual connections are made from the tertiary distribution mains to private consumers and to industrial, commercial, and municipal establishments.

Table 8: Water consumption in urban areas of various developing countries in 1970

Country	Urban consumption levels (lcd)	
	Household supply	Standpipe supply
The Gambia	60-220 lcd	50-150 lcd
Liberia	95-190 lcd	20- 40 lcd
Nigeria	45-230 lcd	45- 70 lcd
Kenya	20-200 lcd	10- 15 lcd
Zaire	30-250 lcd	10- 30 lcd
Jamaica	320-390 lcd	45- 70 lcd
Peru	90-400 lcd	25- 30 lcd
Egypt	100-260 lcd	30- 40 lcd
Yemen	50- 80 lcd	30- 50 lcd
Pakistan	70-180 lcd	20- 60 lcd
India	50-270 lcd	25-100 lcd
Bangladesh	45- 70 lcd	15- 25 lcd
Sri Lanka	170-220 lcd	30- 50 lcd
Indonesia	50-150 lcd	5- 20 lcd
The Philippines	110-540 lcd	30- 60 lcd

Source: World Health Organisation: World health statistics report, Vol. 26. No. 11, (Geneva, 1973)

Frequently private consumers are served by water connections to their individual housing units, although in poorer areas of cities in developing countries public standpipes often serve groups of buildings. Although metering water connections is by no means universal, supplies in developing countries are frequently metered. This may be either by individual meters or by "block metering", i.e. one meter for a complete housing block. Non-metered supplies may be charged at a fixed rate against an assumed consumption, or, as with many public standpipes, may not be charged at all.

In many cities in developing countries water supply systems were originally installed to serve only those parts of the city thought to have the greatest need for safe and reliable water; frequently this was the commercial centre and higher income housing areas. Furthermore, additional investment has often provided greater quantities of water to existing consumers once the original system had become inadequate. Rather less frequently is the distribution system extended or are overloaded or worn out sections replaced.

Not all the water extracted is usefully used by the consumer and losses occur throughout the system. A distinction should be drawn between "system losses", in extraction and distribution, and water wastage, which generally occurs after the water reaches the consumer. Some losses are inevitable such as leakage from pipes and the use of water for flushing the system. These losses can be minimised by checking pipes regularly and operating the system efficiently. Additional losses may come from illegal use and, although such water may reach people with genuine needs, it nonetheless represents a loss of revenue to the water administration. Water wastage is water delivered but lost without real benefit to the consumer, e.g. leaking household fitments or taps left running.

The development of urban water systems is illustrated in the following city examples. These cities currently have water supply improvement projects, and the proposals involved will be discussed below. These case studies are based on work by the authors and cover Cairo and Manila together with two Philippine regional cities, Iloilo and Bacolod in the Western Visayas. The population of the cities in 1980 was 9 million, 6.5 million, 250,000 and 270,000 respectively. The descriptions of the existing water systems, the statistics presented and the details of water supply projects presently proposed or under construction were obtained from the published reports of the consultants involved and from available official publications. [8]

Cairo, Egypt

Water in Cairo is provided by the General Organisation for Greater Cairo Water Supply (GOGCWS) which covers most of Greater Cairo with a population of over 9 million in 1980. GOGCWS is under the jurisdiction of the Ministry of Housing for financial and technical matters and under the Ministry of Local Government for administrative matters. It has

responsibility for the operation and maintenance of
potable and non-potable water supplies for Cairo,
Giza, Shoubra El Kheima and Helwan and provides bulk
water supplies, but not distribution, to Nozha and
Heliopolis.
Water is obtained from ten wellfields and 11
infiltration galleries, most of which are operated at
over 50 per cent above design capacity. Table 9 shows
existing and committed water production for Greater
Cairo and current and estimated future population
within the service area.[9] Cairo however, suffers
from an apparent water shortage with low mains
pressure leaving many consumers without water for
much of the time, and making extensions to the system
pointless. Nonetheless in 1980 the population of
Greater Cairo received the equivalent of 285 lcd. If
the population living in villages beyond the
currently planned distribution system (using shallow
wells) is excluded, then 310 lcd was provided for the
8.3 million people within the service area.
Furthermore some 2.5 million people living within the
service area have only very limited access to potable
water and consume less than 40 lcd. Since
distribution losses vary between only 6 per cent and
10 per cent, Cairo's apparent acute water shortage
must be due to wastage, particularly by those with
service connections.
Government decentralisation policies may well lead
to the total population of Greater Cairo dependent on
existing water sources in the year 2000 being only
14.9 million. Per capita production would then be 300
lcd even without any new investment. This compares
very favourably with many European cities and is
considerably above the long-term target for most
major cities in developing countries. Even if the
population in the year 2000 were 16.2 million, per
capita production would still be 275 lcd.

Manila, Philippines
Water in the Metropolitan Manila Area (MMA) is
provided by the Metropolitan Waterworks and Sewerage
System (MWSS). Its coverage comprises the cities of
Manila, Quezon, Pasay and Caloocan. The service area
includes 21 of the 22 municipalities of the MMA, and
11 contiguous municipalities currently outside the
MMA.
Water for MWSS is obtained mainly from reservoirs
on the Angat river providing a total of about 1,320

Table 9: Population, water production and per capita
consumption for the GOGCWS service area

Year	Population ('000s)[1]	Water production (existing and committed, million litres per day)	Per capita production, (lcd)
1976	8 000	–	–
1980	9 040	2 557	285
1985	10 622	3 997	375
1990	12 354	4 497	365
2000	16 249	4 497	275
2000	14 900[2]	4 497	300[2]

[1] Forecast by American British Consultants (AMBRIC).
[2] If decentralisation is effective.
Source: Internal reports.

million litres per day (mld) which is brought by
tunnel for treatment in Quezon City. In 1977 1,323
mld were available for an estimated population within
the service area of 5.8 million, a per capita supply
of 228 lcd. However, a consultant's report in
1977[10] estimated total losses (water unaccounted
for) of 48 per cent. It also found an average of 8.2
persons served per domestic connection with, on
average, an additional three neighbours buying water
from the owner. The complete service area counted
245,000 domestic connections and 630 standpipes and
each standpipe was estimated to serve an average of
600 people. The total number of domestic consumers
directly served by the MWSS was:

Household installations	2 090 000
Borrowed from household installations	735 000
Water from standpipes	378 000
	3 203 000

In 1977 those borrowing from neighbours consumed 40
lcd (26.9 mld in total) and those using standpipes 35

lcd (13.2 mld in total) including an allowance for
wastage at the standpipe. Those directly served by
connections were therefore consuming some 883.5 mld
(including industrial, commercial and municipal use,
419.9 mld but excluding leakage and theft of 397
mld). Thus 463.6 mld were supplied to domestic
consumers with household water supply, a per capita
consumption of 222 lcd. The muncipal, commercial and
institutional use of 40 per cent of useful water is
very high, suggesting considerable wastage at places
of work.

An analysis of the service records of 400 metered
domestic connections between 1967 and 1975 showed
that with adequate pressure the following assumptions
for domestic water consumption were valid:

Table 10: Domestic water consumption

Annual income level (pesos)[1]	Consumption (lcd)	Consumers per connection
Upper income over 60 000	525	6.6
Middle income 6 000-60 000	235	7.4
Lower income less than 6 000	130	9.0
Weighted average	195	8.2

[1] One US dollar = 7.5 pesos (1978).
Source: Internal reports.

Since ideal conditions of pressure and service
periods do not apply at present, the consultants
estimated an average consumption of 180 lcd for
household connections.[11]

Iloilo, Philippines
    Water in Iloilo is administered by the Metro
Iloilo Water District (MIWD) formed in 1978. The
system pre-dates the formation of the water district
and was previously operated by a private water
company. MIWD is a semi-autonomous body responsible
for the maintenance and operation of the system,
fixing tariffs and billing consumers, although
decisions relating to major system developments are
made by LWUA (the Local Water Utilities
Administration).

The MIWD service area covers Iloilo City
(population 250,000) and the adjacent townships of
Maasin, Cabatuan, Sta. Barbara and Pavia (total
population 10,000). However, the existing service
area excludes large residential areas of the city
which were either recently developed or were ignored
when the system was installed. Water is obtained from
a reservoir (dam constructed 1928) and two
infiltration galleries (constructed in 1962 and
1969). Attempts to develop other sources have failed;
three deep wells constructed within the city were
abandoned within five years due to salinity and
inadequate flow. Water production in 1980 was 18.6
mld of which 10 per cent was used in upstream towns
leaving 16.7 mld for the city. There are
approximately 6,600 service connections within the
city including commercial and industrial connections,
200 to 250 public standpipes and 94 fire hydrants.
Demand exceeds supply to such an extent that system
pressure in the city centre is practically zero
during the day. Of the 94 hydrants only three will
provide water and those public standpipes which work
only do so at night.

The MIWD water supply is supplemented by private
supplies from infiltration galleries, shallow and
deep wells, springs and rainwater. Excluding these
the useful water per capita for the 140,000 persons
within the service area (including industrial and
commercial usage but excluding distribution losses)
was 71 lcd in 1980, or 41 lcd for the whole city.
This figure shows an absolute deficiency since many
people living outside the service area rely on the
MIWD for their drinking water collected either from
standpipes or from private connections inside the
service area, or from vendors. [12]

Large numbers of shallow open wells are used
throughout the city but these are generally brackish
and/or polluted and are not used for drinking water.
Some deep driven wells provide drinking water for a
short time but saline intrusion eventually renders
this water unsuitable. Spring water from the
neighbouring island of Guimaras is brought to the
city by barge and sold to vendors who in turn sell it
on to the consumer. Such water is costly, the
quantities available are relatively small and are
even now almost fully utilised. Bacteriological tests
have indicated contamination in all sources of Iloilo
water, primarily because of the unreliable chlorine
dosing equipment used to treat the raw water.

Bacolod, Philippines

Water in Bacolod City is administered by the Bacolod City Water District (BCWD) which took over from a private company in 1970. The BCWD is a semi-autonomous body responsible for the maintenance and operation of the system, fixing tariffs, and billing consumers, although major system developments are again evaluated by the Local Water Utilities Administration (LWUA).

The service area of BCWD is restricted to the city centre and some wealthier suburbs. The recently completed first phase of a three phase supply project should serve the city up to 1984, but in fact will have to be sufficient for much longer. Water is obtained from springs and deep wells and production has been increased from 20.6 mld to 47.3 mld for the 1980 population of 270,000.

Although this represents a total of 177 lcd, only 25 per cent of the total population is directly served. Those with neither access to a public standpipe nor their own domestic connection obtain water from neighbours, vendors, rain, or one of the 400 to 500 hand-pumped wells. Many of these wells have been closed in recent years because of pollution and they are seldom used for drinking water.

In 1981 production averaged 21.6 mld with leakage estimated at 18 per cent, giving a consumption per capita for those served by domestic connections of 270 lcd (320 lcd including leakage) or 66 lcd (80 lcd) for the whole city. There are few domestic connections (8,800) and many people are probably buying water from neighbours. No figures are available for wastage, and leakage may be greater than it appears as large quantities are apparently being lost[13] since the new investment because of ruptured pipes and blown seals. This is almost certainly due to the failure of pipes and seals under the now vastly increased system pressure. Delivery still relies on the same distribution system and the same household plumbing installed when pressure was much lower.

All these systems show similar features, of which the most important are:

(a) supply is restricted to higher income areas and generally excludes low income housing;

(b) a high proportion of the water extracted (and also of potential revenue) is wasted or lost through leakage or illegal use;

(c) with the exception of Bacolod, where a new supply scheme was implemented recently, the system frequently suffers from very low pressures in the distribution mains.

An apparent chronic and severe water shortage may be due to a real deficiency in supply, as in Iloilo, or excessive wastage, as in Cairo.

The inequality involved in providing mains water only to higher and middle-income areas is typified in Cairo. In 1980 about 4.1 million people were living in buildings without direct access to drinking water.[14] Thus about 45 per cent of the population of Greater Cairo were consuming less than 60 lcd which, after allowing for industrial use, means an average consumption of over 500 lcd by the remaining 55 per cent with private connections. In Manila 2 million people were without access to safe water in 1978 and in Iloilo and Bacolod less than 50 per cent of the population were served either by house connections or by standpipes in 1981.

Water tariffs

Wastage can be significantly reduced, if not eliminated, by appropriate and sensible tariff structures. A differential charging system which provides reasonably cheap water for essential domestic use (say up to 100 lcd) but which escalates rapidly where consumption is over this figure will discourage wastage. Flat-rate tariffs, or charges where the unit cost decreases with increasing consumption, can only result in higher demand, encourage unnecessary consumption and increase wastage. Reduced wastage by middle-class consumers should free greater supply for standpipes serving the poor. Hovever, there is a constant risk of wastage from standpipes where water is provided free. Where the poor live in totally unserved areas and rely on private vendors and wells they are naturally not affected by the level and structure of water tariffs. However, an efficient tariff structure is essential if the water agency is to use its own resources properly and to be able to extend its network.

In Cairo tariffs were not increased during the 10-year period up to 1979. It was estimated in that town that if only half of the existing wastage was eliminated savings of US$200 million (at 1977 prices) in capital investment up to the year 2000 could

result.   More   importantly,   the   essential
redistribution of available water to those in real
need could follow.

Water   tariffs   also   govern   the   financial
performance of the water utility and dictate the rate
at which reinvestment in, and hence improvement and
expansion of, the system can proceed. Tariffs can be
designed to satisfy the water needs of the urban poor
at a cost they can afford while discouraging wastage
and excess.   However, tariffs which the urban poor
may pay, e.g. for standpipe water, should not be so
high that consumers would turn or return to the use
of unhygienic supplies.   Water resources are almost
invariably   such   that   higher   demand   can   only   be
satisfied   at   higher   production   costs.   There   is
seldom, if ever, a reason to deliberately stimulate
demand through low tariffs since the additional
revenue will never pay for the more expensive new
sources required. Furthermore there is no point in
using expensively treated drinking water to flush
toilets, wash cars and water plants. The price the
consumer   pays   for   water   will   largely   dictate
attitudes   towards   its   consumption   and   wastage.
Tariffs furthermore should reflect the increased cost
of drainage and sanitation necessary to dispose of
the waste water generated by improvements in water
supply.

The   tariff   structures   for   the   four   cities
discussed varied considerably. In Cairo in 1979 a
flat   rate   was   applied   to   domestic   consumption
although a progressive rate was under consideration.
Manila in 1977 had a flat rate for up to 30 cubic
metres per month for domestic consumers and a further
charge up to 50 cubic metres. It was proposed however
to differentiate these rates further. In Iloilo and
Bacolod progressive rates were in force rising fairly
sharply in the former but much less so in the latter.

An average low income family of five persons with
a single household tap (if fortunate enough to be
within   the   distribution   network)   is   unlikely   to
consume more than 100 lcd or around 15 m^3 per
month. It can be calculated, using estimates of
household income distribution in the various cities
that, for a household on the tenth percentile from
the bottom of the distribution, expenditure on 15
m^3 per month would amount to 0.5 per cent of
household income in Cairo, 1.8 per cent in Manila,
3.2 per cent in Iloilo and 5.0 per cent in Bacolod.

(These figures are naturally very approximate.)

Thus in Cairo, where water wastage is very high and where it has traditionally been cheaper for consumers to pay for metered and wasted water than for a plumber to repair defective faucets and toilets, water tariffs could be increased considerably without putting water beyond the reach of the poor. In Manila the MWSS doubled tariffs between 1974 and 1977 and has planned a total rise in average revenues per m^3 from 0.5 pesos in 1978 to 1.8 pesos in 1983. In Bacolod and Iloilo annual operating profits should follow tariff increases until such time as higher operating costs and loan repayments fail to match revenues. In both cities 1981 witnessed small operating losses following small profits in 1980. Both cities will increase tariffs in 1982.

Improvement projects

Each city has an improvement project either under consideration or in the course of implementation. Each one is receiving a loan from an international development bank or funding agency. In Cairo a large project is proposed, funded by a loan at easy interest rates. In Iloilo the project is split into three phases, the latter two conditional on the water utility's successfully meeting payments on the loan for the previous phase. Here each phase is relatively small and the interest rates relatively high. Brief descriptions of the major proposals for each city are as follows:

Cairo

The consultants proposed the following programmes approved in principle by the government:[15]

Phase I: (1978-1982), Immediate Phase
         US$ 98.1 million
                                    1978 prices
Phase II: (1982-2000)
          US$689.5 million

This covers extraction, treatment, storage and delivery to major distribution networks only; not tertiary networks or house connections. Furthermore, the Phase I was to be concurrent with projects already in progress (estimated at US$231.2 million) also directed at major extraction and treatment improvements and new pipelines. A further US$576.4 million was considered necessary for a renewal programme up to the year 2000. Total investment up to 2000 would then be US$1.6 thousand million at 1978 prices providing 517 lcd. Since this investment would exclude any improvements in the tertiary distribution system, a further US$1.6 thousand million would probably be required for that and for household connections both in existing unserved areas and in the new areas necessary to accommodate the additional 6 million inhabitants forecast up to the year 2000.

The Master Plan as approved is almost certainly too expensive and inappropriate and fails to address the urgent needs of the 45 per cent of Cairo's population who currently receive less than 10 per cent of the available treated water. None of the current proposals nor existing policies address the real needs of the urban poor in Greater Cairo, but benefit those who already have ample water and are connected to a piped sewerage system.

This is true also of the proposed wastewater disposal project; although it was sensible to prepare a wastewater plan virtually simultaneously with the water plan, proposals for up to 600 lcd by the year 2000 will need very large investments in wastewater disposal. A major centralised disposal system has been proposed with the construction of a 5.5 metre diameter tunnel under central Cairo. Almost incidentally, these same proposals recommend a 0.24 million Egyptian pound pilot sanitation project in the low income unsewered areas (2.5 million people) representing only 0.4 per cent of the total cost of the "Immediate Improvement" phase.

The combined water and sewerage projects would probably cost about US$2,000 per connection, to be recovered from each new household. If beneficiaries received 20-year loans at 12 per cent per annum repayments would amount to 26 per cent of the income of the tenth percentile of families, far more than they can afford.

Manila

A first stage project financed by the World Bank in 1964 only included source development and an improved primary distribution system. It had no provision for secondary or tertiary distribution or for domestic connections and public standpipes. Probably the pressure boosting which followed this

project without improving the secondary and tertiary
system, contributed to the high leakage losses which,
by 1977, reached about 30 per cent of production. In
1977 MWSS prepared a second stage project. Its major
aim was to improve the supply of safe water to the
population of Metro Manila and, in particular, to
extend supplies to the previously unserved urban
poor. It was a two-part project with a total
investment of US$692 million between 1978 and 1983,
eventually serving an additional 4 million people at
an average cost of US$173 per capita and improving
the service to the 3 million with existing
connections. The part to be implemented between 1978
and 1981 comprised source development and
rehabilitation to double average daily production to
about 2,500 mld, the installation of 65 kilometres of
primary and secondary pipelines mainly for slum
upgrading and sites and services areas, institutional
development and the replacement of 140,000 faulty
meters. The second part, 1981-83, comprised 670
kilometres of primary and secondary mains, the
construction of 50 deep wells and the installation of
520,000 domestic and 18,000 commercial water meters.
The MWSS is currently implementing this project in
parallel with a World Bank funded sewerage and
sanitation project. It is doubtful whether MWSS will
have completed all the work on time.

Between 1977 and 1982 it was proposed to increase
connections by 58,440 per year and to replace 140,000
faulty meters. Allowing for bad weather this would
require 370 new connections per day including the
replacement meters. This rate is unlikely to be
achieved. Between 1978 and 1983 an additional 2.65
million people would be provided with household
connections and by 1983 only 0.4 million (5 per cent)
would be served by public standpipes. This assumes
that between 1981 and 1983 at least 50,000 household
connections will be made in slum areas alone and that
the beneficiaries can afford them. No special
provision is made for the wastewater which would be
generated. It is also hoped to reduce the share of
water unaccounted for from 50 per cent in 1976 to 25
per cent by 1986. This includes reducing wastage in
domestic consumption to zero by 1985, although it is
unclear how this can be done. MWSS plans are
summarised in table 11.

Table 11: Proposals for water supply in Manila

	1975	1979	1982	1985	1987

Population within service area: ('000s)

5 258	6 408	7 551	8 423	9 185

Population (percentage) with good access
to mains supply: ('000s)

3 993	5 000	6 110	6 808	7 425
(76.0)	(78.0)	(81.0)	(81.0)	(81.0)

Population (percentage) with good access
actually served by household connections
or standpipes: ('000s)

2 795	4 250	5 866	6 808	7 425
(70.0)	(85.0)	(96.0)	(100.0)	(100.0)

Source: Internal reports.

Iloilo

Proposals have been prepared by LWUA and their consultants under a World Bank loan.[16] Proposals are for a three-phase programme with only the first stage (design year 1982) approved for funding, at US$12.75 million at 1981 prices. The "Immediate Improvement Programme" (IIP) includes seven deep wells to double existing output to 36 mld and primary and secondary mains within the city centre and new middle and upper income "subdivision" development. Later improvements will provide an additional 10.88 mld from six infiltration galleries, further primary and secondary distribution mains and a dam. Finally 216 lcd should be available. No proposals are made for tertiary mains, individual household connections or standpipes nor is any investment in sewerage disposal proposed. The IIP will cost US$12.75 million but excludes tertiary mains and connections. If the population served increases to 200,000 the cost of the IIP alone for new consumers would be US$212 per capita.

Bacolod

Phase 1 of a water supply project costing US$7.5 million (US$107 per capita served) excluding tertiary mains and household connections was recently completed. Further phases are planned to raise availability per person serviced to 166 lcd in 1982 and 158 lcd in 1990. Without these improvements availability will probably fall to 128 lcd by 1990. Phases 2 and 3, like phase 1, would only include new wells, storage and primary and secondary distribution mains. Phases 2 and 3 are in fact necessary to maintain per capita production at its present level. However, no new funds are forthcoming until BCWD has shown its ability to keep up payments on the phase 1 loan and to generate an operating profit. It is clearly totally inappropriate to develop source works and primary and secondary distribution further while the existing rated supply capacity is more than double actual production. Any investment should be directed to tertiary distribution and household connections.

Impact on the urban poor

Each of these cities suffers an apparent water shortage which is most severe in low income areas. Such areas seldom receive mains water and people generally rely on water vendors for drinking water and, where available, on shallow wells for other supplies. In spite of the severe inadequacy of supply in these areas, the proposals outlined above fail by varying degrees to address the needs of the urban poor. In Cairo, a huge investment in supply improvements completely fails to provide appropriate solutions to the needs of the poor. In Iloilo, where about 30 per cent of the population relies almost entirely on water vendors for drinking water, all three stages of the major water project fail to include any specific provision to improve supplies to these people. The recently completed improvements in Bacolod have concentrated entirely on increased water production and primary distribution. As a result less than half of rated capacity is utilised, while the poorest 30 per cent of the population continues to rely on inadequate and expensive supplies from vendors and on polluted wells.

Extensions proposed under these projects are totally geared towards improving supply in the middle and upper income areas. No doubt this is because of a perceived greater reliability in economic returns from middle and higher income families and possibly because of the water utilities' susceptibility to influence from vocal upper and middle income groups. Tertiary networks necessary to serve increasing numbers of potential consumers were excluded from all these projects. In Manila, however, tertiary mains and individual connections were included to the extent that public standpipes were to be installed in low income areas and progressively replaced by household connections. About 12 per cent of the total project cost of $692 million should directly benefit the urban poor. But here the problem is that the huge number of individual installations needed to keep up with the programme are just not being achieved. As a result water supply problems in the low income areas have become even more acute as population density rises.

The inequity of increasing production without extending distribution and without providing individual connections or public standpipes in low income areas can be illustrated by the cost of water to consumers with and without mains supplies. In Iloilo most people without domestic connections or standpipes get drinking water from vendors and other water from shallow wells, rainwater or surface sources. Vendors charge about 80 centavos (10 US cents at the 1981 exchange rate) for a 20 litre can of water, about 40 pesos per m^3. A family of six earning 635 pesos per month (the median income level for slum dwellers) and consuming 20 lcd would be spending 145 pesos per month or 23 per cent of their income. A family of six earning at the twentieth percentile level of 375 pesos per month and consuming only 10 lcd would still spend 72 pesos per month, or 19 per cent of income. For that amount a family of six with a 1/2" household water connection could consume 290 lcd. The proposed supply scheme will raise the currently very low pressure in the existing network so that those with household connections can consume more. However, vendors will continue to pass this water on to the urban poor at vastly extortionate prices.

Drinking water from private wells is generally only available in peri-urban areas. Shallow wells in these cities were found to be either heavily polluted (Cairo and Manila) or suffering from saline intrusion (Iloilo and Bacolod). Drinking water in the semi-rural areas beyond the main system came from hand pump driven wells, or sometimes from protected shallow wells.

Where low income areas are totally excluded from the distribution network, or where mains are not scheduled to reach the area for some years, it may be possible to redistribute existing water. The MINUTE (Metro Manila Infrastructure Utilities and Engineering) project has achieved this in Pateros, a municipality within the MMA. This project is complementary to the major investment described above and aims to improve the provision and maintenance of urban infrastructure throughout the Metropolitan Manila Area. In Pateros the most critical problem was water supply. While this area should benefit from the MWSS project in the long term no provision had been made to overcome immediate problems. The following solutions to increase water supply were considered:

(a) immediate relief by (i) bringing water from MWSS sources into unserviced areas by tanker and (ii) taking private wells into public ownership. These steps would replace the costly and unreliable supply from water vendors;

(b) medium-term relief by the improved use of local groundwater resources and controlled exploitation of aquifers to provide public wells. Consumers would collect water from the wellhead, or short distribution mains to public standpipes and wash-house facilities could be provided. Secondary and tertiary mains proposed under the MWSS project can be brought forward for earlier implementation.

In Pateros, which has a population of 40,000, five elevated storage tanks were proposed, each tank serving public standpipes where residents would collect a rationed supply at a price below that charged by vendors. Tanks would only supply drinking water, other water would still come from brackish wells, vendors and rainwater. The tanks would be filled by tankers or by fire trucks during the night. The quantity of water allowed per capita dictated the number of road tankers and size of storage tanks required and thus the overall cost. For supplies between 9 and 23 lcd the cost remained at 0.7 centavos per litre (compared to 3 centavos per litre from vendors). With such a project capital costs cannot reasonably be discounted over periods of more than ten years. By then major improvements should be completed and the short-term measures redundant.

The same approach to new sources may be used elsewhere. Sometimes local, low cost and small schemes are better and cheaper than large-scale centralised schemes. In many parts of Egypt local artesian wells provide an adequate alternative to the far more expensive centralised extraction and treatment plant with its long and large diameter delivery mains. Certainly this is true in Assiut, presently served by a centralised Nile water supply system.

Conclusions from the case studies
    The most important and significant common factors from the case studies are as follows:
    (a) major new investment in water supply tends to be in existing serviced areas. A likely reason is that utilities expect middle and higher income families to be better payers. The low level of investment in improving supplies for low income communities reflects the other side of the coin. However, in fact, many low income families spend more on the few litres necessary to sustain life than householders with multi-tap systems spend on many tens of times the amount. In Iloilo water from vendors costs 4 centavos (0.3 US cents) per litre compared to about 0.1 centavo per litre for mains water. During the dry season when the groundwater table recedes and there is no rainwater slum households may be forced to pay up to one-third of their total income for their minimum drinking water needs. The situation in informal housing areas of Cairo, Manila and Bacolod is similar;
    (b) utilities give scant attention to considering the need for water where this need is most critical, and how to tailor proposals to meet this need. Water utilities tend to be more concerned with satisfying demands of the middle and higher income groups and in providing them with ever greater quantities. Combined with low tariffs and high wastage this leads, as in Cairo, to sufficient production of drinking water to supply the urban population with access to the system with up to 310 lcd. Indeed in Cairo existing extraction plants and those under construction could provide the essential water needs of Greater Cairo up to the year 2000, yet the current Master Plan proposes to increase production to almost 600 lcd at a cost of about US$300 per capita;

(c) in each case study investment was aimed primarily at increasing production. Encouraging greater economy in water use and extending distribution mains to previously unserviced areas were considered as secondary priorities. In Cairo savings of US$200 million (1977 prices) would follow from halving existing wastage. In Manila, of the current supply to the population with access to the system (1978) of 228 lcd, 110 lcd was unaccounted for, largely through leakage and wastage by government organisations. The proposals for network extensions in Cairo, Iloilo and Bacolod are only for primary distribution, not for extensions to unserved low income communities;

(d) except in Manila tertiary mains and household connections were not included in the proposals. This increases consumption for those who have household connections and delays household supplies for those without. Where proposals are made for new household connections such ambitious installation rates are proposed that they may prove impossible to achieve;

(e) investment in additional volumes of water without extensions to the distribution system or rationalised tariff charges results in either: (i) vastly increased consumption, and thus wastage, among the middle and upper income groups with household supplies, especially when tariffs are low; (ii) increased mains pressure and under-utilisation of the new source. This can occur where tariffs are high, as in Bacolod, and consequently even upper and middle income consumers cannot afford large increases in consumption. Phase 1 of the Bacolod water project excluded tertiary mains or household connections with the result that not all water is utilised and pressure is much higher than before. This in turn causes leakage from old pipes and hydrants and the need for still further investment;

(f) inadequate or poorly graduated tariffs result in high levels of government subsidy and do nothing to discourage wastage. Wastage is also encouraged by inefficient tariff collection and poor metering. Household metering is often considered an essential part of any supply scheme, but adequate maintenance is seldom provided. A high percentage of water consumed thus remains unbilled because of meter faults (e.g. Manila). Costs can often be reduced by block metering with regular revisions of flat-rate charges. Consumers using public standpipes, who are

frequently not charged at all, can face a similar
tariff structure. Both public standpipes and
wash-houses are frequently over-designed and lack
differential pricing systems;

(g) in larger cities institutional complexity
arises from government intervention and fragmented
interests. Thus Cairo has three agencies: General
Organisation of Potable Water, General Organisation
of Sanitary Sewerage and Drainage and the General
Organisation for Greater Cairo Water Supply. These
agencies are controlled by Central Government but
investment priorities and policies are again under
the direct control of three agencies: Cairo
Governorate, Giza Governorate and the Kalyoubia
Governorate. Since Cairo Governorate is the biggest
and richest it gets the lion's share of the water at
the expense of the other two. Furthermore, although
the board of GOGCWS can propose tariffs, it cannot
set them. In 1978 the board proposed substantial
increases in all tariffs (except those for the first
30 m^3 per dwelling per month) but the Central
Government did not agree;

(h) the impact of water supply schemes on drainage
and sanitation is seldom considered. Where sewerage
systems exist in areas with household water supply,
charges for sewerage collection and disposal are
seldom made. This service is generally provided
almost exclusively for the higher income residential,
commercial and industrial areas, who are thus
subsidised by other water users without the benefit
of a sewerage system. Furthermore, the cost of
sewerage systems increases proportionally with higher
water consumption resulting from increased supply.
Failure to consider the implications of water schemes
on drainage and sanitation may result in
environmental problems and sometimes hazards to
public health and hygiene.

Policy options
    A complete change of emphasis for water supply
schemes in urban areas of developing countries is
required:
    (a) where additional water can only be supplied at
a higher average cost (which is almost invariably the
case) and demand at current prices cannot be fully
satisfied, then minimum needs of the low income areas
should be satisfied before the expressed demand of
middle and high income areas;

(b) water tariffs should be set at a level and in a manner which: (i) avoids the need for the water utility to rely on government subsidies; (ii) encourages users to conserve water, avoid wastage at the tap and maintain fitments in good order; and (iii) ensures a minimum supply for low income families either from an on-plot tap or from a well-maintained standpipe nearby at a price they can afford;

(c) the water utility should be responsible for its own financial organisation and management and for policy decisions and investment priorities;

(d) supply projects must be considered together with the drainage and sanitation improvements which additional water usage will require. Householders benefiting from a sewerage system necessitated by high water consumption, should pay for such a system;

(e) the local agency should be entirely responsible for maintenance and cost recovery and should always be involved in the planning and implementation of capital investment projects which are undertaken by a central government agency;

(f) appropriate and understandable technologies should always be used in water schemes and staff should be properly trained to maintain the system. This applies particularly to schemes funded by grants in aid from developed countries which insist on the exclusive use of that country's consultants, contractors, plant and equipment;

(g) increasing water supply is not always the major problem for urban areas in developing countries, redistribution of existing water is. Thus short term schemes to provide water to those without and so achieve some immediate improvements while waiting for new major supply schemes may be worthwhile;

(h) new, low cost, local, small-scale schemes may often be better than large-scale schemes;

(i) urban water projects often show a spiralling pattern of investment in providing water to middle income groups and central city areas:

(1) piped water supply increased;

(2) piped sewerage required when cesspools fail;

(3) households become accustomed to in-house water and install baths, showers and multiple taps, consumption rises;

(4) mains pressure drops and householders complain;

(5) further investment is demanded;

(6) sewers become overloaded and further major investment is needed to cope with the increased volume of waste water.

Unless tariffs are carefully monitored and regularly increased such spiralling costs can only lead to increased inequality of service to the urban poor and oversupply to the more wealthy. There will be high losses within the system and widespread wastage with increasingly inappropriate and high cost levels of demand assumed in the design of new projects.

All the above options are derived from the four cities discussed earlier and are therefore rather city or project specific. From a wider view of global investment for water supply over the next ten years other vital questions should be posed:

- When considering major investment proposals for water supply, should water be treated as a limited resource so as to encourage more appropriate and cheaper projects, to prevent over-use and wastage and to promote conservation and re-use?

- Should proposed investment in major supply projects be regularly reviewed to ensure that these are compatible with the basic needs of the poor and socially disadvantaged sectors and that over-investment in water is not precluding more essential investment in other sectors such as shelter or health?

- Should an international review body monitor the proposed use of international funds for water supply projects so as to prevent over-investment, to promote a more equitable distribution of available funds to the countries most in real need and to ensure that projects are primarily designed to address the immediate needs of the poor rather than the demands of the wealthy?

Notes

1. J.M. Kalbermatten et al.: Appropriate technology for water supply and sanitation, Vol. 1A, A summary of technical and economic options (Washington, DC, World Bank, 1980).

2. J.M. Kalbermatten et al.: ibid, Vol. 2, A planners guide (Washington, DC, World Bank, 1980).

3 R.G. Feachem et al. (ed.): Water, wastes and health in hot climates (London, John Wiley, 1978).

4. World Health Organisation: <u>International drinking water standards</u> (Geneva, 1971).

5. World Bank: <u>Village water supply</u>, A World Bank Paper (Washington, DC, 1976).

6. J.M. Kalbermatten, op. cit.; R.G. Feachem, op. cit.; and G.F. White et al.: <u>Drawers of water</u> (Chicago, Chicago University Press, 1972).

7. J.M. Kalbermatten et al., op cit., Vol. 1A.

8. The analysis of proposals and the conclusions reached represent the personal, professional views of the authors. No inference should be drawn that they in any way reflect the views of the specialist consultants who were responsible for project preparation in the various cities. The opinions expressed by the authors are entirely their own and do not necessarily reflect the views of their firm, of local officials in the countries or of any international funding agency.

9. American British Consultants (AMBRIC): <u>Cairo waste water master plan immediate implementation proposals</u>, Report prepared for the Overseas Development Administration, United States Agency for International Development and Government of Egypt (London, 1980).

10. Camp Dresser and McKee: <u>Manila water supply proposals</u>, Reports prepared for the Metropolitan Waterworks and Sewerage System, Philippines and the United States Agency for International Development/ World Bank (Washington, DC, 1976-78).

11. ibid.

12. Gilmore Hankey Kirke Partnership: <u>Regional cities development project, Iloilo City proposals</u>, Report prepared for the Government of the Philippines and World Bank (London, 1982).

13. Gilmore Hankey Kirke Partnership: <u>Regional cities development project, Bacolod City proposals</u>, Report prepared for the Government of the Philippines and World Bank (London, 1982).

14. American British Consultants, op. cit.: Agency for International Development: <u>Immediate action proposals for housing in Egypt</u>, Ministry of Housing and Reconstruction (1976) and Doxiades Associates: <u>Egypt urban development project: Study for lowest income housing</u>, Report prepared for the Ministry of Housing and Reconstruction, Egypt and World Bank (Washington, DC, 1977).

15. E.S. Parsons: <u>Cairo water supply master plan</u>, Report prepared for the United States Agency for

Interational Development and Government of Egypt (Washington, DC, 1979).

16. C. Lotti and Associates: Metro Iloilo water district water supply proposals, Report prepared for the Local Water Utilities Administration, Philippines, and World Bank (Washington, DC, 1980).

17. Gilmore Hankey Kirke Partnership: Metro Manila infrastructure utilities and engineering programme, Report prepared for the Ministry of Public Works, Philippines, and World Bank (London, 1980).

7 HUMAN WASTE DISPOSAL IN URBAN AREAS

by J. Pickford

Introduction

This chapter discusses a very personal matter, sanitation. Clearly adequate sanitation is essential in reaching and retaining satisfactory health levels. Good sanitation need not require running water but it does call for education to understand its use. There are many means of achieving adequate sanitation with very little or no water.

A world-wide problem

Human activity results in a wide variety of wastes of which the greater part are those from extraction and manufacturing industry and from agriculture. At the domestic level human wastes are mainly of three kinds - excreta, wastewater and solid waste. It is those which are considered in this chapter. The removal and disposal of excreta, wastewater and solid waste are inter-related. For example, where sewerage sullage and excreta are usually, but not invariably, removed together. In some more prosperous homes the putrescible part of garbage (vegetable peelings, left-over food and the like) is discharged with sewage through a sink disposal unit. An adverse relationship exists in developing countries, where refuse blocks the flow of sullage in sewers and in drains.

The waste most associated with humans is of course their own bodily waste - their excreta - faeces and urine. Because excreta presents health risks and is for most people culturally obnoxious its removal and disposal is particularly important. In almost every part of the world waste disposal presents problems. Because it is waste, people do not want to bother with it; the sooner it can be forgotten the better. The problems vary. In many of the older cities of North America and Europe a major problem is that sewerage systems built in the later years of the nineteenth-century or the early years of the

153

twentieth are now nearing the end of their lives and
the cost of repair or replacement is fantastically
high. In the poor developing countries the problem is
often to provide sanitation for the first time by
methods which are economically acceptable.

In this chapter particular attention is given to
waste disposal in places visited by the author. It
seems likely that these places are typical of the
situation throughout the Third World. Except for a
few prosperous oil-rich countries of the Middle East
the problems and the underlying causes seem the same.

The single factor which has had most effect on the
present waste conditions and which will cause most
future problems is the phenomenal growth of Third
World urban communities. A ten-fold increase of
population since 1945 is not unknown and doubling of
the urban community in less than 20 years is
usual.[1] As far as sanitation and general
environmental well-being are concerned, one of the
most serious consequences of rapid urban expansion
has been the growth of squatter settlements and slum
areas in run-down city centres. Lack of proper
sanitation is not restricted to squatters. Often many
of the people now enveloped by urban sprawl once
lived in rural conditions. They then used the fields
for the "call of nature" - fields that are now
covered by houses and factories.

The Water Decade
A series of international conferences led to the
designation of the 1980s as the Water Decade. First
came the Conference on The Human Environment at
Stockholm in 1972 when the Secretary General, Maurice
Strong, spoke about Third World cities and the need
for drinking water being greater than the need for
food. Then in 1976 the Habitat Conference in Canada
passed a resolution aimed at providing all the
world's population with clean water, an objective
which was ratified at the Water Conference in
Argentina the following year. So the years 1981 -
1990 have been set aside as the International
Drinking Water Supply and Sanitation Decade. The
addition of "sanitation" to the title of the Decade
is significant. It recognises that for human health
and happiness adequate sanitation is as important as
good water. So the expanded goal is clean water and
decent sanitation for everyone by 1990. As far as the
Decade is concerned "sanitation" is usually taken to

mean removal and disposal of human excreta. Sullage and solid waste disposal are not included.

Even before the launching of the Decade in November 1980 it was recognised that any achievements would be at a national level rather than world-wide. The United Nations agencies could only suggest, encourage and promote. No special water and sanitation organisation was formed and no funds were set aside specifically for the Decade. It was hoped that more international aid would go to the sector, but this would be for specific projects; it would not be put into a Decade basket from which it could be passed to deserving countries. In any case the amount of money needed was uncertain. Pressure from the media led the Decade organisers to give an umbrella cost estimate and US\$ 6,000 million has been suggested. The actual cost will depend on the level of service provided. Since it must come from a variety of local and international sources, the overall cost is not particularly significant. Whether the highest or lowest estimates prove realistic the cost is high, but insignificant compared with what Barbara Ward called the "annual haemorrhage of resources to manufacture the instruments of death".[2]

It would have been pure but unfortunate fantasy to hope that the Decade could release billions of dollars of international largesse. Nevertheless the Decade can achieve something of greater value: an awareness of the need for water and sanitation so that individuals, local bodies, governments, non-government organisations and international agencies all work together towards the goals. Most national plans admit that there will not be complete coverage for sanitation during this Decade. Many millions of the rural people will not be provided with satisfactory latrines by 1990. If some progress is made the impetus should continue and when goals for water have been reached greater effort can be devoted to providing sanitation for all as well.

Sanitation statistics

For the launching of the International Drinking Water Supply and Sanitation Decade the United Nations Development Programme published figures showing the number of people requiring water and sanitation. In the previous decade 47 per cent of the urban population of developing countries had no access to adequate sanitation. In rural areas 87 per cent had

no access, giving an overall figure of 75 per cent.
By 1990 there will have been a substantial increase
in population. By adding this increase to the numbers
without sanitation the requirement for additional
provision during the Decade is as follows:

Table 12: Population without adequate sanitation, in
1990 (forecast) in millions

	Urban	Rural	Total
Asia and the Pacific	355	1136	1491
Africa	130	342	472
Latin America	212	120	332
Europe (including Algeria and Morocco)	30	30	60
Middle East	20	25	45
	747	1,653	2,400

Source: in World Water (London, T. Tedford Ltd.) Nov.
1982.

These statistics are by no means reliable or
accurate. In a few countries there have been detailed
surveys of the true requirements, but many of these
have been recent, carried out after the compilation
of the global Decade figures. Some countries had
reliable information from the 1971 census. In many
others even the present population is uncertain.
Apart from the difficulty of carrying out an accurate
survey with limited administrative resources, there
is often a bias for one reason or another. For
example it is likely that in some places census
figures are "adjusted" for political reasons: regions
or states within the country want to gain political
muscle by showing that their populations are large.
Elsewhere there was physical movement of people at
the time of the count: city dwellers return to their
villages which they regard as their true homes. Many
people deliberately avoid the census-man because they

fear it will result in taxation or because they are
squatters with no legal tenure for their homes.
So the figures for existing need are often little
more than intelligent guesses. Growth of population
is even more uncertain. Who can tell the effect of
family planning schemes or whether the rural to urban
drift will continue. And what constitutes an "urban"
area? Does a community of 15,000 people count as
urban? In places where the population density
gradually decreases with distance from the centre the
limit of the "urban area" is likely to be merely an
administrative   boundary   with   little   physical
significance.
    As far as sanitation itself is concerned there are
particular problems. Some countries regard a pit
latrine as inadequate whether it is in a rural or an
urban area. Others count pit latrines as satisfactory
in rural areas but not urban, and yet others include
all pit latrines in the satisfactory category.

Lack of adequate sanitation
    Whatever   the   statistics   show,   the   sanitation
available for large parts of the urban population of
most developing countries is deplorable. The early
morning sight of bare backsides alongside roads,
canals, railway lines and drains is a well-known part
of the Indian scene. Such indiscriminate defecation
(to give it its official title) is by no means
restricted to India or even the Indian subcontinent.
It is common throughout the Third World. Even where
adults use latrines, children are often prohibited
and expected to "find somewhere to go". Household
latrines are impossible for people without houses:
the major cities of India have hundreds of thousands
of pavement-dwellers.
    Nepalese towns are an example of widespread open
defecation on a small but intense scale. For example
in a town with 6,000 people not far from Kathmandu
there is only a handful of houses with any kind of
latrine. The remainder of the population use open
defecation. For the women there are two defecation
fields which no male may approach, and the men use
other defined areas. Right in the centre of the town
alongside the school there is a defecation lane
largely used by children. It is almost impossible to
walk along this lane without treading on excreta.

One stage up the sanitation ladder are "dry latrines". The squatter area of Baldia in Karachi is an example which is described in detail only because improvements are mentioned later. It is by no means untypical: dry latrines of one kind or another are widespread.

A typical dry latrine in Baldia is against an outside wall of the plot, either in the yard or as part of the dwelling itself. If in the yard it may have a door; if part of the house it may only be screened by a curtain. The latrine consists of two plinths with a lower space between. The user places his feet on the plinths and defaecates into the space between. Usually a container of some kind is placed there: empty battery cases are favourites. With luck the container is emptied before it overflows, but more often it is full to overflowing by the time the sweeper calls. The sweeper tips the contents of the battery case into a larger container of his own, typically an 18 litre (4 gallon) kerosene tin with the top taken off. If the battery case has overflowed, or if there is no container in the latrine, he removes the faeces literally "by hand", assisted by a brush. Many sweepers have bicycles with large bins hung from the handlebars. When the bins are both full the sweeper pushes his bicycle to an open space on the outskirts of the area or to a dry nullah in the town itself. Excreta spills on the way. At the tipping point fresh excreta is tipped on that already dumped forming stinking pools. In the monsoon the pools are washed down the nullahs which pass between built-up areas.

Bucket collection is a slight improvement on the dry latrine. In colonial times it was operated in a systematic way in many countries, often using prisoners or labourers from other countries. It is still widely practised in West Africa and elsewhere. Ideally a clean bucket is brought to replace each full one every night. So excreta removed at night is known as "nightsoil". The full buckets are taken to a depot where they are emptied and thoroughly cleaned. In practice a nightsoilman usually empties full buckets into a larger container which he brings with him. He does this just behind the latrine, almost inevitably spilling some nightsoil in the process. The process fouls the nightsoilman and his clothes with resultant health dangers. (Figure 5)

Figure 5

Bucket collection

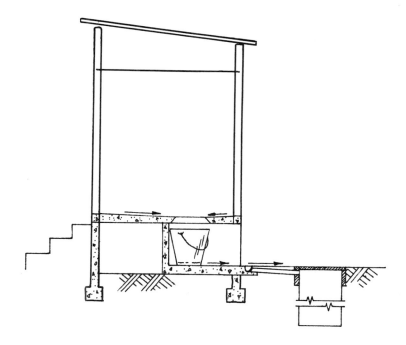

In Cairo, and doubtless in many other towns, unsewered areas are served by a vault system. The vault is a small waterproofed tank into which excreta and water used for anal cleaning are usually passed via a short pipe. Alternatively the vault may be under the latrine. The vault when full may be emptied by the women and children of the household who dump the contents in a nearby drain or canal, or on vacant land. Some vaults are emptied by paid collectors who remove the contents in a tank mounted on a donkey-hauled cart. Rarely is a municipal or private vacuum tanker used.

A similar vault is used in Japan and in the Republic of Korea. The vault is accessible from outside the premises by a small door not unlike that often used for removing buckets from bucket latrines. The collector traditionally uses a scoop to empty the vault taking the excreta away in wooden buckets carried on a yoke. After storage the excreta is poured onto crops as a fertiliser.

Another local variation for removing excreta from premises by hand is the "long-drop". The long-drops of Sana'a in Yemen have been described in detail[3] but there may well be other cities which use the same method. Latrines are built in the upper storeys of tall buildings over a shaft which extends to ground level. Urine and washing water is discharged by spouts into the street. Faeces collect at the base of the shaft, from which they are removed from time to time. Traditionally the material was dried on roof-tops and used as fuel to heat bath water.

By far the most common method of disposing of excreta is through some form of pit latrine. A pit latrine may take various forms including those shown here. The essential feature is that faeces decompose in a pit in the ground from which liquid percolates into the underlying and surrounding soil. The pit may be lined with brickwork or other material to prevent collapse of the sides, but the lining should allow liquid to pass; often it is of honeycomb construction. Urine and water used for anal cleaning thus seeps into the soil. Sometimes waste water used for bathing and other household purposes is also discharged to the pit. Soluble products of faecal decomposition pass to the soil leaving an organic residue which is similar to good earth. Pits can be bad. Poor construction and lack of lining often lead to collapse of the sides and hence of the latrine building. Floors made of sticks are sometimes attacked by termites or rot, and then collapse. The most crude form of pit has only sticks or rough boards across the hole so there is ready access for flies and mosquitoes; the faeces may be visible to users and the latrines may be extremely malodorous. Small pits with a large number of users fill quickly and have to be replaced. High water-table adds to the problems, since a deep pit is impossible unless it is of the bore hole variety. (Figure 6)

However, there are hundreds of thousands of entirely satisfactory pit latrines. Some good patterns of pit-digging and latrine-construction seem to be traditional. The particular case of East African pits, of which the author has personal experience, is detailed later.

In the underprivileged areas (low-cost housing squatter settlements and slums) there is sometimes a variety of excreta-disposal practice. Typically some people have no latrine; others use the local

traditional method, whether it is dry latrine,
bucket, vault or pit; others often attempt to provide
their own septic tanks or even a community built
sewer. Such sewers are usually too shallow and too
flat and there is insufficient water to provide a
reasonable flow, so the sewer blocks and itself
becomes a danger to health.

Figure 6

Pit latrine

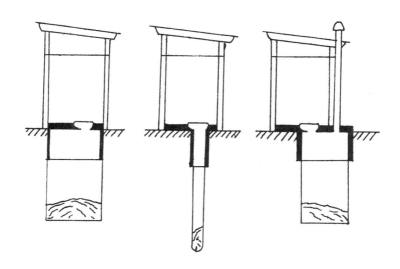

Health effects of poor sanitation
   It has been realised for many years that a high
proportion of mortality and morbidity in developing
countries is associated with what was usually called
"watercarried" disease. Cholera and typhoid, can be
carried by water, as can hepatitis, dysentery,
gastro-enteritis and diarrhoea. Awareness of the
dangers of polluted water led to the provision of
public treated water supplies in industrial

countries. It was assumed that a major factor in improved health and increased life-expectancy was pure drinking water. The provision of safe, clean water continues to be a major priority for developing countries and is the primary objective of the Water Decade. However, there has been in recent years an increasing understanding that safe water supplies alone do not eliminate, or even greatly reduce, the incidence of these diseases. The reason is that the common diseases from the excreta of a sick person pass by some means to the mouth of someone else: transmission of the disease is by a <u>faecal-oral</u> route. Water may be contaminated by germs (pathogens) derived from a sick person's excreta and so reach other people, but there are other routes. The danger from some of these routes can be reduced by washing – for example by washing hands after defecation. Hence an ample quantity of water, even water of less-than-satisfactory quality, helps to reduce these diseases. So too does health education by persuading people to take such measures as washing their hands before preparing food.

Other excreta-derived diseases do not pass on through the new host's mouth. There is, for example, bilharzia, which affects hundreds of millions of people in the Third World. The route of bilharzia transmission is from excreta via a freshwater snail and through the skin of someone in contact with water – someone planting padi, bathing, washing clothes or simply wading through a stream to get from one side to another. With hook-worm (which affects even more hundreds of millions of people than bilharzia) the point of entry to the new sufferer is again through the skin – usually the feet of people who cannot afford or do not use shoes or sandals.

The common feature of all these diseases – from cholera to hookworm – is that their transmission starts with excreta. So obviously the best way of preventing transmission is to so deal with human waste that it ceases to be a transmission route – i.e. to provide good sanitation.

Malaria is a water-related disease because mosquitoes use water for their life-cycle. General environmental improvement, by eliminating lying water, can help to reduce malaria. Good excreta disposal has no effect. On the other hand, another type of mosquito (the <u>fatigans</u>) prefers polluted water and is known to thrive in wet latrines. It passes on Bancroftian filariasis which can lead to elephantiasis.

Hookworm and bilharzia have already been mentioned as examples of excreta-source infections. Both are types of worms, or helminths. There are many other varieties of worm which infect hundreds of millions of people. Roundworm, or ascaris, presents particular difficulties because the eggs are resistant to an unfavourable environment and are very persistent. Roundworm eggs may still infect people after nearly a year, and can reside in soil on which excreta has been placed. Other worm infections are passed on in uncooked meat or fish.

The worm infections are not lethal in the way that cholera is. Death is not sudden and dramatic. Nevertheless the worm diseases are debilitating and may hasten death from other causes such as measles. In areas short of food they are obviously associated with malnutrition, which is a major killer in many countries.

Methods of waste disposal:
Externally-selected methods
  Sewerage
    The removal of human excreta from WCs through a piped system is now customary in the industrial countries. Properly-built, properly-maintained and properly-used sewerage has many advantages. From the user's point of view the excreta disappears without nuisance. There is no smell and no flies. A flush toilet, whether of the pedestal or "Asian" squatting-plate type, is easy to keep clean. Sewerage can deal with sullage - the wastewater from bathing, laundry, kitchens and even car washing - and with industrial waste water. From a technical point of view it is possible to install sewerage in almost any area. However impermeable the soil, however flat the land, whatever the level of groundwater, and for any housing density, sewerage is feasible, although pumping is often necessary. What is more, the technology is known and there is no shortage of information about sewerage itself and the treatment of sewage. If there are insufficient local engineers for design and construction, consultants can easily be found to do the work.

    It is not surprising that, with all these advantages, sewerage is selected for the disposal of human waste by the western-trained engineers, medical

officers, administrators and politicians of the Third
World. Until a few years ago United Nations agencies
also advocated sewerage. Nothing else would be good
enough.

Sewerage is fine in certain conditions. It is
completely appropriate for prosperous cities and
towns with ample water supply, in whatever continent
they are - east or west, north or south.

But sewerage is not appropriate for the majority
of people for whose welfare the Decade was launched.
It is rarely suitable for the poor - for the
squatters, the slum-dwellers, the underprivileged.
The exceptions are areas where there are existing
sewerage systems provided for the better-off, which
already have an adequate flow for self-cleaning.

Sewerage is not appropriate for poor urban
communities for several reasons. The first is cost.
On average the full annual cost of sewerage is about
a quarter of the average wage in developing
countries. Of course no particular case exactly fits
"the average". Actual costs may be higher or lower
than the average, and the incomes of local people may
be greater or less than the average of all developing
countries. Nevertheless, it is undoubtedly true that
the cost of sewerage is unacceptably high for the
majority of Third World urban populations.

A second factor is the need for enough water for
flushing a water-carried system. The smallest
quantity for effective sewerage is 50 litres per
person per day (lcd). Some engineers suggest that the
minimum should be 75 (lcd) of which 50 (lcd) is
simply for flushing. The exact figure is in any case
irrelevant as far as many underprivileged people are
concerned. If they are lucky they get running water
from public standpipes not too far from their homes.
Millions of people, even if they have access to
public standpipes, cannot rely on a delivery of water
because water comes through the pipes intermittently.
For example in South-east Asia over 90 per cent of
supplies are intermittent. So when water is actually
available there are long queues. Water is not
available for enough hours in the day to obtain the
water needed to flush WCs. Even if the water supply
could be improved the question has to be asked: is
there justification for the high cost of obtaining
and treating water to make it drinkable and then
using it to flush a small amount of excreta along a
sewer? In many places water is scarce. Abstraction

for communal supplies means less water for
irrigation. As more water is demanded more distant
sources have to be used and the cost goes up.

Then there is the likelihood of abuse of
water-flushed sewerage systems. All over the Third
World there are sewers which are so blocked that
there is no flow, or the actual discharge is much
less than the design capacity. One reason for this is
the material used for anal cleaning. Where water is
used there is no difficulty, nor is there where
people use proper toilet paper. But for the poor it
is unthinkable to spend money on toilet paper when
there is not enough money for food and other
necessities. So newspapers and other used papers are
used - hard stuff which blocks drains and sewers.
There is abuse of sewerage too because of inadequate
refuse collection: manhole covers are lifted to dump
rubbish in the sewers.

Another disadvantage of sewerage is that
construction and maintenance have to be carried out
by public bodies. It has been noted that attempts by
communities to provide their own sewers are dismal
failures. The only exceptions are where there is
ample gradient and a surveyor or engineer gives
technical guidance. In many congested areas in town
centres and squatter settlements the streets and
alleys are narrow and anything but straight, making
construction of sewerage difficult and costly.

For inland cities in developing countries there is
another disadvantage of sewerage which is often
forgotten by those trained for western technology.
From the disease-transmission point of view
conventional sewerage and sewage treatment is not
satisfactory. In industrial countries the primary aim
of sewage treatment is reduction of oxygen demand and
this is usually achieved by trickling filters or the
activated sludge process. A good well-run
conventional wastewater treatment plant reduces the
number of bacteria to one -tenth or one- hundredth.
However the treated discharge from the plant is still
highly charged with micro-organisms of faecal origin.
These include disease-carrying pathogens if there is
illness of the faecal-oral-transmission kind amongst
the sewered population. If the treated plant effluent
is discharged to a river from which water is taken by
people living downstream and these people drink the
river water without treating it first, then there is
an obvious health danger.

Other types of waste disposal

In industrial countries the most common method of dealing with excreta in unsewered areas is the septic tank.[4] It is said that there are over 30 million septic tanks in the United States alone. Septic tanks work well where there is ample space for drainage of the effluent into permeable soil. The treatment processes in septic tanks are aided by high temperature, so their performance is better in the tropics than in countries with cold winters.

However, conventional septic tanks suffer from the same disadvantages as sewerage. (Figure 7) Their cost is high and they depend on extravagant use of water to flush faeces from water closets to the tanks. The septic tanks themselves provide only partial treatment of sewage and their effluent has to be discharged to a drainage field in permeable soil. They are therefore generally unsuitable for high-density housing where the soil is impermeable or the water-table is high.

Figure 7

Septic tank

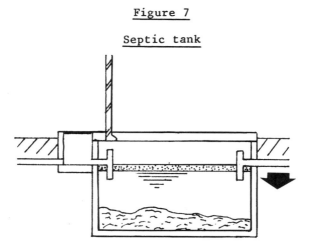

Very similar to the septic tank in its operation is the aqua-privy. (Figure 8) The fundamental difference is that whereas the waste to a septic tank comes from WCs along household drains, excreta is deposited directly into an aqua-privy from a latrine immediately above. As a consequence water is not required merely for transportation and an aqua-privy operates satisfactorily provided enough water is added each day to make up for losses due to

evaporation and leakage. Some interesting types of
aqua-privy have been designed over the years with
varying success. In the late 1940s pre-cast concrete
aqua-privies were constructed in the West Indies and
seem to have been successful.

Figure 8

Aqua-privy

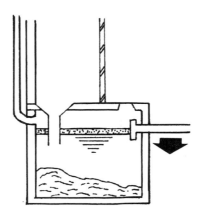

Another interesting and unusual form of aqua-privy
incorporating prefabrication techniques was the
hexagonal unit provided in bustee improvement schemes
in Calcutta by the Calcutta Metropolitan Development
Authority (CMDA).[5] Similar pre-cast concrete panels
were used for the chamber and superstructure. Not
surprisingly, the cost of these units was
comparatively high. CMDA found that they could cover
the whole cost of a two-chamber pour-flush latrine
for less than 75 per cent of the aqua-privy cost.
With aqua-privies the users had contributed the
remaining 25 per cent of the cost.

Incidentally, aqua-privies have proved technically
suitable for public and communal latrines for a long
time. The question of household versus communal
latrines is discussed below, but the point made here
is that from a construction and operational point of
view aqua-privies are quite suitable for
multiple-user latrines.

Technical information on low-cost sanitation
   There is now a world-wide interest in low-cost
sanitation as the appropriate technology for under
privileged urban communities. It is often referred to
as something new. Yet most of the systems now being
advocated have been available for years, for example
in the World Health Organisation technical report on
excreta   disposal   for   rural   areas   and   small
communities[6] published a quarter of a century ago.

Recent World Bank initiative
   During the past few years the World Bank has taken
a remarkable initiative with regard to low-cost
sanitation. Some very comprehensive studies have been
undertaken using United Nations Development Programme
funds. The   Canadian   International   Development
Research Council and other multilateral and bilateral
agencies have also been involved. Resulting from
these studies the Bank has published a series of
excellent volumes containing a wealth of valuable
information about technical, economic, health and
sociological   aspects   of   sanitation.[7]   The
culmination of the advice contained in these volumes
are algorithms by which a selection can be made of
sanitation technology. There is detailed advice for
various aspects of the selection process including
the method by which systems can be compared
economically. Another recommendation defines the
tasks for feasibility studies divided between the
sanitary engineer or public health specialist, the
economist, the behaviour scientist and the community.
The community advises the behaviour scientist at
various stages of the study and finally selects the
preferred alternative. Another valuable discussion in
the   publications   is   regarding   the   sequential
upgrading of alternative technologies with the aim of
eventually providing everyone with either a sewered
pour-flush toilet or a vault emptied by a vacuum
truck. Several systems which have not been tried on a
large scale are proposed and the ventilated improved
pit latrine (VIP) is given particular attention.
   The greatest merit of the Bank's publications is
perhaps that they offer to those concerned in the
planning and execution of sanitation schemes very
comprehensive guidelines which can be universally
applied. For a country, region or city which plans to
"provide sanitation" they are ideal. They enable a
group of outside engineers, economists and behaviour

scientists to decide on suitable forms of low-cost sanitation even if their previous experience is confined to "conventional" North American or European practice.

Local adaptation

It can be seen that one of the merits of the World Bank publications is that they provide methods of selection which can be applied in any developing country and if followed carefully presumably give the same results in similar circumstances. Some such circumstances can be fairly clearly defined: for example there is a preference for sitting or squatting while defecating, and the anal cleansing material used. Even in these matters it is unwise for an "outsider" to be categorical. Before the start of the Dar-es-Salaam household survey described later it was said at the briefing meeting in London that 60 per cent of the population was Moslem and used water for anal cleaning; 40 per cent was Christian and used paper. This was based on advice from a sociologist who had recently worked in the United Republic of Tanzania. When the results of the survey came in it was found that virtually 100 per cent of those without WCs used water. The minority had adopted the habits of the majority.

A criterion in the selection of appropriate sanitation is often given as "acceptability". This is a very difficult factor to assess; humans are extremely adaptable animals and can readily accept all kinds of different environments. Those who have moved from rural to urban surroundings have already accepted fantastic changes. The whole way of life – housing, transport, pattern of work, access to schools and so on – is quite different in an urban environment from what immigrants experienced in their villages or scattered farms. So if people have been able to adapt in other ways there is no reason why they should not adapt in their sanitation habits – given the impetus to do so. The impetus is what is often lacking.

Similarly, "ability to pay" or "affordability" is suggested as a gauge of the suitability of alternatives. Here again, how can affordability be reliably measured? When squatters in a modern city are asked their income a low figure is often given because it is expected that survey information will be used for assessing taxes. If a head-of-household or his wife is asked "Would you pay so much for a proper latrine?", the answer depends almost entirely on the respondent's expectations. If they are eager for improved sanitation they are likely to say they will pay more than they can really afford. If they expect a free service or subsidy if they claim to be poor, the answer given will be that they can afford hardly anything.

In some situations a good way to ascertain acceptability and ability to pay is to examine what has already been done or to try out a pilot scheme. The past habits of latrine construction may give a foundation on which improvements can be based and give an indication of the amount of effort which local people are willing to devote to sanitation. Pilot studies may similarly show what can reasonably be achieved. However, there is a danger of "reading too much" into pilot schemes. Usually the conditions are not typical of what has to be done on a larger scale. For example, the input of technical, sociological and educational expertise is often quite great. The monitoring which is an essential part of a pilot scheme makes it special. A great deal depends on the skill with which the organisers of the pilot scheme are able to enrol the interest and enthusiasm of the beneficiaries. Too often such a scheme is seen as coming from outside and to be irrelevant to the local situation. It is an outside job. An example was mentioned at a recent conference.[8] In Egypt a government official visited a household latrine which had been built as part of an externally-financed improvement project. The latrine was scrupulously clean. On further examination the official realised that it had never been used. He asked the lady of the house why. "Oh", she said to this representative of the government, "this is yours, not mine".

Anecdotes abound of the use of externally-provided latrines for storage of wood, straw, crops and for children's sleeping. Obviously in all these cases the fundamental deficiency is the desire for a latrine on the part of the householders. They regard provision of latrines in the same way as someone living on the ground floor of multi-storey flats thinks of stairs or elevators: very fine, but irrelevant.

Even when latrines are valued they may be considered as a convenience suitable for adults, or for men only. The author had a similar experience to that reported by the Egyptian official. On a visit to a "pilot" scheme in Africa a latrine was unlocked by a householder for inspection. It had been built a year or so before and was found to be perfectly clean with no nuisance from smell, flies or cockroaches. It was obviously used regularly and the householder was full of praise for the fine latrine with which he had been provided. He was asked how many people used it. "Just me and my wife". Seeing several children playing in the yard, it was assumed that the householder had omitted to mention them because he had misunderstood the original question. But no. The man-of-the-house was obviously surprised that children were considered as possible latrine-users. Naturally they went outside and defecated wherever they wanted to and wherever they happened to be. The latrine was seen as providing adult privacy. This attitude towards children's defecation habits is common. Even where there is some understanding of the dangers of disease from excreta it is often thought the children's excreta is harmless.

Similarly, in some male-dominated cultures, latrines are reserved for men and older boys. Women, girls and young boys must find their own place to defecate. For example in an urban area visited by the author he found satisfactory latrines provided as a matter of course by the householders even though their "houses" were poor mud-walled places. These latrines were reserved for males: the women and girls used the cow-sheds.

Just as male-only latrines were provided here "as a matter of course", in other places there are millions of household latrines provided for the use of all members of the households. The latrines themselves may be good, bad or indifferent. The crucial starting-point is that many urban people already see the need for sanitation. Given this lead over those to whom a latrine is viewed as unnecessary much can be done to provide a satisfactory system. We will therefore look in detail at some urban areas of which the author has experience.

Dar-es-Salaam

A characteristic of the dwellings here is that most are single-storeyed with a fairly standard plan. A "household" often consists of several family units - on average between three and four families share the dwelling and also share a yard at the rear where much of the social life of the household takes place. As in many other countries with a warm or hot climate, cooking is generally carried out in the open yard near the kitchen. The latrine or latrines are built off the yard not far from the kitchen. Sometimes two latrines are provided - one for men and one for women, or one for adults and the other for children. In general the latrine building is spacious, because it is used for bathing following defecation, although in some dwellings a separate bathroom is provided.

The majority of latrines are built over pits; many pits are large and some have been in use for 20 years or more without filling. When pits do fill another pit is sometimes dug alongside. The method of emptying into a second pit has been customary in the old island town of Lamu off the Kenya coast for a couple of centuries at least and has been studied in detail. The bottom of the new pit is dug until its base is below the bottom of the latrine pit. Then some of the blocks lining the latrine pit are removed. The semi-liquid contents of the latrine pit flow into the new pit and consolidated solids at the bottom are removed by hand. The lining blocks are replaced, the new hole topped up with soil, the latrine slab is replaced and the latrine is ready for several years' further use.

The soil in Dar-es-Salaam varies a great deal. That in areas where pits are large and long-lasting is reasonably porous with a low groundwater level. Elsewhere there are impermeable clay layers, some of which are saucer-shaped with resultant shallow perched aquifers. Here it is impractical to dig large deep pits. Small pits are therefore usual, and these fill quickly, with considerable inconvenience to householders because the municipal tanker system is overtaxed, and anyway householders cannot always find the ready cash to pay for a tanker service.

A carefully-planned household survey was carried out to provide data from which recommendations for upgrading could be made. The survey covered 311 households in 14 areas unserved by the sewerage system. Some of the information gained during the survey has been mentioned: the composition of households, the almost complete use of water for anal cleaning and the widespread use of household latrines. The majority of these latrines were provided by the householders themselves and there appears to be a substantial body of private contractors available for those not able to do the actual construction. Pits are usually lined with concrete blocks, lumps of coral or other material. For the lining of small pits oil drums are common in all countries, and some ingenious alternatives were found. For example old truck tyres placed on top of each other were very satisfactory, besides using waste material whose disposal is sometimes difficult.

In areas with a high water table there were found to be a number of "mound" latrines, some of which were quite large. One had a pit of about 2.5 metres diameter; several were about 2 metres by 4 metres in plan. Generally these "mound" latrines have elevated walls rendered inside and out with cement, but a few have the "mound" of earth which is usual elsewhere.

In spite of this wealth of successful local experiences the "external" agencies working in Dar-es-Salaam at one time concentrated their efforts on trying to introduce new ideas and latrines which are locally unfamiliar. Trial compost latrines were built and many proved to be completely unsatisfactory: those which did not collapse emitted an appalling stink. This was due to improper use. To operate properly a compost latrine must be fed with a regular supply of carbonaceous material and must be kept dry. In spite of plenty of well-thought-out posters extolling householders to put all their vegetable waste in the compost latrines, nothing like enough was added. People who have been brought up with pit latrines have learned from an early age to avoid depositing any waste in the pit as it would then fill more quickly. Similarly pit latrine users in Dar-es-Salaam are accustomed to urinate in the pits and to allow water used for anal cleaning to go in. Some use the latrine as a bathroom.

Reed's Odourless Pit Latrines were tried without much success. Another innovation has been the World Bank's VIP, the ventilated improved pit. The type of VIP proposed was well-designed. Its capital cost was comparatively low because the pit is small and the superstructure of minimum dimensions. Some components of the VIP were designed for mass-production with consequent reduced cost.

For those people who had previously no latrine, or whose old latrine was bad, an externally-financed VIP has attractions. In practice it was found that there are two serious drawbacks to the VIP compared with the "traditional" local version. One is that the small pit is justified on the assumption that there

would be a good public pit emptying service. After
VIPs had been built an investigation to find the best
method of emptying was started. The second difficulty
was the size of the latrine building, the
superstructure. Although the design materials and
construction of the new latrines were all good, the
space inside was a minimum to reduce costs. The
people had been used to ample space and naturally
felt unreasonably confined in a tiny cell. To them a
small but otherwise satisfactory latrine was
infinitely worse than a spacious room. The lesson to
be learned is that for successful innovation the new
latrine must be appreciated as better by the users.

Baldia, Karachi
    The dry latrines of this squatter area were
obviously bad from almost every point of view, and
the local people realised that they were bad. They
were not the only unsatisfactory factor in life for
these "squatters". Water was scarce, streets unpaved,
refuse was not collected. There were not enough
schools, a negligible local health service, virtually
no public transport and so on. Added to these
troubles, the owners could not be certain that they
would be able to keep their houses because they had
no right to the land. So sanitation received a low
priority.
    A European country had been involved for many
years in a study of the area. Geographers,
sociologists, town planners and the like had spent a
decade studying the area and its people. Now they
were ready to provide money for physical improvements
- roads and drains, water and latrines. Especially
latrines. However, there was no clear idea as to what
kind of latrine or how any improvement programme
should be implemented. Tens of millions of rupees
would be made available, if only someone could decide
how to spend it.
    Advice was sought regarding a suitable type of
latrine and a large long-life pit was proposed for
areas with suitable subsoil. Estimates of cost were
prepared and agreed, but still nobody had any idea
who could spend the money. There was no communal
organisation covering the whole area - certainly not
one which could deal with millions of rupees. The
municipal authority was unwilling to be involved for
three perfectly good reasons. Baldia was an unplanned
squatter area and as such came outside the normal

municipal system. The proposed latrines would be within individual householders' plots and were therefore not a municipal responsibility, just as WCs have to be provided by householders in areas where the municipality lays sewers. Then to provide latrines for one squatter area while nothing was done for other squatters could lead to endless political trouble. Similarly the provincial and national governments could certainly not become involved in spending the money since urban sanitation was a legally defined municipal responsibility. So the millions of rupees were not spent: no programme could be agreed and the expatriates went home, taking the offer of money with them.

Fortunately for Baldia the issue was taken up by a few individuals and organisations. The United Nations Children's Fund (UNICEF) took a lead and provided some funds — not vast sums, but enough to get something done. The plots were defined and leased, so that householders now had some security. A welfare group, the Pakistan Jaycees, provided technical and managerial guidance, and organised contracts for some of the earliest UNICEF-funded latrines. A group of social work postgraduates became interested, as an academic project. The Department of Social Work at Karachi University, like the Jaycees, became agents for UNICEF. Their policy was slightly different, although the difference was fundamental to the whole project. Jaycees' pits were provided to householders complete: the contract included digging the hole, lining it and providing cover slab, squatting plate and water-seal. The Social Work Department, on the other hand, required householders to dig their own pits. In some cases neighbours helped with the excavation. In one part of Baldia a cricket team did valuable work. Originally they simply wanted to use a street for cricket practice. The street had pools and streamlets of excreta. Some householders had built pits in the streets for offset pour-flush latrines, and the masonry tops of the pits obstructed the cricketers' pitch. Amongst the social work students was a mature lady of great determination and ability, who became the pivot about which the various parties turned. She was later appointed Community Organiser. She worked with the cricketers, one of whom was a mason. Members of the team dug pits: UNICEF funds were used for materials; the mason built the lining and cover slab. Once mobilised in this way, the

cricket players formed the nucleus of a welfare
society, whose aims were the improvement of the area.
   With regular technical advice from Jaycees, very
occasional visits by UNICEF-supported advisers from
abroad and on-the-ground enthusiasm of the society
encouraged by the community organiser, the
outside-funded latrine programme grew. More
significantly, householders who were not selected for
the UNICEF latrines built their own to the same
pattern. The actual design of the latrine gradually
changed. Fairly early on a local construction
technique was introduced. The first design provided
by the Water and Waste Engineering for Developing
Countries (WEDC) Group from Loughborough, United
Kingdom, was for a large pit with a lining of
sand-cement blocks and a reinforced concrete slab.
The latrine itself could be either over the pit or
outside, connected to the water seal by a short pipe.
The Baldia linings employed a local system for
building "tandoori ovens". At the top the diameter
was gradually reduced; the idea is known in the
building industry as "corbelling". In this way the
slab is much smaller, saving cement and reinforcement
bars - both of which were in short supply. Then
during another visit by an adviser from the WEDC
Group there was four-sided discussion. Taking part
with the WEDC man was the mason responsible for much
of the early construction, who was now becoming the
technical organiser; there was the lady community
organiser; and there was a representative of the
local community.
   The aim was to reduce cost. It was decided that
pits would still be large - about 2 metres diameter
and 3 metres deep. An innovation was to line the pit
with undressed stone - pieces of rock obtained from a
local quarry. This was readily available and cost
little more than US$1 for a cartload. The most
regular shaped blocks would be set aside and the
remainder used for lining the lower part of the pit.
Only the smallest amount of cement mortar would be
used. Then the top metre or so would be built with
the set-aside regular pieces of stone laid in cement
mortar and corbelled like a tandoori-oven to give a
small opening at the top, just big enough to fit a
manhole cover made on site. Because many houses
already had a "dry" latrine the pit would be dug in
the yard, so avoiding the demolition of the latrine
building. However, when a new latrine building was

needed and the householder did not want to use
pour-flush, the pit could be under the building.
   The actual use of pour-flush water-seal latrines
created difficulties at first. These difficulties are
typical of the kind of social, community and personal
troubles that beset sanitation programmes. The water
supply for Baldia was notoriously bad and every
tin-full needed time and effort to obtain. So the
owners of the new pour-flush latrines grumbled
relentlessly about the water-seal. By following the
meaning of the term pour-flush, latrine users were
pouring water carefully into the bowl. They found
they needed a lot of water to clean it after
defecation.
   So the community organiser and university social
work department staff and students visited the new
latrine owners. They explained, and demonstrated,
that a small quantity of water thrown into the bowl
was much more effective than a large quantity poured
in. Instead of difficult-to-get clean water,
wastewater could be used to clean the bowl. The
important thing was to keep the latrine clean at all
times.
   The latrine construction programme and the social
consciousness which had been aroused by the
activities of the community organiser, the social
work students and the local welfare society led to
all kinds of other improvements. People became aware
of the effect of the environment on their health. As
UNICEF participated in the latrine programme
particular attention was devoted to children. There
had been a high infant mortality rate and a large
number of deaths at childbirth. So the local women
who performed the functions of midwives were given
elementary training. Literacy classes for women
followed instruction in home crafts. The physical
environment was also improved. Some street lights
were installed. A few additional public water taps
were made available. Some roads were paved. Some
drains were provided. Most important of all in its
potential for further improvement was the attitude of
the people who had learned to work with each other
and with the municipal authorities for the common
good of the community.

Unsewered areas of Cairo
   Cairo is characteristically a city of high-density
tall buildings. The majority of the people live in

apartments rather than the small household units of the other places we are considering. As seen in the previous chapter Cairo is blessed with an ample water supply derived from the river Nile. It is comparatively prosperous and has been able to attract a fair amount of foreign aid. So for most of Greater Cairo sewerage has either already been provided or is planned. Sewerage is the appropriate form of sanitation.

But inevitably in a Third World city whose growth is rapid, there are areas which miss the progress. There are several districts in the greater city which retain some of the characteristics of rural life. Some are still true villages separated from the main urban sprawl by fields. Others are pockets of poverty surrounded by industry, commerce and multi-storey apartments. A traditional form of sanitation in many unsewered areas is a form of vault or cesspit. This is a small chamber, usually built of brick and sometimes with a concrete base. Excreta from pour-flush latrines passes through short lengths of pipe to chambers. Some of these are emptied by the occupants. It is the practice for this unpleasant task to be undertaken by women and girls, who may themselves be barred from use of the latrine. It is more usual for the chambers to be emptied by contractors who use the ubiquitous kerosene tin to carry the contents to a donkey-hauled tanker. The tanker may be discharged to a canal which is used for water supply further along.

The people in these areas, seeing that other Cairoenes are connected to the public sewerage system, are often desperately keen to be sewered themselves. In some areas they have laid pipes which have soon become clogged because of inadequate flow and insufficient fall. Conventional sewerage is rarely satisfactory if built without competent technical supervision. With proper advice a combination of chambers and sewers can overcome the difficulties of low-flow and slack gradient because the solids settle in the tanks, and there undergo some biological decomposition. It is, of course, essential that the accumulated solids are removed from the tanks: desludging is necessary as the chambers become, in effect, small septic tanks.

Another way of improving the traditional system is to provide hygienic facilities for the disposal of solids whether derived from the usual self-contained

tank or from a chamber connected to the local sewer.
Tipping depots can be provided on the municipal
sewers or at the sewage treatment works.

Patna[9]

A non-profit-making organisation which has had
remarkable success in providing sanitation is the
Sulabh Shauchalaya Sansthan (SSS). It originated in
Patna in the State of Bihar in India and has since
extended its activities to other Indian States and to
Sri Lanka. The movement began as part of the
celebrations commemorating the centenary of Gandhi's
birth, with the initial object of freeing sweepers
from the degrading work associated with dry latrines
- removing excreta and carrying it through the
streets on their heads. The SSS (now called Sulabh
International) acted as an intermediary between the
state government and the householders. Funds had
previously been allocated for latrine conversion -
that is, converting dry latrines to pour-flush pit
latrines. The State could make grants for 75 per cent
of the cost of conversion. However, no local or state
organisation had been responsible for implementation
and the funds were diverted to other activities. SSS
acted for the householder, built the pits and
latrines and provided the 25 per cent of the cost not
covered by the grant. This was given to the
householder as a loan repayable to SSS, who charged
10 per cent to pay for their own expenses.

The detailed construction of the pits varies
according to the space available, but all have two
pits about a metre across and a metre deep. The pits
are used alternatively by blocking the pipe to one of
these pits. It has been found that one pit lasts a
family between two and five years depending on the
number of children and the nature of the soil. SSS
guarantees to undertake any repairs in the first five
years, and empties full pits on payment of 25 rupees
(about US$3). In some places the householder can sell
the mature excreta as fertiliser for as much as 40
rupees.

The idea of double pit pour-flush latrines is not
new, although some details of the SSS plans are
original. What is new is the success of the scheme,
whereby a private organisation has built tens of
thousands of latrines in a short time. SSS has also
built public latrines for which they provide 24
hours-a-day attendance and for which a small charge

of 10 paise (one United States cent) is made. For
this the user is given some soap powder for washing
after defecation.

Calcutta

There is nothing new about the need for sanitation
in Calcutta. For a couple of centuries and more its
alleys and squalid hovels have been spoken of as the
worst in the world. Since the partition of India in
1947 the situation has steadily become worse as
hundreds of thousands of migrants and refugees pour
into the metropolis. The squatter areas and slums –
the "bustees" – have cried out the need for proper
sanitation. The task of changing the environmental
condition of these areas has been laid on the
Calcutta Metropolitan Development Authority, CMDA. In
the later years of the 1970s the bustee improvement
programme made good progress. Space was at a premium
(the population density is amongst the highest in the
world) and CMDA was anxious to serve as many people
as possible with the available funds. It was
therefore decided to adopt a modified communal
system. Communal latrines in general become filthy
and unusable unless there are attendants available
throughout the day and night. On the other hand,
"households" are small in Calcutta. There are many
single-person families because men often come to the
city for work leaving these families in their
villages. So it was decided to provide single-unit
communal latrines. One latrine was provided for every
25 people. With so small a community sharing a
latrine it was hoped that the people would themselves
arrange for cleaning. Generally the scheme seems to
have worked well.

The choice of technology was original, but the
latrine had several disadvantages. It was the
cleverly-designed aqua-privy latrine made from
pre-fabricated concrete panels already described. The
first snag is the size of excavation required if the
tank is below ground. In much of Calcutta groundwater
is close to the surface, and in these places it is
impracticable to dig sufficiently deep so the chamber
is only partly below ground level and the whole
structure becomes very high. The latrine has to be
reached by steps with obvious disadvantages for old
people and young children.

The main disadvantage relates to the disposal of
effluent. Like a septic tank, an aqua-privy only

provides partial treatment. Where there is plenty of space the effluent percolates into the ground through a porous drain system. In Calcutta's congested bustees this is obviously impossible. It was difficult enough to find space for the latrines. So the effluent from many of the latrines was led into the surface-water drainage system - the open monsoon drains. The effluent from aqua-privies is very strong since only a little water is added, and it is highly charged with micro-organisms including disease-carrying pathogens. Disposal of sludge was also given insufficient attention. During the first couple of years there was no need to bother about this, but when the sludge level approaches the top of the chamber the effectiveness of settlement decreases and eventually if sludge completely fills the tank to overflow level there is virtually no treatment at all. It was intended that the aqua-privies should be emptied by tanker-lorries. However, many of the latrines are inaccessible to large lorries and the only realistic way of removing sludge is to bale it out. The sludge is a mixture of old inactive and harmless material with excreta which has only just been deposited.

Later the provision of aqua-privies was abandoned in favour of two-pit pour-flush latrines similar to those built in Patna and other parts of India. These are cheaper than the aqua-privies, and the CMDA was able to cover the whole cost of two-pit latrines at less cost than the 75 per cent grant previously made for the aqua-privies. (The remaining 25 per cent has been a loan to the people.) Pit latrines have no effluent problem since liquid percolates into the ground, and the two-pit system ensures that the sludge when removed is entirely decomposed and so is quite safe to take out by hand.

Factors determining the choice of appropriate
means of upgrading traditional methods
When the various systems of excreta removal and disposal are looked at together it can be seen that by far the most common of the successful schemes is some form of pit latrine. Exceptions are the Vietnamese compost latrines and the Japanese vault and tanker system. These exceptions have special requirements which prevent their widespread adoption, at least in the immediate future. The "secret" of the success of compost latrines lies in keeping the

material dry and adding extra carbon either in the form of ashes or vegetable matter. Composting requires care and a tradition of using both urine and faeces as fertilizers. If the latrine-user needs the collected urine and the composed faeces and carbon material for his own crops he may be willing to make an effort to ensure that the latrine is properly operated. To some extent this attitude towards compost may be due to traditional agricultural policy.

As far as pit latrines are concerned, there are now basically two satisfactory types. One is the large pit. Ideally this is large enough to last the household "for ever". It has been suggested that the period of seven years often referred to in the literature of many cultures has the meaning of "eternity" and so a long-life pit must be large enough to last at least seven years. Many people who dig long-life pits have a more realistic view of "permanent", and so there are the pits which give no sign of filling after more than 20 years. In fact there are indications that with suitable surrounding soil and enough water to keep the excreta wet a state is reached where the reduction of sludge volume by consolidation and decomposition balances the volume of added excreta.

The second satisfactory type is the double-pit, which again in some places is traditional in a crude form. A light superstructure built of local material such as bamboo could easily be moved to a second pit when the first one became filled. When the second pit was filled re-excavation of the first pit was easier than digging in virgin soil. The "modern" twin-pit VIP or pour-flush latrine is merely an improvement of the same basic idea, the fundamental difference being that the "improved" pit is lined so that with successive re-excavation the side walls remain intact rather than gradually collapsing.

Methods of anal cleaning are crucial in the selection of appropriate systems of excreta disposal and the development of traditional methods. Of the people who need to be provided with proper sanitation during the International Drinking Water Supply and Sanitation Decade a high proportion clean their backsides with water. Water-cleaning is preferred throughout India and in Moslem countries. Most people in these places already use water: others would like to, but water is scarce or can only be obtained with difficulty - for example by walking a long distance.

Provision of accessible water supplies to these people is likely to receive priority over sanitation, so in long-term planning it can usually be assumed that water will either be available before sanitation is considered, or will be provided as a package with improved sanitation. For people who use water for anal cleaning some type of pour-flush or water-seal latrine has advantages and is likely to be "acceptable", although it may be necessary to accompany latrine construction with a user-education programme such as that at Baldia.

Where there is a local tradition of providing dry latrines with well-built walls and roof (whether within the house or as a separate building) pour-flush latrines may be considered as a logical development, as often there can be a "conversion" from dry to pour-flush without demolition of the latrine room or building.

People who have no latrines at all, and therefore "traditionally" defecate in the open air, may object to using latrines with walls and roofs. To some extent this can be overcome by making the latrine room large so as to reduce the feeling of confinement when using the latrine. Similarly, there is no reason for persuading people to build minimum-size latrine rooms if they are in the habit of using a spacious room. This particularly applies, as we have seen in our consideration of Dar-es-Salaam, where people are accustomed to bathing in the latrine. It is common practice for householders to build their own superstructure whatever the mechanics and funding of the sanitation programme. Why persuade them to build a minimum-size room if they want to build a big one and are willing to provide the extra material and labour?

Arguments about the relative merits of household and communal latrines often arise when considering people whose present practice is to defecate in a common place like a defecation field or the banks of a stream. It has been reported that when household latrines have been provided in these circumstances the people continue to use the common ground because of the social aspects. A woman was reported to have said, "All day long I am confined to my home and family. The only time I get away from them and can gossip with other women is half an hour before dawn when we all go to the field to defecate". Communal latrines may satisfy this need for social evacuation of the bowels.

On the other hand there are many obvious advantages in a household latrine and disadvantages in a communal latrine. The greatest disadvantage of communal latrines is the difficulty of maintaining them in a clean and sanitary condition. Because they are communal no individual user feels responsible for cleanliness. So generally it is only those latrines with well-supervised attendants which are well-kept. In latrines without attendants the individual squatting plates or pans remain fouled and may become so disgusting that users do not enter the cubicles. The passages leading to the cubicles are next used and if the latrine is still not cleaned the whole building becomes revolting and people use the area around the latrine for defecation. Examples of unsatisfactory communal latrines can be seen (and smelled) throughout the world. Even in industrial countries public latrines without regular attention often become filthy.

The communal latrines at Patna are kept clean by attendants paid by an admission charge of 10 paise. The Oxfam sanitation units in the refugee camps of Bangladesh are all well-kept, because attendants are paid from Oxfam funds. For the Ibadan "comfort stations"[10] an attempt was made to pin responsibility for maintenance on the community served. At first the scheme worked well but before long many of the communities gave up their responsibilities. Householders became unwilling to clean the latrines themselves or share the cost of paid attendants. In other West African towns there have been communal latrines for 60 years or more and they are therefore accepted as quite normal. Some are well-designed, well-built and well-maintained.

Apart from the difficulty and cost of maintenance the greatest disadvantage of communal latrines, and consequently the greatest advantage of household latrines, is the inconvenience of having to walk some distance - say up to a couple of hundred metres - to a communal latrine. This is no great hardship for a healthy person who can attend to the call of nature regularly - say first thing in the morning. But during illness, especially illness accompanied by diarrhoea, it is obviously much more convenient to have a latrine at home.

Apart from those communities who habitually excrete socially, most people prefer privacy. For some people, particularly women, privacy is essential. Whilst most communal latrines provide privacy by having partitions between the cubicles, a user can be seen going into the building, which is embarrassing for some people. So to overcome this embarrassment some communal latrines, like the Ibadan comfort stations and many others in West Africa, are multi-functional. Part of the building is set apart for bathing and for washing clothes.

Conclusion: The need for flexibility

In preparing programmes for the International Drinking Water Supply and Sanitation Decade there is a natural tendency to look for methods which can be applied anywhere. International planners up to the mid-seventies assumed that the solution for all towns and cities was conventional sewerage. Similarly it would be convenient if a single system could be used for all the 2,400 million people who need sanitation by 1990 – or at least for the 747 million town-dwellers whose sanitation must be improved if the Decade's objects are to be met.

From a technical point of view it is possible to decide on a limited range of options and to provide rules for deciding which option is most appropriate. The World Bank in publications for the Decade has done this admirably. These rules are ideal for engineers trained in the conventional way. They make selection of technology into the solution of mathematical equations. Put in x and y and you get an answer z. The equation can allow for non-technical data. A "yes or no" answer to the question "is this option acceptable?" enables acceptability to be included in the equation.

However, when schemes in different parts of the world are examined it can be seen that successful improvement of sanitation is not a simple matter. It does not depend on engineering alone, nor economics nor management nor sociology alone. There must be combined effort, and each part of the selection process must be interwoven. Diagrams produced by the World Bank show a pattern of separate inputs: the sociologist deciding what system will be "acceptable", the engineer providing a design and the economist dealing with what is "affordable". For most projects there is very little chance of such a range of experts. Too often when specialists are available, they compete instead of working together. The attempt to find a perfect solution can be disastrous, because there are so many factors which are outside the range of the standard formula.

We have seen that efforts by outsiders to provide a good system have sometimes failed whereas in other places satisfactory latrines have been constructed with no guidance. So there needs to be a much keener appreciation of previous local sanitation. Wherever there are existing satisfactory latrines, that satisfactory type should be adapted locally and modified by improvements that take account of the local traditions in latrine construction and latrine usage. Sociologists may claim a proprietory right to interpret traditional ways. Unfortunately training in the social sciences is often just as irrelevant to effective sanitation programmes as is training in conventional engineering practice. There is a professional "mystique" amongst sociologists, just as there is amongst engineers and economists. The fundamental requirement for successful sanitation may be a change of attitude amongst professionals as well as amongst the people whose sanitation is to be improved. This new and desirable attitude includes a readiness to learn from people who do not understand professional "mystiques".

Usually at present the education of professionals and semi-professionals is contrary to this - rather it is in development of a specialist culture which is completely removed from the reality of appropriate low-cost sanitation. The key to appointment and promotion on the staff of colleges and universities is "academic performance", which has to be based on "research". Examination of academic publications shows that the subject matter is seldom related to anything which would really help the urban slums. Even the language cannot be understood by those who are not already experts. Unusual "technical" words are used to describe quite ordinary things. So a different type of advanced training is required. It must be one in which the full-time worker in this field of sanitation learns about the dangers of specialisation.

The basic requirement of successful sanitation improvement may be that those responsible take account of, and work with, the ordinary people who will benefit. There must be real co-ordination of all the factors which influence the selection of the most appropriate system. Knowledge of engineering must be added to management and economics and health and human science and institutional organisation and so on. But underlying it all must be a readiness to learn from others and to realise that what the local people do on their own without outside guidance is likely to be most effective in the long run.

Notes

1. D.J. Dwyer: People and housing in the third world cities: Perspectives on the problems of spontaneous settlements (London, Longmans, 1975).
2. B. Ward: "The sanitation revolution", in World Health (Geneva, World Health Organisation), Aug.-Sept., 1980, p. 9.
3. J.F. Jackson: "Sewerage, sewage treatment and refuse disposal for the city of Sana'a", in Proceedings, Fifth WEDC Conference on collaboration in water and waste engineering for developing countries (Loughborough. WEDC Group, 1979) pp. 55-84.
4. J. Pickford: The design of septic tanks and aqua-privies, Overseas Building Notes (No. 187, Watford, Sept. 1980).
5. A. Pacey (ed.): Sanitation in developing countries (Chichester, John Wiley & Sons, 1978), p. 148.
6. E.G. Wagner and J.N. Lanoix: Excreta disposal for rural areas and small communities, Monograph Series No. 39 (Geneva, World Health Organisation, 1958).
7. J. Kalbermatten et al: Appropriate technology for water supply and sanitation (Washington, DC, World Bank, 1980).
8. Proceedings, Seventh WEDC Conference on water, people and waste in developing countries (Loughborough, WEDC Group, 1981) p. 15.
9. B. Pathak: Sulabh shauchalaya (hand flush water seal latrine): A simple idea that worked (Calcutta, A. Pathak, 1981).
10. P.A. Oluwande: "Development of the aqua-privy for urban sanitation", in Proceedings, Second WEDC Conference on water, waste and health in hot countries (Loughborough, WEDC Group, 1975) pp. 109-117.

8 SCHOOLING FOR THE CHILDREN OF THE URBAN POOR

by S. Chitnis and C. Suvannathat

Introduction

This chapter discusses the role of formal schooling policies. It is based on two case studies, for Bangkok and Bombay. While there are similarities between these two cities clearly not everything which is good for one will apply to the other. Furthermore some recommendations which may be valid for them both need not be so elsewhere. They both are areas where schools are, by and large, physically available. The same would not have been true in some parts of Africa. In both cases also the possibility of at least free tuition exists. Again this would not apply everywhere.

Of all the various urban basic needs services to be discussed, schooling may appear the most conspicuous failure. Schooling in principle holds out the promise of equality of opportunity and, finally, of increased social equality. Yet in poor urban areas none of this is being achieved. This requires some explanation. Unlike in rural areas, in the towns children are commonly fairly close physically to schools. Schools are generally bigger, which is usually associated with improved educational performance. Teachers should, in principle, be more willing to accept urban than rural postings, so one common problem of rural schooling should be removed. Yet school drop-out and repetition rates are as high as in rural areas. Of course, there are contrary factors at work. The poor urban family's need for cash income may be so intense that child work is encouraged. Both parents may be working outside the home so that sibling care forces absence from school. Furthermore the ethos of some urban slum communities may be against schooling despite the clear advantages which a completed primary or secondary education brings in the labour market and despite everyday displays that illiteracy means poverty (and poverty means illiteracy). Frequently nonetheless the children of the urban poor fail to complete even four years of schooling, instead they repeat a couple of classes because they fall below the school's official standard and then drop out. Conversely they are often absent for long periods and then fail to return at all. As a result schooling plays little role in developing greater social equality.

There are a number of possible, broad explanations for the failure of urban school systems to integrate the children of the poor within them. One is that the home background of these children in terms of material and cultural deprivation can only be compensated for by extensive pre-school programmes, which are almost certainly too expensive for general application. Another explanation is that nothing the school system can do will ever be fully effective so that only the complete removal of urban poverty would guarantee, say, universal achievement of primary education. A third explanation is that schools reflect the dominant white collar culture with which many slum children will be uneasy. Such children will have difficulty in conforming and may, indeed, not do so. Finally is perhaps the optimistic approach that a better distribution of school resources, if that could be obtained, plus abstention from pushing fancy new school subjects, might do much to equalise educational chances and school performance.

This study hardly presents a final answer to these questions although it sheds light on many issues. The study is based on reports specifically focusing on two major Asian cities, Bangkok and Bombay. There is no doubt that the picture they paint is generally applicable to other major Asian cities. The next section concentrates on a statistical presentation of the school situation in Bombay, paying particular attention to drop-outs and repetition. After that a range of associated factors which characterise the schooling problems of the urban poor is reviewed. The final section discusses possible action.

Schooling in greater Bombay

Bombay was one of the first cities in India to adopt a policy of free and compulsory primary education (1927), and its Municipal Corporation has provided free primary education since 1907. Out of a current total of 2,036 schools in Bombay, 1,298 (with 73 per cent of primary and secondary pupils combined) are financed and managed by the Municipality. They serve the needs, not only of the population speaking the State language, Marathi, but also of migrants from other States. Except for two schools run by the Central Government all the others are owned and conducted by private management. These include religious or caste organisations, missionary societies, charitable trusts, private educational foundations, industrial houses and companies, etc. Only 51 out of the 765 secondary schools in the city are owned and managed by the Municipality; the majority come under private bodies.

Some private schools, both primary and secondary, are "aided" with State funds. Others are "unaided". Municipal schools charge no tuition fees at the primary level and only a nominal fee at the secondary level. In contrast, all, except the very few private schools that have been established as charities, charge tuition fees ranging from four or five rupees a month to upwards of 200 rupees per month in the most elite and generally unaided schools.

In principle all schools in India are structured for uniformity, and by implication, equality of academic programmes and facilities. Uniformity is obtained through conforming to the syllabus and textbooks prescribed by the State Department of Education. Schools, furthermore, have no control over the final certification of their students. The school leaving certificate examination at the end of ten years of school as well as the higher secondary school or junior college examination two years later are conducted by the State Boards of Education. However, differences creep in through the manner in which each management administers its programme. There are differences in the physical facilities provided, in the emphasis on English language and on subjects like science and mathematics, in the range of general knowledge given to students, in the quality of teaching and of supervision of academic work, in the extra-curricular activities to which students are exposed and in the social and intellectual climate that the school management creates. Superiority in these factors pays off, not only in the all-round development of students, but also in the quality of their examination performance. This in turn improves and secures a student's access to university, particularly to the prestigious courses and exclusive institutions for technical and professional education.

The quality of the extra-curricular and other facilities that the school management provides is at least partly a function of the funds available. High fees not only ensure "exclusiveness", they also guarantee superior physical surroundings, better teaching aids, laboratory, library and other academic facilities, a smaller teacher-student ratio, more varied choice in courses, more diversified and better organised extra-curricular activities, etc. Parents who can afford to do so, send their children to private schools that offer these "extras". The schools then gain students from home backgrounds favourable to schooling. In contrast, the free municipal schools and the private charity schools are used by the mass of children from working class backgrounds, who are generally first generation learners, from educationally disadvantaged homes.[1] These schools are confronted with pupils who are altogether unprepared for the discipline of schooling and who have very little or no help from their homes. Irregular attendance, poor performance and heavy drop-out combine to create a school climate that is hardly conducive to survival within the school system, much less to achievement and performance of the quality required for higher education.

Since children from the socially and economically disadvantaged families in Bombay are largely in municipal schools, it is necessary to focus on these schools to understand the schooling of the poor. However, overall school enrolment in the city will first be examined.

Data on the 6-11 years age group are available in the quinquennial survey of school enrolment of the Municipal Corporation.[2] The 1981 Census estimates the population in the compulsory school age (6-11 years) to be about 623,000 and claims that 98.5 per cent of this group is at school. It further reports that the number of "non-attending" children in this age group, which stood at 13,368 at the time of the census, fell to 8,767 by the time the census report was written (March 1982) as 4,601 children subsequently joined school after an intensive school enrolment drive that accompanied the census.

However, in the census data the term "non-attending" is ambiguous and vague. It can apply to three categories of children: (a) those who have never been enrolled at school, (b) those who are enrolled but who do not attend school regularly, (c) those who have dropped out of school. Those in the last category may continue on the schools rolls or their names may have been struck off the school register. The children themselves may or may not be aware of the exact situation and may or may not consider, and describe, themselves as enrolled at school. Thus the census data on this subject cannot be used without further clarification. Inquiries with the census authorities on this point were not particularly illuminating. The authorities indicated that enumerators listed as "non-attending" were all those who were "not currently enrolled" at school, i.e. at the point of the census. Asked to specify whether drop-outs were included among those "not enrolled", they were uncertain. Presumably, the listing depended on how the children and their parents saw the situation. It is possible that most drop-outs consider themselves to be "enrolled" at school regardless of whether they "attend" or not.

The census figures must thus be taken with reservation and the reality of school enrolment in the city must be examined in more specific terms. It is necessary to find out how many of those who enter school complete their education and how many drop out. It is also necessary to know how many attend school regularly, pass the annual examinations and progress through to successively higher standards. We will make an effort to do so below.

School retention and drop-out survey

Official data as provided by the State Department of Education are generally used to estimate "retention". Such data give total school enrolment from Std. I, which constitutes the entry point, to Std. X, the terminal point. Taking, for example, the academic years 1971-72 to 1980-81 students enrolled in Std. I in 1971-72 should, if they progress smoothly through each year of school, be in Std. X in the year 1980-81. The 73,996 students enrolled in Std. X in the year 1980-81 could be regarded as those who "survived" up to the terminal point of school. Similarly, the 135,542 students enrolled in Std. V in 1975-76 could be viewed as those who completed the primary stage terminating at Std. IV. The rate of retention up to completion of Std. IV would then be 69 per cent for girls and 75 per cent for boys. Up to completion of Std. IX and entry into Std. X, it is 36 per cent for girls and 42 per cent for boys.

These figures must, in the absence of more detailed data, be accepted as a rough measure but they do not really tell us much, either about retention or about drop-out. They have not been adjusted for "failure" in each standard, both from the batch enrolled in Std. I in 1971-72 and from the backlog of failures from earlier batches, or for "fresh admissions", i.e. those who may have joined school after the initial entry point at Std. I, possibly coming from outside the city, or for "transfers" of children moving away from the city. We have no clue to the necessary size of the adjustment for failures and fresh admissions and transfers. But if these adjustments were made the percentage of retention could well change significantly.

Meanwhile, data from a major study on drop-out and stagnation in municipal schools being completed by the Education Department of the Bombay Municipal Corporation,[3] indicate a very high incidence of drop-out. This study covers a highly representative sample of 95 (7 per cent) of the 1,298 municipal primary schools and offers a detailed follow-up of students admitted to Std. I during the academic years 1972-73, 1973-4 and 1976-77. Forty-five of these 97 schools provide schooling up to Std. VII. Others provide education only up to Std. IV. The sample of the former schools was stratified to distinguish those with a relatively "better" performance record from those with an "average" performance record. Data are given in table 13. Students from the two upper primary schools constitute batches A and B in the table and students from the lower primary schools constitute batch C.

The table indicates that only 18 to 24 per cent of students had completed Std. IV within the stipulated period of four years. An even smaller percentage, only 9 per cent from batch A and 11 per cent from batch B, had completed the seventh standard within the regular seven year period. A large number, 39 per cent from batch A, 30 per cent from batch B and 44 per cent from batch C, failed and were held back before completing Std. IV. A smaller number, 5 per cent in batches A and B, failed after completing Std. IV. These failures, a total of 44 per cent in batch A, 35 per cent in batch B and 44 per cent in batch C are "stagnating" in lower classes.

As many as 32 per cent of students from batch A, 35 per cent from batch B and 24 per cent from batch C

Table 13: Enrolment, drop-out and performance of municipal school students in Bombay[1] in percentages for each year

Batch	Academic Year	Std.	Left with certificates	Left without certificates	Passed and promoted	Failed and held back
A enrolled 1972-73	1972-73	I	1	22	55	22
(17 schools)	1975-76	IV	9	32	20	39
	1978-79	VII	14	33	9	44
B enrolled 1973-74	1973-74	I	3	26	63	8
(25 schools)	1976-77	IV	11	35	24	30
	1979-80	VII	18	36	11	35
C enrolled 1976-77	1976-77	I	3	18	55	24
(55 schools)	1979-80	IV	11	25	18	46

1 Data cover a total sample of 97 municipal schools. The data refer to the end of the year in question, i.e. for Batch A in 1978-79, 14 per cent of the original, 1972-73 enrolment had left with certificates, 33 per cent without certificates, 9 per cent passed Std. VII in the time intended and 44 per cent were still in school in other standards.
2 Drop-outs.
Source: Special survey by Education Department, Bombay Municipality, 1981.

had left without school leaving certificates and, presumably, had dropped out of school before they reached Std. IV. A small, one per cent in batches A and B dropped out, thereafter. As many as 9 per cent to 11 per cent of the students, in each of the three batches, left with school leaving certificates before completing Std. IV. A small 5 per cent in batch A and 7 per cent in batch B left with certificates after they had cleared the Std. IV examination. It is to be hoped that these students, 14 per cent from batch A, 18 per cent from batch B and 11 per cent from batch C, were admitted to other schools. But we have no information on this.

Since the Municipal Corporation data provided no details on the status of those who failed, some primary data were collected from one of the three municipal schools observed specifically for this report. These data may not be representative for all municipal schools; nevertheless they illustrate the likely form of stagnation. In this school 395 children were enrolled in Std. I in 1975-76. After seven years (i.e. in 1982) only 22 (5 per cent) had reached Std. VII. As many as 244 (62 per cent) had dropped out or left school with transfer certificates, at various points. The remaining 129 (33 per cent) had failed repeatedly and were lingering in the lower classes as follows:

	No.	Per cent
Std. I	Nil	(–)
Std. II	3	(2)
Std. III	12	(9)
Std. IV	18	(14)
Std. V	55	(43)
Std. VI	41	(32)
Total	129	(100)

Thus 33 (8.4 per cent of the original enrolment) of those who joined Std. I in 1975-76 were both still in school and had still to complete primary school in 1982. No-one knows how long it will take them to do so nor how long the 96 students (25.3 per cent), stuck in Stds. V and VI, will take to be promoted to Std. VII and to complete that level. Will these students finally finish school? Or will repeated failure undermine their future? If so, at what cost to themselves and their families?

We also asked certain élite and middle class schools about drop-out. It appears that drop-out is a problem of schools that serve the poor, the working class and the lower middle class. It does not seem to exist in schools that serve the middle and upper middle classes. Even the problem of failure affects them only marginally. This is for several reasons. Students are better prepared for schooling when they enter school. They go on to attend school more regularly and are better supervised both at school and at home. Schools alert parents if they notice a child's poor or declining performance. Parents in turn readily provide extra coaching to save their children from losing a year. In some schools the students' performance is so closely watched and controlled that, at least at the primary level, annual promotion is automatic.

While drop-out constitutes total withdrawal from school, irregular attendance may be viewed as partial withdrawal, particularly when it occurs continuously. A cursory observation of poor childrens' schooling reveals their poor attendance. Unfortunately, there is very little systematic information available. Both the State Department of Education and the Education Department of the Bombay Municipal Corporation collect data on school attendance. But these data are presented in an aggregate form, which conveys very little. For this report specific data were collected from one municipal school and are presented in table 14. Again these data may not be representative but they illustrate the problem.

The table shows that between 10 and 20 per cent of the students are usually absent for more than 10 days a month in Std. I, Std. II and Std. III throughout the year. Another 5 to 10 per cent are absent for between five to nine days. The share absent for more than ten days a month falls in the higher standards. Nevertheless absenteeism is quite high throughout the school particularly at the beginning of the school year in July.

The table gives absenteeism as a percentage of "average" enrolment. In municipal schools enrolment, for each class, is not constant throughout the year. Students are admitted and drop out at any point. Enrolment is generally lowest at the beginning of the year in July and August, increases between September and December and declines thereafter. In Std. I, in the school shown in the table, it was 339 in July, 394 in August, 406 in September, October, November and December, dropped to 386 in January, and stood at 367 in February and March. Enrolment obviously picks up as the academic year advances. It declines from January onwards, possibly because seasonal employment attracts children away, or because their interest flags after a few months of school.

In addition to the problems of drop-out, failure, stagnation and absenteeism, a further major shortcoming in the education of poor children is their late start. In India a child is normally expected to enrol in Std. I as soon as possible after the fifth birthday. Of 393 admissions to the first standard in 1975 in one municipal school, 153 children (39 per cent) were 5 years old, 145 (37 per cent) were 6 years old, 50 (13 per cent) were 7 years old, 24 (6 per cent) were 8 years old and 21 (5 per cent) were between 9 and 12 years old. Late start and repeated failure combine to cause inordinate delay in the education of poor children. Table 15 gives the age composition of children in Stds. I, II, III and IV in the school mentioned. Only between 51 to 61 percent of the children in Stds. I-III and 71 per cent of the children in Std. IV are in the appropriate age group. Stds. I, II and III seem, in particular, to have a large percentage of over-age children. Few, however, are over age in Std. IV. This suggests that Stds. I, II and III constitute difficult hurdles to cross. Given the high percentage of failure in Std. I and indeed in Stds. II and III, it may well be that children from poor families are eliminated before they reach Std. IV.

The massive incidence of failure and drop-out in municipal primary schools is devastating evidence of the quality of the school performance of poor children and, of course, of the social and economic problems they and their families face. There are a few other indicators of performance and they too are revealing. Each year the State Government awards 250 merit scholarships to Std. IV children. Not a single municipal school child ever qualified for a scholarship in the 20 years up to 1977–78. In that year the Corporation began special classes to coach selected students. Sixteen thousand five hundred and seventy-seven children were prepared for the

Table 14: Children absent by standard and month in percentages

	July	Aug.	Sept.	Oct.	Nov.	Dec.	Jan.	Feb.	Mar.	
3-5 days	8.5	5.6	4.0	1.2	6.2	6.6	4.1	3.8	8.7	4.9
Standard I: 6-9 days		5.0	3.8	1.2	1.7	3.0	0.5	2.3	4.1	10.6
10+		30.6	15.7	17.3	13.8	20.2	19.0	21.2	13.9	2.2
Standard II: 3-5 days		4.0	7.1	8.9	4.8	6.8	7.5	4.9	1.9	2.2
6-9 days		1.7	1.8	3.0	0.6	2.4	2.7	2.5	2.2	15.0
10+		28.2	19.2	11.9	10.7	16.2	16.4	14.8	14.7	4.3
Standard III: 3-5 days		3.5	8.3	3.5	4.3	6.2	6.7	1.5	2.0	2.4
6-9 days		0.8	1.2	1.6	3.5	3.5	1.9	1.2	0.4	8.7
10+		16.5	11.1	10.9	10.95	12.4	11.1	11.2	9.4	5.7
Standard IV: 3-5 days		5.7	4.8	10.3	1.2	13.5	11.1	6.9	9.6	1.2
6-9 days		2.8	3.6	2.4	1.6	1.6	1.2	1.2	2.9	2.5
10+		17.0	12.3	5.1	4.3	6.3	9.1	7.7	5.3	4.0
Standard V: 3-5 days		0.4	5.4	5.3	0.4	12.6	6.6	9.1	7.2	0.4
6-9 days		4.6	3.1	1.4	-	5.0	4.6	3.9	1.6	1.6
10+		15.5	4.2	3.4	3.8	5.7	5.4	5.5	3.6	4.0
Standard VI: 3-5 days		8.8	4.2	7.7	1.6	12.8	2.8	8.6	9.7	-
6-9 days		3.1	5.8	1.7	-	5.6	3.9	3.4	3.4	4.6
10+		17.5	11.1	7.7	3.8	10.0	7.8	6.9	2.9	1.9
Standard VII: 3-5 days		10.1	6.4	13.5	-	18.2	6.4	5.5	3.8	2.9
6-9 days		1.8	4.6	4.5	1.8	5.4	2.7	0.9	0.9	4.8
10+		17.4	8.3	-	7.2	8.2	5.4	8.3	8.6	

Source: Primary data collected.

high while grade repetition from school failure led to a wide range of age and abilities in any one class. These made the teacher's job more difficult and reduced the pupil's willingness to learn. Grade repetition in fact inhibited academic growth and caused dropping out. Furthermore, in Thailand, the bureaucratic nature of the school and examination system were major disincentives for children to stay on in school.

Research studies examining the effect of community factors stressed such variables as the economic status of the community, its consciousness of educational values and its responsibility towards the school. These qualitative indicators were related to the school's intellectual atmosphere and the pupils' level of school performance. In communities without these three variables low school attendance and neglect of the school as a focal point of community activity resulted, yielding low intellectual stimulation and a low level of pupil performance in school.

Finally, the causes of educational wastage in the form of low achievement levels, school failures or repetition and dropping out were seen to be a combination of social, economic, psychological, educational, administrative and sometimes political factors. These might be derived from the pupil himself, his family, teacher and school or community. Nevertheless, all factors were generally closely interlinked. In addition it was stressed that low pupil achievement was the cause of school drop-out. Among the inter-related factors associated with school performance, the child's socio-economic status (as best represented by father's occupation) and his or her related problems such as health and learning, type of child rearing, parent's degree of support and encouragement for children to go to school and stay in school, grade repeating, teacher's qualification and standard of instruction, teacher's positive perception of child's ability, school organisation and the community's consciousness of educational values were the best qualitative indicators of school achievement levels among the urban poor.

This general analysis for Bangkok is confirmed by findings in Bombay. Prominent among family based inadequacies is their poverty which operates as a handicap to education in many ways. Firstly, children need to earn. According to the Census of India of expenditure of 72 rupees; (ii) factory workers with per capita expenditure of 103 rupees; and (iii) small establishment workers, who are the best off (per capita expenditure 117 rupees). The average of 4.03 years of education among casual workers is lower than the average for factory workers and workers in small establishments (6.01 years).

Explanatory factors

A synthesis study prepared for Bangkok reviewed the large number of factors associated with poor school performance of the children of the urban poor. One first finding of the study concerned the causal relation between school drop-out and low school achievement. It established that the cause of drop-out was mainly low levels of achievement, thus it is school achievement levels during the early years which must be raised if drop-out is to be eliminated. This, of course, tallies with experience in Bombay and is probably generally valid.

The Bangkok study synthesised a wide range of evidence on school achievement and its relation to various factors, namely: (a) pupil characteristics; (b) family factors (including socio-economic background); (c) teacher and school factors; and (d) community factors. Among pupil characteristics it was found that low achievement levels were linked to the absence of pre-schooling, to lower levels of intellectual ability measured by cognitive complexity, lower levels of aspiration and attention to learning. The general health, as measured by average height and weight, and nutritional status of low achieving pupils was low. Few pupils had regular exposure to newspapers, books, radio and television. Only a small percentage of their parents had more than the compulsory four years' of schooling. Besides, the children appeared to have irregular school attendance and longer periods of school absenteeism, a less intellectually complex and a less analytical style of thinking than scholastically successful children, less tolerance for delayed gratification, an inability to finish homework, poor health maintenance habits and both physical and mental health problems leading to consequent learning problems.

As far as family background factors are concerned it was often found that the urban poor or other disadvantaged pupils' socio-economic background was

strongly   associated   with   their   scholastic
achievement. Father's occupation was so important
that it could stand for all socio-economic background
variables.   The   most   important   factors   affecting
school achievement were home atmosphere, household
language, types of child rearing, parental education
and family size. The urban poor pupils were generally
surrounded by environmental characteristics which led
to   a   non-intellectual   home   and   neighbourhood
atmosphere. Moreover poor practices in child care and
rearing were found to be negatively related to the
health   of   pre-school   children,   reducing   their
readiness for school. All this caused the children to
adapt poorly at school. This finding was by no means
surprising. Child psychologists had known it for
years. Urban poor pupils were also from minority
groups whose household language was not Central Thai,
the medium of instruction at schools.

In addition, children from a lower class culture
and   low   income   families   had   usually   learned   a
linguistic form favouring a more concrete word usage
than   had   the   middle-class   child.   This   made   the
problem of moving through the stages of conceptual
development and learning various subjects, especially
the   Thai   language, more   difficult.   Very   closely
related   to   academic   backwardness   were   some
undesirable psychological traits which certain types
of child rearing in urban low income families had
developed. Urban poor children were more likely to be
brought up with control and psychological punishment
rather than with love and reasoning. This developed
some psychological traits which inhibited academic
growth rather than enhancing it.

Poor school performance is also related to certain
teacher and school factors. It was found that in
schools where disadvantaged children were taught by
less qualified teachers, educational wastage in forms
of grade repetition, drop-out, and low level of
achievement resulted. The less qualified teachers are
those without a teaching certificate, those who had
shown job dissatisfaction, poor mental health, lack
of initiative, and inability to assume their expected
roles and associated responsibilities. Studies also
directly or indirectly revealed that teachers' low
perception of children's ability led to conflict and
frustration and poor academic performance. In Bangkok
it was observed that the quality of teaching was
often very poor, curriculum standards were set too

high while grade repetition from school failure led to a wide range of age and abilities in any one class. These made the teacher's job more difficult and reduced the pupil's willingness to learn. Grade repetition in fact inhibited academic growth and caused dropping out. Furthermore, in Thailand, the bureaucratic nature of the school and examination system were major disincentives for children to stay on in school.

Research studies examining the effect of community factors stressed such variables as the economic status of the community, its consciousness of educational values and its responsibility towards the school. These qualitative indicators were related to the school's intellectual atmosphere and the pupils' level of school performance. In communities without these three variables low school attendance and neglect of the school as a focal point of community activity resulted, yielding low intellectual stimulation and a low level of pupil performance in school.

Finally, the causes of educational wastage in the form of low achievement levels, school failures or repetition and dropping out were seen to be a combination of social, economic, psychological, educational, administrative and sometimes political factors. These might be derived from the pupil himself, his family, teacher and school or community. Nevertheless, all factors were generally closely interlinked. In addition it was stressed that low pupil achievement was the cause of school drop-out. Among the inter-related factors associated with school performance, the child's socio-economic status (as best represented by father's occupation) and his or her related problems such as health and learning, type of child rearing, parent's degree of support and encouragement for children to go to school and stay in school, grade repeating, teacher's qualification and standard of instruction, teacher's positive perception of child's ability, school organisation and the community's consciousness of educational values were the best qualitative indicators of school achievement levels among the urban poor.

This general analysis for Bangkok is confirmed by findings in Bombay. Prominent among family based inadequacies is their poverty which operates as a handicap to education in many ways. Firstly, children need to earn. According to the Census of India of

1971, as many as 37 per cent of Bombay children aged 0-14 are engaged in work for pay or profit. In fact in many cases it is the children who keep their families on the upper side of the "wolf line". Parents may therefore see little immediate alternative to their children working full or part time. But work interferes with school, either by discouraging enrolment altogether or by making for poor attendance and drop-out. In one school in Bombay students were absent en masse each time a neighbouring factory had a peak period of production.

In a more direct way poverty implies food deprivation, resulting in continual hunger, malnutrition and ill-health. One investigator in Bangkok[6] reported the direct and indirect effects of physical illness on the developing child. Illness forbade the young child from continuing his normal activity while pain suffered can lead to his misunderstanding and misinterpreting his parents' intentions. Cerebral pathology could disturb the child's consciousness and ability to learn. In older children, illness such as cardio-pulmonary disease, blood dyscrasia, renal and endocrinal disorders make school attendance irregular and can lead to emotional problems. Another study in Bangkok[7] indicated that children's intellectual ability was related to nutritional status and to height and weight. While no significant intellectual difference was observed between groups of high income and low income children with normal nutrition, the intellectual ability of the under-nourished low income group was significantly lower.

In the city of Bombay poverty also means houselessness, or at best a meagre shelter. Children living on pavements and in hutments are exposed to harsh heat in Summer and to continuous wind and rain during monsoons. For almost four months a year they are often in damp or wet clothing, for weeks on end. Even those who have shelter live nevertheless in places where toilet facilities are negligible, where drains are clogged, flooded and overflowing, where there is no drainage or sanitation at all and certainly without a corner to sit and study or a light to read by at night.

In Bombay "leaving school for change of residence" is a common occurrence. This reflects frequent shifts in residence. Children are pulled out of school as their parents move from one construction site to

another, or from one slum to another as their
"illegal" shanties are demolished, or as they are
"evicted" from their slums in "slum clearance"
drives. Children also move back and forth from
village to city if their families fail to find work.

Studies in Bombay have also stressed "cultural
deprivation" as a factor discouraging success at
school, including children's inability to formulate
or to deal with abstract concepts, inability to
classify, comprehend and to recognise patterns, poor
articulation and limited ability to handle language.
This in turn arises out of their total unfamiliarity
with the language used at school, which is altogether
different from the "lower class" dialects that they
speak at home. They are also unfamiliar with the
artifacts, apparatus and the modes of interaction
that they are required to use at school.

Finally table 16 shows reasons "non-attending"
children in Bombay gave for leaving school. It can be
noted that non-attending girls outnumbered boys by
some 13 per cent.

Other school factors enumerated in Bombay as
discouraging school enrolment include the following:
physical inadequacies, i.e. no playgrounds,
workrooms, etc.; drab surroundings and poor
maintenance; few visual aids and teaching materials;
a tendency on the part of teachers to attribute the
poor performance of children to "poor capacity" or to
the "indifference of parents" and the inability to
recognise fully the implications of their social
deprivation for their performance; a failure to build
upon the capacities of children from working class
backgrounds, to harness the unique maturity that
exposure to poverty and to life in the raw cultivates
in these children, and conversely, the practice of
forcing them through moulds and paces set for middle
and upper class children from white collar
occupational and professional homes; a failure to
provide textbooks and a curriculum fitting these
children's interests and to work with them through
the spoken dialects of their illiterate subculture
and to help them graduate to the concepts and
language used in formal education; a failure to adapt
school timings and terms to the needs of children
with other obligations to fulfil, i.e. younger
siblings to take care of, etc.; the failure to enable
these children to cope with the fear and uncertainty
that they must inevitably suffer, as their home lives

are continuously marked with sickness, death,
disruption, unemployment, usury and uncertainty of
every kind; the teachers' inadequacy to teach complex
subjects to students whose social backgrounds
strengthen learning difficulties; the prevalence of
bureaucratic practices and procedures that cripple
the initiative of school teachers, administrators and
children alike and often inhibit illiterate parents
from enrolling their children at all.

In this last context it can be mentioned that in
Bombay at least the entire education system managed
by the Municipal Corporation is headed by a single
education officer with total responsibility for its
administration. Every innovative action, every small
decision, every small transfer of teachers,
supervisors or administrators has to have her
personal approval and sanction. Decentralisation in
the organisation and administration of the municipal
school system is urgently required. Similarly the
ethos of this administration seems to rest on total
deference, awe and fear of disapproval. It is visibly
difficult for creativity, initiative, drive and
confidence to flourish. As individuals, the persons
in the system are capable of empathy and concern. But
the ethos of the organisation in which they function
is not conducive to dynamism and involvement. There
are also serious organisational problems in utilising

Table 16:. Reasons for non-attendance in Bombay
           in percentages

Reason	Boys	Girls
No school nearby	15.0	13.7
Looking after siblings	18.6	25.2
Household work	18.4	26.5
Need to earn	17.9	9.9
No clothing, pencils, etc.	11.3	9.9
Illness	3.4	3.4
Vagabond or truant	5.2	1.5
Married	-	0.4
Physical disability	4.0	2.2
Lack of interest	6.2	7.3
Total	100.0	100.0

Source: Bombay Municipal Corporation: Quinquennial
census of school-age children, 1981.

and absorbing the assistance and aid offered by voluntary bodies. A few such organisations have done excellent work, others have found it extremely difficult to be accepted. Much as they try to, they find it impossible to break through the bureaucratic barriers and to help. Similarly in Bombay organisations like the British Council or the Ford Foundation have given assistance to improve the teaching of science, mathematics or languages, but their contributions remain isolated. This may be because they are essentially limited as "pilot projects" or "experimental programmes". But it is also possible that the lack of dynamism within the system, the lack of a spirited involvement on the part of the mass of teachers, supervisors and administrators and rigidities of different kinds are to blame.

Steps to take

It is doubtful if working through the education authorities alone can ever solve the problems surrounding the school performance of the children of the urban poor. Thus in Thailand it has been stressed that changes within the family environment are essential. Among the urban poor parents are unable to create a stimulating environment which will lay strong foundations for their children's emotional health and intellectual development. Means to enrich and stimulate the intellectual and emotional world of deprived and less privileged children are as follows:

(a) Changing child-rearing practices. Regardless of the family's socio-economic and cultural background a "democratic" environment can be created by combining love-oriented, reasoning-oriented, psychological punishment-oriented and control-oriented methods of child rearing.

(b) A greater balance in parental roles between mother and father should be emphasised. Verbal interest and expression in child care on the father's part are not enough.

(c) Parental aspirations and expectations should be based not only on the family's financial condition, but also on the children's own interest and abilities, which are rarely considered by lower class mothers.

(d) To ensure that each child can fully benefit from his or her own individuality and unique family experience, both parents should concentrate on the significance of total family relationships.

(e) Parents should realise that the social and emotional aspects of child growth and development are as important as intellectual and physical aspects.

No doubt these points are generally valid, not only in Thailand. Adult education programmes are therefore essential to inculcate changed parental attitudes towards child development. However, no doubt they will be difficult to achieve.

In Thailand it is also stressed that beneficial changes can take place within schools. Competent teachers who have confidence in their students are those who strive to teach all dimensions of a good education. But without such competence and confidence, children will not learn even if the textbooks are available, school supplies are adequate, the school large and the class small. Many features of Thai teacher training are still unsuitable to the real needs of Thai society. Important amongst these are the bureaucratic nature of the school administration, ineffective school-community relations and a cognitive rather than affective orientation in teacher training. Some remedial steps can be taken. Thus, more individualised and more field-based components can be gradually incorporated into teacher training. Since the inadequate adjustment of the school curriculum to the psychological and social needs of young children is frequently mentioned as a cause of wastage a better adapted curriculum should be developed.

In addition in Thailand it is suggested that techniques of teaching and class management specifically for urban poor and disadvantaged children should be developed alongside the revised curriculum. Teachers should encourage pupils to perceive classroom tasks more positively by their own influence and example. In addition compensatory education schemes and programmes for urban poor and disadvantaged children should aim at overcoming specific learning problems. For example, the idea of a "reading mobilisation year" can be adopted in the total school programme geared towards the improvement of Thai language reading.

Finally, in all poor countries the free supply of textbooks, guidance and counselling services, medical and health services, food and school lunch services and free clothing are all necessary items. However, close supervision is needed to ensure adequate and efficient use of these aids.

In Bombay, organisations such as Nirmala Niketan, the school of social work affiliated to Bombay University, has built an excellent programme reducing drop-out and failure and advancing the progress of children from poor families at municipal schools. The programme provides family counselling services, sponsors financial aid, provides exercise books and evening study centres, organises school preparation sessions a month ahead of admissions to Std. I in June, and organises special classes with Std. I children to improve retention. But these programmes cover only a small fraction of the municipal school population. The School of Social Work covers only 15 schools with a population of 9,617 primary and secondary school children, 1.05 per cent and 3.2 per cent, respectively, of all municipal school children at those stages of education. Moreover, the nature of the help these programmes offer requires a heavy investment of time and calls for rare personal qualities. Such programmes wherever implemented require a sensitive understanding of the problems and the situation of the children and of the schools in the target group. This calls for patience, tenacity and adaptability. Results are slow, strategies have to be tested, retested, revised and varied. In fact, in Bombay, the School of Social Work, which has operated its programme for ten years, already finds that its success has dropped considerably at the school where it first started. As the pioneers of the programme moved on to extend it elsewhere, the staff left behind could not retain the earlier dynamism.

In Bombay again the Corporation itself has fairly comprehensive plans for improving school effectiveness. More schools will be built so that each child is within walking distance. There is also a scheme for "open learning", or non-formal education for "out of school" children, schemes for vocational education, action aimed at a shift from rote learning and almost exclusive use of the didactic method of teaching to the multi-media approach, to include the use of television, tape recordings, and packages for programmed learning. Plans for qualitative improvement cover programmes for in-service teacher training. There are schemes to produce material for programmed learning, for better laboratories and libraries, for incentives to students for reading, writing, speaking, comprehending, cultivating good health and work habits, programmes for improving the school environment, for more effective supervision, and for improved methods and equipment for classroom teaching.

Valuable as they are, Bombay experience suggests that, as a general rule, plans and programmes of this nature for better teachers, a better curriculum, more supplies, are not likely to yield the results desired unless they are supported by more basic action. It is firstly necessary in those areas where it does not in practice apply to implement compulsion. However, since experience clearly indicates that it is totally unrealistic to expect all children to attend school as full-time students, it is necessary to develop alternative facilities for working children. A basic requirement is for school classes at suitable hours. A syllabus would need to be covered in two or three hour school days instead of the normal six to seven hour school days. For Bombay the following table provides some clues as to when and for how long students who are forced to earn in order to supplement their family incomes could participate. The table shows significant differences between the preferences of girls and of boys, which must be considered.

Table 17: Alternative education for out-of-school children in percentages

| Suitable time | Working children | | Non-working children | |
	Boys	Girls	preferred duration	preferred duration
Any time	21.7	15.7	1 hr: 7.1	0.9
Morning	11.8	10.2	2 hrs: 61.4	28.3
Afternoon	14.7	40.3	3 hrs: 17.7	24.3
Evening	25.5	10.4	Over 3 hrs: 3.5	29.9
Night	16.8	2.6		
No response	9.5	20.8	No response: 10.3	16.6
	100.0	100.0	100.0	100.0

Source: A. Jacob: Educating out-of-school children: A survey of Dharavi slum (Bombay, Tata Institute of Social Sciences, 1979).

It would be naive to imagine that in Bombay or elsewhere such children will make use of new facilities developed unless they are provided with strong incentives and motivation to do so. Experience suggests that incentives should be in the liveliness of the programme offered and in its visible relevance to the children's upward mobility. Incentives should be strong enough to make it worthwhile for working children to attend school at the end, or the beginning, of a working day.

A further point which applies to usually all Asian cities concerns the existing gap between schools for the well-to-do and schools for "others". In all major cities the better educated and otherwise privileged families place a high premium on the education of their children and strive hard for quality in the schools their children attend. In contrast, they do nothing to improve schools for the masses. One possible way of channelling their interests and resources to the advantage of others would be to create a social class mix. Naturally this is likely to be difficult if not impossible. A further requirement is for much greater involvement of other groups, businesses and voluntary organistions in the education of the poor. In Bombay, for example, such involvement has weakened in the three decades since Independence, a part of the larger malaise of the decline of the capacity for self-help and the increased tendency to lean heavily on the government. Programmes such as those discussed above for Bombay cannot be expanded or extended without public support, finance and help. Industrial and business houses, voluntary organisations, public spirited individuals, must be drawn on for necessary support. Business and industry encouraged, of course, by suitable tax exemptions, has shown interest in financing rural development projects and health and family planning programmes in rural and urban areas. Similarly women's organisations and student groups have helped in a variety of welfare programmes. They could do more to stimulate community development and assistance in education programmes. Such assistance in building up nurseries and day-care centres for pre-school children would be beneficial.

In general terms there are other ways in which private employers can help overcome the education problem. One way would be through adult education courses for their employees. Another would be day-care services for the employees' younger children thus freeing their siblings from this task. But those steps would probably inevitably be restricted to larger and better paying enterprises. In Bangkok the helpful role which nurseries can play is also stressed. In addition health care programmes usually need to be extended to urban poor households in all Asian cities, both to build up children's health levels and to educate parents on child health and nutrition. Family planning programmes aimed at reducing household size may also have a general role to play. Finally community leaders everywhere have a responsibility to encourage school attendance, support school improvement projects and stimulate home visits to identify potential and actual school drop-outs and, if possible, organise relief and assistance.

At the policy level a number of general points can be made of universal applicability. One of these is the necessity for better estimates of the numerical size of the education problem. The statistical concepts on which data collection is based are often hazy and confused and the extent of school enrolment is probably often exaggerated. On the other hand aggregate statistics nowhere demonstrate the amount of in-school repetition and the considerable age-range in class. If statistics do not reveal the extent of the problem, and generally it requires micro-level studies of the type reproduced here from Bombay to do so, then policy makers will not see the urgency of remedial action.

Generally it would not appear that the education of the children of the urban poor is seen as a policy problem by educational planners. Hardly ever is the content of a primary school curriculum reviewed in terms of its difficulty or appropriateness for children from different socio-economic groups. The result, naturally, is that education planners are likely to take their own cultural frame of reference as the norm to which others must gradually conform. In the long run this may be acceptable. In the short run, as we have seen, children of the urban poor can be brought up to that level only by intensive and expensive efforts. But, more commonly, such children drop out of the education race soon after it begins. Of course, in many countries a common practical question is whether a high standard of universal primary education is indeed possible. It may be argued that something lesser, more non-formal in character, may be all that the mass of the urban, and rural, population can currently hope for. But to act on that basis would be to give in to the current social division between the privileged and the rest and to deny all hope of equality of opportunity. In this way a definite and deliberate policy for early childhood education aimed at developing sound knowledge among underprivileged children is essential.

Notes

1. As an illustration, a comparison of a municipal with an élite school showed over two-thirds of pupils in the former from households with incomes of below 500 rupees in 1981. In the élite school no household income was below 600 rupees.

2. The authors are grateful to the Municipal Commissioner of Greater Bombay and to the Education Officer of the Bombay Municipal Corporation for sharing these data, even before they have been compiled in the official report.

3. These data were obtained directly from the Education Department of the Municipal Corporation.

4. B. Prakash: <u>Pattern of employment among slum dwellers of Bombay</u>, Draft report for the International Council on Social Welfare, Regional Office for Asia and Western Pacific (Bombay, Tata Institute of Social Sciences, 1981) (mimeo).

5. L. Deshpande: <u>Bombay's labour market</u> (University of Bombay, Department of Economics, 1979) (mimeo).

6. S. Thanaphum: "Health problems affecting intellectual and emotional development of Thai children" in <u>The child and adolescent in a changing Asian world</u>, Second Asian Forum on Child and Adolescent Physciatry (Manila, 1979).

7. U. Hongmuen: <u>The relationship between intelligence and the nutritional status indices of pre-school children in day care homes in Bangkok</u>, Master's thesis, Srinakharinwirot University (Bangkok, 1977).

9 IMPROVING THE MOBILITY OF THE URBAN POOR

by G. Roth

Introduction

This final sectoral chapter raises the issue of transport. The urban poor frequently face very difficult problems of journeying between home and work, or school, or hospital visits. Some of these problems can be overccome if, for example, effective medical units are widespread, as disccussed in the chapter on health care, or if good schools are close by. However, some problems relating to travel will remain so that the most suitable and effective form of official intervention in transport planning and implementation merits debate.

It has been said that "The importance of urban transport lies fundamentally in its contribution to the large economies of scale and specialisation associated with urban growth. transport facilities expand the options for work and give access to health, education and other amenities."[1] Scale economies and access to urban amenities are particularly important to the urban poor, yet the urban poor in developing countries often travel under appalling conditions. In Rio de Janeiro, some workers travel four hours to and from work, and spend 25 per cent of their income on public transport fares.[2] In New Delhi travellers often come to blows attempting to board delayed municipal buses,[3] while in Dhaka passengers regularly travel on the roofs of buses.

Some of these difficulties may be inevitable in low-income societies, or in rapidly expanding cities. But in many cities - in both developed and developing countries - transport problems are exacerbated by rules and regulations that discourage the provision of low-cost, high-quality transport services, which the majority of the population can afford. To that extent transport can be readily and rapidly improved, without major expenditure of public funds.

This chapter indicates some ways for municipal authorities to identify and relieve transport difficulties, especially those facing low-income travellers. To the individuals concerned mobility is important for the activities it facilitates. To city authorities the improvement of mobility is also likely to promote the following objectives:

(a) to provide direct employment in the urban transport sector;

(b) to increase employment in the urban area by easier access to the workplace;

(c) to stimulate other urban activities, such as education, entertainment and trade, that improved transport encourages.

Transport needs of the urban poor

Any discussion of the transport needs of the urban poor must recognise that travel is intensely desired by all income groups in all societies. If travel were a commodity, like potatoes or margarine, that people consume less as they get richer, then the better-off would, for example, live near their places of work so as to reduce their amount of travel. To the author's knowledge, all the recorded evidence points the other way: richer people travel more. Table 18 illustrates this, showing the travel of different income groups in the city of Salvador, Brazil.

Rising incomes are associated with more travellers per household, more trips per traveller and a longer daily distance travelled. Clearly travel is not indulged in for its own sake; it is an activity derived from people's desire to expand their activities over wider and wider areas. People travel for work, for commerce, for social intercourse and for entertainment. As they get richer they have more opportunities to interact with others and their need for travel increases.

While detailed measurements of urban travel have been made in developed countries, and in some of the richer cities in developing countries, including Brazil and Singapore, very few measurements appear to have been made in the poorer cities of developing countries. There is, in particular, an almost complete absence of information on non-motorised trips, possibly because the studies are carried out by consultants who apply the methods and models used in Western cities where the movement of pedestrians and cyclists can be of minor importance and is often

Table 18: Daily travel characteristics in Salvador, Brazil
Average for all household sizes

Household income in 1975 Cruzeiros per month	Under 417	417-834	835-1,251	1,252-2,085	2,086-3,336	3,337-4,587	4,588-5,838	5,839-8,340	8,341-12,510	Over 2,510
Travellers per household	1.4	1.8	2.2	2.7	2.9	3.1	3.2	3.2	3.5	3.8
Trips per traveller	2.9	3.0	3.0	3.3	3.6	3.6	4.0	4.3	4.6	4.9
Average door-to-door travel speed (km/h)	10.8	12.0	12.0	12.0	13.2	13.2	13.8	12.6	14.4	15.0
Time per traveller (minutes per day)	103.1	106.2	108.0	111.1	116.7	114.8	116.9	125.0	124.4	121.0
Distance per traveller (km/day)	18.2	21.9	21.8	22.6	25.1	25.4	27.2	26.0	30.0	30.1

Source: Colin Buchanan and Partners (unpublished).

ignored. These groups therefore tend to be ignored
also in transport studies in developing countries,
despite their considerable significance. It is also
difficult and costly to obtain information on
non-motorised trips. Nevertheless, some studies have
been made, and the results obtained in India,
Indonesia and Nigeria allow us to glimpse the travel
conditions of the very poor.

Travel characteristics in Delhi
     From 1978 to 1980 the (United Kingdom) Transport
and Road Research Laboratory and the (Indian)
Association of State Roads Transport Undertakings
undertook household surveys in two contrasting
socio-economic areas of Delhi in order to identify
the characteristics of travellers and of the public
transport serving them.[4] The two areas chosen were
Nand Nagri and Janakpuri. Both are on the outskirts
of Delhi, approximately 20-25 kilometres from the
city centre but, while Janakpuri has mainly middle-
and high-income residents, Nand Nagri is a low-income
resettlement area. The household characteristics of
the two communities are as follows:

Table 19: Household characteristics: Nand Nagri
          and Janakpuri

	Janakpuri	Nand Nagri
Household size	4.9	4.9
Students per household	1.7	0.9
Employed per household	1.5	1.5
Monthly household income, rupees	1 594	446
Monthly per capita income, rupees	325	91
Monthly household expenditure, rupees	1 107	401
Expenditure on transport, rupees (and per cent)	145 (9.0)	50 (11.0)
Share of households with personal transport non-motorised) (per cent)	62.0	29.0
Share of households with children of school age not attending school (per cent)	-	28.0

Source: Transport and Road Research Laboratory:
Supplementary report No. 673.

As can be seen, the share of expenditure on transport was higher in the poorer community. Data were obtained on all regular trips undertaken daily by household members in both communities although, unfortunately, total travel was not recorded. Table 20 shows the daily trip rate per household for educational and employment purposes and for regular daily trips undertaken by housewives.

Table 20: Household daily trip rates excluding non-regular trips: Nand Nagri and Janakpuri

	Janakpuri	Nand Nagri
Daily trips per household:		
For employment	3.06	3.15
For education	3.34	1.80
By housewives	0.43	0.20
Total	6.83	5.15
Average daily trip rate per capita	1.39	1.05

Source: As for table 19.

A "trip" was defined as a single direction movement, e.g. from home to work, therefore household members undertaking such journeys would make at least two trips per day. All travel modes, including walking, were included. The number of daily trips in the high-income community was significantly higher than in the low-income community for education, less so for housewives and very similar for employment. Vehicle ownership was closely associated with income (see table 19). Of the vehicle-owning households in Janakpuri, 50 per cent possessed a bicycle, 45 per cent a motorcycle or scooter and 5 per cent a car. In comparison, in Nand Nagri 98 per cent of vehicle owners owned a bicycle and the rest a motorcycle or scooter. The association of higher levels of vehicle ownership with increased trip making is logical and is consistent with findings in other cities.

The characteristics of educational trips in Nand Nagri and Janakpuri are shown in table 20.

Table 20: Educational trips: Nand Nagri and Janakpuri

	Janakpuri	Nand Nagri
Percentage of students using:		
Bus services	49.0	6.8
Walking	41.0	92.0
Cycle rickshaw	6.0	0.4
Other	4.0	0.8
All modes average journey distance (km)	4.7	1.4

Source: As for table 19.

While almost half the students in Janakpuri travelled by bus, nearly all those in Nand Nagri walked. Almost all the students in Nand Nagri went to the local school, the average distance being 1.4 kilometres. A significant number of Janakpuri students travelled to schools distant from their homes, the average distance being 4.7 kilometres for a one-way trip.

Of the students who used bus services, those from Janakpuri waited an average 9 minutes to board a bus and then travelled for approximately 30 minutes in the bus, a distance of 9.5 kilometres; their total journey time averaged 53 minutes. In comparison the small percentage of students who travelled by bus from Nand Nagri, estimated a waiting time of 19 minutes and an "in vehicle" time of 40 minutes, for an average distance of 15 kilometres. Total journey time, one way, for the Nand Nagri students, was estimated at 77 minutes.

The breakdown of employment trips by different modes for the two communities is given in table 21. The great majority of workers in both communities travelled to work by bus. The residents of Nand Nagri used the bus because the distances to work were usually too great for cycling or walking; only the DTC (Delhi Transport Corporation) service was available to them. In contrast, the workers from Janakpuri had the option of using charter buses, e.g. buses hired by groups of like-minded workers to provide themselves with better services. The characteristics of travel by the different bus services are shown in table 22.

Table 21: Employment trips: Nand Nagri and Janakpuri

	Janakpuri	Nand Nagri
Percentage using:		
DTC bus services	50.8	81.4
Charter bus services	30.9	–
Personal motorised vehicle	10.6	–
Bicycle	2.3	5.1
Walk	2.8	9.3
Other	2.6	4.2
All modes average journey distance (km)	15.8	15.9

Source: As for table 19.

Table 22: Employment trip characteristics: Nand Nagri and Janakpuri

	Janakpuri Charter bus services	DTC services	Nand Nagri DTC services
Average waiting time (min.)	3	17	23
Average "in vehicle" time (min.)	42	41	45
Average total trip time (min.)	60	73	85
Average distance travelled (km)	19	16	18
Average fare (paise)	79	63	53
Average fare per km (paise)	4.16	3.94	2.94

Source: As table 19.

While the users of charter buses travelled farther than those in the DTC buses, their total travel time was less, because of the lower waiting time. Travel by DTC buses involved substantial waiting times,

particularly for travellers from Nand Nagri whose
total trip time to work averaged 85 minutes, more
than those from Janakpuri despite similar trip
lengths.

Only 10 per cent of Janakpuri residents travelled
by motorised private transport, cars, motorcycles or
scooters, although 31 per cent of households
possessed such vehicles. The buses were said to be
cheaper and it appeared that many of the personal
vehicles were used only for social and leisure
activities while, for the journey to work, travellers
were more concerned about saving money than saving
time. Over 94 per cent of those interviewed in both
communities suggested that the DTC bus services could
be improved. In both communities greatest priority
was placed on more frequent service with the second
priority the provision of direct service without
interchange. The high priority placed in Nand Nagri
on "enforce discipline at queues" reflects the fights
that occurred daily at the bus stops as passengers
attempted to board. At Janakpuri the number of
passengers waiting at bus stops was considerably less
than at Nand Nagri.

The picture emerging from this study is that, of
the two communities, those with the lower incomes
spent a higher proportion of their time travelling
and a higher proportion of their household income on
travel. The low-income community was utterly
dependent for motorised transport on the municipal
bus service, the middle-income community less so,
because of the charter bus services. The incidence of
non-work trips was far higher in the high-income
community than in the low-income one.

Travel time in Nigeria

Another aspect of travel by the urban poor is
given by G. Banjo.[5] Banjo reported the results of
an interview of travellers in the two major cities of
Nigeria, Lagos and Ibadan. Respondents were asked the
amount of time they typically spent on specified
activities. The results are summarised in table 23,
which gives separate figures for respondents engaged
in supplementary employment in addition to their main
employment.

In Nigeria's major urban centres those without
supplementary employment typically travelled 3.3
hours per day, while employed respondents with

Table 23: Allocation of time in Lagos and Ibadan
          (in hours)

Activities	Employed respondents not engaged in supplementary employment			Employed respondents with supplementary employment		
	Lagos	Ibadan	All	Lagos	Ibadan	All
Main employment	8.2	8.2	8.2	7.7	7.6	7.7
Supplementary employment	–	–	–	2.6	2.8	2.6
Subtotal	8.2	8.2	8.2	10.3	10.4	10.3
Travel to work and back	1.5	1.3	1.4	1.2	1.0	1.1
Travel for other purposes	1.8	1.9	1.8	1.3	1.2	1.3
Subtotal	3.3	3.2	3.2	2.5	2.2	2.4
Other	12.5	12.6	12.6	11.2	11.4	11.3
Total	24.0	24.0	24.0	24.0	24.0	24.0

Source: G.A. Banjo: op. cit.

supplementary employment travelled 2.5 to 2.2 hours per day. These figures, which are similar to those reported in Delhi (where the work journey alone ranged from 2 hours to 3 hours a day) by far exceed the time spent by travellers in developed countries (see table 24). In Nigeria supplementary employment seems associated with less travel. This may be because those who have spent over three hours a day travelling have no time or energy for further employment. This may be another example of the poor travelling more and getting less.

Table 24: Mean daily travel times for selected locations (in minutes)[1]

	Travel to work and back	Travel for all other purposes	Total
Lagos, Nigeria	89(45)	107(55)	196
Ibadan, Nigeria	77(42)	108(58)	185
Belgium	65(52)	60(48)	125
Kazanlik, Bulgaria	56(48)	61(52)	117
Olomouc, Czechoslovakia	58(49)	61(51)	119
Six cities, France	50(51)	49(49)	99
Osnabruck, Federal Republic of Germany	45(44)	58(56)	103
Hayerswerda, German Democratic Republic	61(57)	46(43)	107
Gyor, Hungary	62(58)	45(42)	107
Forty-four cities, United States	49(43)	65(57)	114
Lima-Callao, Peru	89(51)	74(49)	173
Reading, United Kingdom	–	–	86
London, United Kingdom	–	–	88
United Kingdom	48(69)	22(31)	70
Washington, DC	–	–	73
Bogota, Colombia	–	–	94
Singapore	–	–	79

[1] Values in brackets are percentages of daily travel time.

Source: Quoted in G.A. Banjo: op. cit.

Trip patterns in Indonesia

A household study carried out in Bandung[6] indicates that, in that city also, travel increases with income. The trip rate pattern by income group is shown in table 25.

Table 25: Household trip rate by monthly expenditure group[1]

| Trip Purpose | Monthly expenditure group | | | | | | | |
	1	2	3	4	5	6	7	All
Work	1.1	1.2	1.2	1.5	1.2	1.2	1.7	1.3
Education	0.5	1.0	1.6	2.4	2.6	3.1	3.7	1.9
Shopping	0.6	0.7	0.7	0.7	0.6	0.8	0.9	0.7
Other	0.5	0.2	0.4	0.4	0.5	0.5	1.3	0.5
Total	2.7	3.1	3.9	5.0	4.9	5.6	7.6	4.4

[1] Excluding return trips. Expenditure group 1 is the poorest.

Source: Kusbiantoro: op. cit.

The data show a clear tendency for trip rates to go up with income for each trip purpose; the most striking change is for education trips. High incomes in Bandung are no doubt associated with larger households, which tend to include many in the student age group. Among the higher income groups most of these go to school or university while in the lower income groups a number do not go to school at all. For work trips the results can be interpreted as indicating that, in general, the household head is the only active worker at all income levels, except the very highest.

Walking trips predominate among the lower income groups, exceeding 80 per cent in the lowest income group. The proportion of walk trips declines as income increases, falling to about 25 per cent of all trips for the highest income group. The proportion of bicycle trips also declines over most of the range, but less sharply. Trips by bus seem to peak at income level 5, and to decline thereafter, while trips by car and motorcycle rise steadily from that point. Similar patterns are observed in other countries.

Travel times in Bandung are relatively similar for all income groups, but travel distances increase with income. This is particularly noticeable for education and shopping trips: the higher-income groups travel by motorised transport to higher-level urban facilities beyond their local areas. Low-income groups, on the other hand, particularly people who cannot regularly afford motorised transport, are confined to their localities.

The following conclusions may be drawn from the data reported on urban travel in developing countries:

(a) There is a tendency for the rich to travel further, more often and faster than the poor. Other things being equal the rich tend to make more and generally longer trips.

(b) Households in urban India spend about 10 per cent of their income on travel, with the very poor spending a higher proportion than those better off. (Car-owning households in Western countries tend to spend an even higher proportion on travel, about 12 per cent, but the share spent on travel by non-car owning households is low, about 3 per cent.)

The time spent on transport by low-income groups tends to be greater than that of high-income groups in the same society. One exception to this tendency is Salvador (Brazil) where average daily travel time appears to rise with income (see table 18). (This is said to be because of the city's unusual configuration of land use.) In international comparisons higher-income groups tend to spend a minimum of about one hour per traveller per day,[7] while lower-income groups spend more. Higher income groups can afford to place a higher value on time relative to other forms of consumption than can the poor.

In summary, the urban poor tend to spend more of their time and money on travel than do the rich but, nevertheless, they achieve a lower level of mobility. They pay more and get less. Before considering how to set about improving the mobility of the poor, it is necessary to review some of the technical factors associated with urban transport, both private and public.

Technical factors relating to public transport

It is generally believed that public transport can only be provided, at a financial loss, by public monopolies operating large fleets of large vehicles. This is not so. Reference has already been made to the privately chartered buses in New Delhi, which can provide a service superior to that of the local authority. There are numerous other examples of unsubsidised, high-quality, low-cost, public transport services. Many, but not all, are provided by small operators using small vehicles. The most famous of the "informal" public transport services are probably the "jeepneys" of Manila (so called because the original vehicles were ex-US army jeeps left in Manila after the Second World War), but the dolmus of Istanbul, the minibuses of Kuala Lumpur and Hong Kong, the matatu of Nairobi, the becak of Indonesia, are known to all students of transport.[9] These systems can compete successfully against conventional buses, although the reasons for this have not been clearly understood. They can be discussed under the following headings: private vs. public ownership; small vehicles vs. large; size of operational unit; route associations.

Private vs. public ownership

That publicly owned bus companies make losses is not entirely surprising, since the systems taken over by public authorities tend to be those that private operators find unprofitable. However, losses under public ownership tend to rise rapidly, at a rate that bears little relation to increases in levels of service. A few examples can illustrate the point.

(a) Buenos Aires: Buenos Aires, the capital of Argentina, has a population of 9 million living in an area exceeding 1,500 square miles. It has a variety of transport modes, the most important being the "microbus" (or "collectivo" in local jargon), used for 54 per cent of all trips and 75 per cent of public transport trips. The collectivos were developed in the 1920s as taxis used by groups of passengers, with the fares being paid by each passenger individually. These taxis ran on fixed routes chosen by the driver. The shared taxi quickly showed certain advantages and was favourably received by the general public because of its flexibility, higher speeds and greater frequencies than the underground and electric tramways. The collectivo vehicle developed from a 7-seater to an 11-seater; subsequently to 14 and 17 seats, finally reaching 23 seats, the typical current unit.

The microbuses offered stiff competition to the tramways and underground systems and this caused the government to establish the "Corporate Enterprise" in 1936 which was supposed to have had a total monopoly over public transport services. Nevertheless, several microbus lines remained in existence until 1951, when a national enterprise, "Transportes de Buenos Aires", took charge of all services, including those of the "Corporate Enterprise". However, the service operated by the "Transportes de Buenos Aires" deteriorated rapidly both in quality and financially. By 1959 it was losing US$120,000 per day. In 1962 the situation became intolerable and "Transportes de Buenos Aires" was dissolved. All transport services, except the underground railway, were turned over to private companies. Trams and trolley-buses were replaced by regular full-size buses. However, many of these were subsequently replaced by the 23-seat microbuses. These still operate profitably and provide a superior level of service.

(b) Private buses in Calcutta: One of the largest, densest and poorest cities in the world, Calcutta supports a population of some 10 million in an area of less than 600 square miles. Private buses first appeared in the city towards the end of the nineteenth century but were banned in 1960 when all bus services were vested in the Calcutta State Transport Corporation (CSTC). The CSTC suffered from managerial and financial problems and, in 1966, was paralysed by strikes. In response to public demand before the 1966 elections, and to its need for ready cash, the Government of West Bengal sold permits which enabled 300 private buses to operate. These operated at a profit, although they charged the same fares (equivalent to about 0.50 US cents per mile) as the loss-making CSTC and worked inferior routes. By the late 1970s some 1,500 regular private buses were operating in Calcutta, in addition to about 500 private minibuses. Today, private buses account for about two-thirds of all bus trips in Calcutta, without subsidy. Meanwhile, the CSTC, which operates the best routes at the same fares, is subsidised to the equivalent of US$1 million a month.

The success of the private bus operators has been attributed to three factors:

(1) Keeping their vehicles on the road: when a private bus breaks down, it is repaired, often on the spot, with parts bought if necessary on the black market. The CSTC, in contrast, has to obtain spare parts officially and only half of its buses are generally in operation.

(2) Fare collection: the private bus crews (who are paid a percentage of the takings) make greater efforts to collect the fares than do CSTC employees.

"Fare evasion" is estimated to be 25 per cent on CSTC buses and negligible on private lines.

(3) Higher labour productivity: the State Corporation's manning levels, at 50 employees per bus (1980) is one of the highest in the world.

A key factor in the success of private buses in Calcutta is the route association. These associations, generally one for each route, were formed voluntarily and spontaneously. Each owner retains control over the operation and maintenance of his vehicle and receives the takings it collects. The associations have rules to govern relationships between members, for example, vehicles must run on time. This is important because a bus running late tends to pick up more than its "fair share" of passengers, at the expense of the bus following. Owners of buses which do not keep to time are fined and fines are distributed among the other members. It has been reported that the fines are sometimes proportional to the delay, at the rate of so many rupees a minute, and paid directly to the owner of the bus following.

Calcutta's private bus operators vividly demonstrate that, given a suitable organisational framework, privately operated buses can provide and expand transport services without subsidy, despite the inability of a municipal monopoly to do so.

(c) Thailand: Bangkok in the early 1970s had 24 franchised bus companies, all of which charged a basic fare of about 4 US cents. The biggest company, the Nai Lert, was consistently profitable. A distinguishing characteristic was that most of its buses, all single deckers, carried a crew of three, one driver and two fare collectors. In 1976, after recommendations by European consultants, the government decided to amalgamate the 24 companies and to create the "Bangkok Metropolitan Transport Authority" (BMTA). Shortly after the buses were taken over by the city, fares were raised by 20 per cent and the system started to operate at a deficit. By 1979 the BMTA was losing the equivalent of over US$25 million a year, while an estimated 7,000 privately owned minibuses were running at a profit. The main reasons for the switch from profit to loss seem to have been improved working conditions and higher wages to bus crews and reduced utilisation of vehicles.

Experience world-wide suggests that public transport operators have higher costs than private operators, even when providing similar services, because they have less flexibility in making the best use of their resources, and because of higher labour costs. In transport, as elsewhere, the discipline of living within one's budget applies a constant downward pressure on costs, a pressure that is all too easily relieved by the availability of public subsidies.

Small vehicles vs. large

An established (but questionable) principle of public transport operation is that large vehicles are more economical to operate than small ones. The supposed reason is that, with labour costs accounting for over two-thirds of bus operating costs, smaller vehicle operations would require substantially more labour in order to meet peak demand. This argument, although perfectly logical, may be questioned for two reasons.

The capital cost <u>per seat</u> of a bus seems to increase with the size of vehicle. Thus operators in San Juan, Puerto Rico, can expect to pay US$17,000 for a minibus seating 17, but US$140,000 for a full-size bus seating 50, i.e. a full-size bus can cost three times as much per unit of passenger capacity. This is because small vehicles can be mass produced and bought "off the shelf" while large ones tend to be assembled as separate units and made to special order. But there is a second reason favouring the small bus which, while more subtle, may be more important. For a given route capacity, small buses provide more frequent service and therefore involve less waiting time per passenger. This factor may be ignored by a franchised operator who has to bear the costs of his crew but not the waiting time of his customers. Hence the preference of monopoly operators for big vehicles. However, where competition is allowed, transport operators have to respond to the needs of the passengers, who dislike waiting for buses. Small vehicles providing a frequent service reduce waiting time. Thus when private bus operators took over the municipal service in Buenos Aires in 1962 one of their first actions was to replace the large municipal buses by smaller ones. More generally, whenever a private operator is free to choose the size of his vehicle he generally chooses

something less than a full-size bus. The small bus
has other advantages: as it holds fewer passengers,
it is easier to fill with people starting at one
point and wishing to travel to another, so it tends
to stop less frequently than large ones. And, being
more manoeuvrable, it can often make its way more
quickly along congested roads.

Thus, while a bus operator might like to provide a
service using a small number of large buses,
preferably crowded, with passengers obliged to wait a
long time for the bus's arrival, the public often
prefers the speed that can generally be provided only
by small vehicles.[9]

Size of operating unit

Some businesses require large firms. Others, such
as a restaurant or hairdressing business, can be
successfully provided by a single operator, a family
firm, or a small partnership. The unit supplying
public transport ranges from the one-man bicycle
rickshaw in East Asia to fleets of thousands of buses
in cities such as Sao Paulo, Seoul, Bombay and
Bangkok. Numbers of employees per bus also vary
widely, from under two in Australia to 58 in the
Office des Transports en Commun du Zaire (OTCZ) of
Kinshasa (as only about 50 per cent of the OTCZ buses
are on the road at any time, the staffing works out
at 116 people per operating bus). Attempts have been
made to assess the effect of fleet size on the
efficiency of public transport but the results are
not conclusive. A study in the United Kingdom
reported that unit costs increase with fleet size,
while the opposite effect was found in India. It is
sufficient to note that there is no clear evidence
that larger bus fleets result in lower costs or
higher profitability.

On the other hand, there is clear evidence that
large bus fleets make financial losses, under the
same conditions that small operators, owner-drivers,
make profits. Although operators the world over are
reluctant to admit to making profits, the pressure by
small firms to obtain permits to provide transport
and the prices at which permits in some cities change
hands, or are hired out, is a sure indication of
profitability.

The reasons for the financial success of the small
transport firm, be it a haulier, a taxi driver or a
bus operator, are well-known and typical of other

types of small business in the service sector. The
owner is usually willing to work longer and less
regular hours than would a paid driver in a large
fleet. He will clean his own vehicle (or ask family
members) and is likely to do routine servicing and
maintenance himself. He will not have his own depot
but will service his vehicle on the street or at a
local garage. His record-keeping will be minimal;
just sufficient to keep the tax inspector at bay. He
will make a greater effort than a paid driver to
collect fares from passengers and to ensure that the
amount collected does not get lost on the way. An
extra driver can be employed if two shifts have to be
run a day. Some facilities, such as a two-way radio
service, can be purchased centrally, without the
owner relinquishing control of his vehicle.

There is also evidence that with an appropriate
organisational structure, small firms can provide a
high level of service over a wide area. Taxis are a
case in point. While some may be operated as one-man
(or one-woman) firms and some in large fleets, there
is no need for any formal co-ordination to achieve an
acceptable level of service. Taxis find their way to
where the business is most profitable. A single
operator cannot cover a whole route, but a route can
be covered by a large number of individual operators
organised, if necessary, in a route association. In
passenger transport the basic operating unit is the
vehicle and, as the taxi business proves, the owner
of even one vehicle can operate at a profit.[10]

Route associations

To provide the most effective transport service
each unit must, however, work within an appropriate
organisational framework. A taxi has to be recognised
as available for hire and, if it intends to carry
more than one person, its destination must be clearly
indicated. The intending passenger should know the
likely fare and where vehicles can be readily found.
Some of these characteristics are provided by the
route associations which are to be found in many
cities in the developing world.

In a route association each vehicle remains under
the control of its owner, both for driving and
maintenance and for the disposal of income earned.
Only the route is shared, i.e. the member of the
association plies a specified route, in conjunction
with others, thus offering a frequent service. Fares

are generally but not invariably fixed by the association: in Hong Kong and Istanbul, for example, higher fares are charged in peak periods. In Buenos Aires the route association ("Empresa") must stick to fare levels fixed by the public authorities. As an example of a route association, further information about the Empresa may be of interest. The Empresa is the formal employer of the drivers and assumes all responsibility arising from the labour laws. Vehicle owners choose and replace their drivers and pay the vehicle's operating expenditures. Income goes to the vehicle owners who either turn it over to a common fund for equal distribution among Empresa members or for pro-rating according to the mileage run by each vehicle or through some other method chosen by the Empresa.

The Empresas offer several advantages: each member is directly responsible for the operation of his vehicle(s). The public benefits from competition between different Empresas. New Empresas can be formed with a minimum of formality. Labour productivity is high: on average, each microbus employs three persons to drive, maintain and repair it. Each vehicle produces 1.2 to 1.5 million passenger kilometres per year so that average labour productivity is around 450,000 passenger kilometres per year, about three times that of conventional bus services.

The precise organisation of a route association varies from city to city. Any group operating a route has an interest in limiting its numbers and in ensuring that its members work harmoniously together. Conditions are therefore imposed on entry (possibly an entrance fee) and rules prevent members from "stealing" traffic from following vehicles by travelling behind their schedules. However, in many cities (including Buenos Aires, Calcutta and Hong Kong) route associations compete with one another so that no group has a monopoly over an entire route.

The importance of track or right-of-way

While informal public transport can often out-perform conventional systems it cannot give a high-quality service without an adequate "track", or right-of-way, which only the public authorities can provide. Exclusive "busways", roads reserved for buses, can provide high-capacity routes at relatively low cost, but very few have been built. The best known in developing countries are in Curitiba (Brazil), Port-of-Spain (Trinidad) and in Abidjan (Ivory Coast) where an existing road has been converted to exclusive bus use.

Should, then, cities rush to provide exclusive busways or railways to relieve their transport problems? Not necessarily. Urban infrastructure is costly and new facilities should not be introduced until existing ones are used to the maximum. Traffic management measures used for this purpose include:

Roadway management: one-way streets, "tidal flow" and other measures increase the capacity of street networks at modest cost.

Signalisation improvement: installation of traffic lights and, where appropriate, linking them by computer control, can significantly improve traffic flow and reduce energy consumption.

Preferential treatment for public transport: if the object of traffic management is to maximise the safe flow of people rather than of vehicles it can include measures to give priority to high-occupancy vehicles, buses, minibuses or any vehicle carrying more than a specified number of people. In the Singapore area licensing scheme, for example, vehicles with four or more occupants are exempt from paying the license fee. Special lanes for buses are another example of preferential treatment. Some operate continuously, some in peak periods only; some are exclusively for buses while others, such as those in Bangkok, are also for minibuses.

Parking controls: without controls valuable street space is taken up by parked cars, severely reducing the capacity of the street network to facilitate movement. Furthermore, free street parking discourages the provision of off-street parking.

Facilities for pedestrians and cyclists: facilities for pedestrians and cyclists are essential for the urban poor, who are often confined to these modes. But they are also important for the non-poor. Safe crossing places, broad footways, and segregated cycle-ways should be considered essential in all urban areas.

For a detailed review of traffic engineering measures readers are referred to the publications cited at the end of this chapter. Suffice it to say that these measures are of major importance to improving urban mobility, as any traveller to Cairo can testify. The area of space devoted to streets in

Cairo, about 30 per cent, is about the same as in many Western cities; that travel conditions in Cairo are poor is largely due to less efficient use of available facilities. This is reflected in the proportion of street space taken up by parked cars; by low standards of intersection control and the less than adequate lane markings which do too little to assist driver discipline.

An agenda for action
Given the travel needs and the technical factors described above, the list of measures to improve the mobility of the urban poor should include: (a) the collection of relevant information; (b) improvement of pedestrian and bicycle facilities; (c) implementation of traffic engineering measures; (d) removal of restrictions that prevent the poor (and the non-poor) from offering services to others; (e) planning for urban expansion; (f) selective investment in additional infrastructure.

Collection of relevant information
Those disadvantaged by inadequate mobility must be identified to be helped and they cannot be identified without surveys of the travel habits of different income groups. Such surveys should establish mobility "norms" in the study area and seek out those groups whose mobility is below the "norm". The travel disadvantaged cannot be found by counting automobiles on streets or people in buses. They can best be found by asking people in their homes about their travel patterns, as in the New Delhi surveys described above. The key data to obtain are the total daily distance travelled, the mode and purpose of trips and the total time and money spent on travel, per household and per traveller. Surveys need not be large, 30 households can generally furnish a representative "travel profile" of a social group.

Improvement of pedestrian and bicycle facilities
The private transport modes most relevant to the urban poor are walking and cycling. A considerable amount can, and should, be done to improve conditions for pedestrian and bicycle travel. The primary need is to separate these modes from motor traffic, for example, by providing adequate footways and separating them from motor transport. Pedestrian crossing points over busy streets should be provided:

a recent transport improvement programme for Bombay included pedestrian bridges and tunnels. Safe bicycle facilities can yield substantial benefits in cities suitable by terrain, and by climate, for cycling. (The World Bank recently financed 2 kilometres of bicycle tracks in Sfax and 15 kilometres in Madras.)

Implementing traffic engineering measures
    Prime attention should be given to measures that assist pedestrians, cyclists and public transport. Many of the measures that speed public transport will also assist private cars but they should not be despised on that account. Attention to street parking is essential to safeguard traffic flows. Rationing parking space by price can produce substantial city revenues from those who can well afford to pay and also enables off-street parking facilities to be provided commercially.

Removing restrictive regulations
    Once traffic management has squeezed the maximum benefits from the road network, authorities should use the labour and initiative of the city people, preferably of the poor, to improve transport services. In many cities effective participation by the poor is prohibited by regulations. In Indonesia, for example, the low-cost, frequent services of the becak (three-wheeled bicycle rickshaw) are being displaced by a wide variety of motor transport, including subsidised municipal buses. Four hundred thousand becaks were licensed in Jakarta in 1964, but only 14,000 in 1978. It was claimed that becaks impeded other road users, were inappropriate to the image of a modern city and an affront to human dignity. Nevertheless, the income of a becak driver is five times the rural wage.[12] The treatment of the becak in Indonesia is reflected the world over in a tendency to restrict informal, "unincorporated" transport and to encourage the more formal "corporate" units.[13]
    As was shown above "informal" modes of public transport can provide cheaper and better quality services than regular buses and trains. City authorities should take full advantage of what they offer and not suppress them in order to protect more costly and less effective conventional services.

Planning for urban expansion

Many cities in the developing world are doubling their populations every ten years. They also have to contend with increasing motorisation, which is closely associated with economic growth. Some of the difficulties can be mitigated by advanced planning of transport and land use. Detailed land-use plans are expensive and, in many cities, impossible to implement. However, the preparation of "broad-brush" sketch-plans, which define corridors of growth, industrial areas, universities, airports and other major publicly determined land uses, can be undertaken relatively cheaply.[14] As the direction of city development is strongly influenced by the provision of transport infrastructure, city authorities control a powerful tool for guiding urban growth. The expense of building roads, railways, etc., ahead of time would normally be unacceptable, but the reservation of appropriate land need not be costly and should be undertaken whenever possible.

Selective investment in infrastructure

Even when, as a result of traffic management and other measures, existing infrastructure is used to its best advantage, there comes a point when additional investment is necessary to accommodate urban growth. Indeed, under a well-planned system, investment is likely to constitute a continuous improvement programme. Officials in expanding cities are under immense pressure to sanction a variety of expensive schemes, ranging from underground railways to sleek suspended monorails. A useful ploy in dealing with proposals for high-cost revenue-producing schemes is to allow the promoters to bear the financial risks. "Our beloved city could use a metro costing zillions?" The mayor might declare "of course it could". "And all the expenses will of course be recovered from the farebox? "Of course, of course - so the city will give permission to you, Mr. Promoter, to go and build it, and operate it, and charge what you will for the use of it, but not one cent will you get from public funds, nor will your new system be protected from competition by other modes." Officials should insist that any system proposed to them should be realistically compared to alternative modes. Except in very special situations, buses and minibuses on freeways are likely to rival any alternative in terms of capacity, cheapness and flexibility.[15] The costs of infrastructure, to the extent possible, should be financed by users. It is thus particularly important to devise mechanisms to charge car users the costs of roads built for their use. Bangkok is constructing a network of toll expressways and Singapore collects the equivalent of US$2 from low-occupancy vehicles entering its central area during the morning peak periods. New charging methods investigated by the International Bridge, Tunnel and Turnpike Association, and others, may help cities in all countries to recover the full costs of road provision from road users.[16]

An example from Kenya

The principles discussed in this chapter may be illustrated by a proposed programme to improve urban transport in Nairobi and Mombasa. The objectives of the programme would be: (a) to conserve energy; (b) to improve transport at moderate cost; (c) to meet the transport needs of poor people, both for public transport and for pedestrian facilities.

The programme would include five components:

Traffic management measures

These are measures to discourage private cars from passing through the central area while at the same time giving preferential access to public transport. Bus lanes, exclusive bus streets and bus priority phases at signalised junctions would be provided within the central area and its approaches. Junctions would be equipped with traffic signals and co-ordinated by a central area-wide traffic control system in order to provide priority for buses and minibuses along the "bus only" streets and to regulate traffic flow at junctions controlling access to the central area. The parking meter control zone would be extended to discourage long-term on-street parking and to provide adequate short-term off-peak parking space for retail and commercial activities.

Major public transport corridors serving the central area and the industrial area would be widened within existing rights of way. Junctions along these corridors would be equipped with traffic signals. Certain junctions which are heavily congested during peak periods would be redesigned and equipped with traffic signals.

Pedestrian facilities and traffic safety

Footpaths, pedestrian traffic signals, and footbridges at critical safety points would be provided along routes used by residents of low-income areas to reach the central area, the industrial area, local markets and other community facilities. Some 15 kilometres of routes would be improved specifically for pedestrians. A further 30 kilometres of footpaths are incorporated within the measures described above.

Improved road access in low-income areas

Improvements would be made to access roads within low-income settlements. The works include new paving, surface water drainage, the construction of seven bridge culverts over water courses, a pedestrian bridge over the railway line, the surfacing of footpaths and street lighting.

Road maintenance improvements

Road and street-lighting maintenance equipment and improvements to the existing depot and workshop facilities would be provided to enable Nairobi to maintain its existing road network adequately and the facilities would be improved through the enlargement of the engine shop, provision for a security fence and replacement of old equipment. A road improvement programme would be carried out over three years to stop the further deterioration of the road network.

A minibus fund

A minibus fund would be established and administered by a Kenyan financial institution. Not less than two-thirds of the fund proceeds would go to existing owner-operators with the other one-third available for individuals (such as existing drivers) who do not currently own a minibus but wish to operate one. Only vehicles which comply with acceptable specifications could be financed. Loans would be repayable over three years probably at 14 per cent per annum in 72 equal semi-monthly instalments with no grace period. Eligible beneficiaries would be required to make periodic monthly payments to a renewal fund aimed at the purchase of a new vehicle after three years. The minibus programme also provides for the upgrading of informal repair facilities. Basic shelters, services, and tools in approximately 100 open worksheds serving 200-250 mechanics would be provided.

Summary

This chapter has suggested (a) how the travel needs of the poor people can be identified relatively to norms in their communities and (b) cheap and effective methods of improving the mobility of the poor and the non-poor.

The starting point was the observation that travel is an activity intensely desired by all income groups in all known societies; people do not travel less as their wealth increases. Evidence from Latin America and the Far East is consistent with measurements in developed countries: that rising incomes are associated with more travellers per household, more trips per traveller and longer distances travelled per day. To travel further, faster modes of travel are chosen. While the poorest have to walk, higher income groups use various, more costly, transport modes, ranging from the bicycle to the private car. Most of the data on urban travel, in both developing and developed countries, relate to motor travel and hence exclude the travel of the very poor, who are unable to afford regular motorised public transport. Evidence from Nigeria and India suggests that the very poor, whose main transport mode is walking, spend a great deal of time on travel but cover comparatively short distances. The amount of money they spend on travel is small, but can be a high proportion of disposable income.

In many cities public transport can be improved with negligible investment on the part of the city authorities. High-quality service at low cost can be obtained from minibuses, shared taxis and other "informal" transport modes, which can often provide superior service at a lower cost than conventional bus or railway systems. "Informal" public transport modes are particularly useful to the urban poor both because they provide employment and because they are often the only public transport mode that can penetrate to the areas where the poor live.

The chapter described measures that city authorities can take to improve the mobility of the urban poor, and illustrated some of them with the example of a proposed project to improve urban transport in Kenya. The main conclusion of the chapter is that there is no need to invent new transport modes to help low-income people to travel in cities. There is a need to allow, and possibly encourage, private individuals to respond to the mobility needs of their neighbours by providing them with services at prices they can afford.[17]

Notes

1. World Bank: Urban transport sector policy paper (Washington, DC, 1975).
2. M.M. Webber: Potential urban transport projects in Brazil, Report prepared for the World Bank (Washington, DC, unpublished).
3. D.A.C. Maunder, P.R. Fouracre, M.G. Pathak and C.H. Rao: Household and travel characteristics in two residential areas of Delhi, India, 1979, Supplementary report 673 (Transport and Road Research Laboratory, 1981).
4. D.A.C. Maunder, et al, op. cit.
5. G. Banjo: Activity travel patterns in Nigeria, Paper presented to the 13th Annual Conference of the British Universities Transport Studies Group (1981).
6. Kusbiantoro: Bandung: Travel demand analysis and its policy implications, Thesis submitted to the University of California (Los Angeles, 1979).
7. G. Roth and Y. Zahavi: "Travel time 'budgets' in developing countries", in Transportation Research, (Pergamon Press, New York) Vol. 15A, No. 1, Jan. 1981.
8. Jamieson Mackay and Partners: Personalised public transport in cities in South-east Asia, Report to the Transport and Road Research Laboratory (London, 1979).
9. A.A. Walters: Costs and scale of bus services, World Bank Staff Working Paper No. 325 (Washington, DC, 1979).
10. C. Feibel and A.A. Walters: Ownership and efficiency in urban buses, World Bank Staff Working Paper No. 371 (Washington, DC, 1980).
11. Institute of Traffic Engineers: Transportation and traffic engineering handbook (Englewood Cliffs, New Jersey, Prentice-Hall, Inc., 1982); and P. Midgley: Urban transport and traffic management - how to maximise benefits and avoid unnecessary investments, Paper prepared for the International Road Federation, Fourth African Highway Conference, Nairobi, 20-25 Jan. 1980 (Washington, DC, World Bank).
12. G. Roth and Y. Zahavi, op. cit.
13. P. Rimmer: Urban public transport in Southeast Asia (forthcoming).

14. Y. Zahavi: The UMOT project, Report No. DOT-RSPA-DPB-20-79-3 (Washington, DC, United States Department of Transportation, 1979).

15. Transportation Research Board: Transit planning, Transportation Research Record No. 559 (Washington, DC, 1976).

16. R.S. Foote: "Prospects for non-stop toll collection using automatic vehicle identification", in Traffic Quarterly, (Eno Foundation for Transportation, Westport, Connecticut) Vol. 35, July 1981, pp. 445-460.

17. L. Grava: Locally generated transportation modes of the developing world, Part 2 of Urban transportation economics, proceedings of five workshops held in 1976 and 1977. Special Report No. 181 (Washington, DC,Transportation Research Board, 1978).

10 CONCLUSIONS

by P.J. Richards

The contributors to this study have covered the most important aspects and problems of urban basic needs satisfaction. Each contributor has discussed a distinct sector (with perhaps the exception of the chapter on building codes which partly, in that sense, overlaps that on housing), one with which he or she is professionally familiar, and each approach has been startlingly different. The subject matter is naturally largely responsible for the range of approaches. There is, of course, a world of difference between planning a water supply project costing thousands of millions of dollars, scheduled to last for 20 or 30 years, and promoting the installation, and use, of appropriate and cheap sanitary facilities. An awareness of the failings of current building codes leads in one direction and an awareness of the obstacles besetting current education systems in another. Recent housing policies demonstrate a number of mistakes and misconceptions. Reviewing urban health care systems in a historical and world-wide context naturally generates a different set of insights on their function and future. Familiarity with the deficiencies of many urban transport systems promotes certain views for their improvement. However, perhaps it is more important to ask whether the contributors share a consensus on the nature of urban poverty and low levels of basic needs satisfaction and on appropriate responses within their own fields of professional competence. What assumptions therefore are perhaps implicit in each separate discussion?

Most of the chapters in the study refer explicitly to the inter-connection of the factors causing urban poverty and low welfare levels and responsible for transmitting these from generation to generation. Poor housing, poor sanitation, malnutrition, inadequate and low quality water supplies, low family

incomes, the need for older children to earn or to
care for their younger brothers and sisters, the
absence of adequate waste disposal, the proliferation
of disease and inadequate health surveillance and
primary health care all frequently go together. The
effects of an inadequate domestic and household
environment marked by malnutrition, illiteracy, debt
and squalor are intensified by ineffective,
inefficient and sometimes corrupt urban management in
its broadest sense. Urban households alone can hardly
solve their basic needs problems, nor, as some
contributors make clear, can better management within
urban areas of health, water, sewerage, transport,
housing or education projects and programmes solve
these problems without community participation,
education and training.

Not surprisingly perhaps it is the contributors to
this study on health and on education programmes who
take the widest view of urban poverty. Ebrahim
explicitly looks at Asian urban poverty in the
context of the ability of today's industrialised
countries to have solved the worst of their own urban
poverty problems during the last century. This
success he ascribes to higher incomes, social
security, universal primary education, comprehensive
health care and urban renewal. Western (or
"Northern") health programmes were in their early
days an example of deliberate social engineering
which brought about a major social transformation and
which most developing countries would like to copy.
But they are caught up in their own contradictions,
e.g. massive expenditure on major hospitals and not
on primary health care, training for health personnel
based on the concept of curative and not preventive
medicine, free enterprise advertising which distorts
food consumption patterns and increases malnutrition
and the countries' inability to achieve universal
literacy in any meaningful sense. Furthermore even
the "Northern" model has not achieved equality of
access to health care, let alone equality of health
status. What can be done is perhaps to encourage a
more radical approach to the analysis of community
health problems, ceasing to view health as just the
avoidance of disease, and, in the delivery of health
programmes, building up more participation and
community involvement to ensure timely immunisation,
surveillance and care.

In urban education programmes, as to some extent in urban health programmes, some rural experience can be drawn on in providing solutions to urban problems. Underachievement of the children of the urban poor in education mirrors the situation in neglected and remote rural areas where the provision of schooling hardly affects social mobility or intellectual achievement. Yet in urban areas there are few problems of physical accessibility to schools and indeed overall financial resources are more satisfactory than in the countryside. Nevertheless levels of absenteeism and drop-out in some urban areas are extreme. To some extent deliberate remedial teaching can bring poor urban children back into the mainstream of schooling once they have dropped out or failed to pass on to higher grades, but the necessary effort to achieve this would be immense. Furthermore no remedial teaching can compensate for the necessity for young children to contribute to family incomes. More attention to parental and adult education is also suggested as a means of improving child rearing and child upbringing practices, in the hope that in this way both parents' and children's attitudes towards education would become more positive. All of these suggestions require greater, more efficient and more sensitive forms of intervention transplanted into education programmes. The education chapter also refers specifically to bureaucratic obstacles to the more efficient management of education programmes, especially the centralisation of all authority for the towns both of Bangkok and Bombay in one administrator. Devolution of authority away from this level is clearly distrusted.

The approach taken in the chapter on housing policies is pragmatic and, for all that it stresses the magnitude of the housing problem of the poor and its very probable recent deterioration, it displays some optimism. Partly this optimism comes from reviewing the successful experience of Hong Kong and Singapore. However, their relatively high income levels apart, these two countries do demonstrate what intense political will and good administration can achieve. However, the high income levels are crucial in achieving universally good housing. The chapter sees a role for all the possible forms of government intervention in low income housing, for direct construction, for sites and services programmes and for slum and squatter area improvement. All the way through, however, Yeh stresses that the big problem is the availability of serviced land; in the long run where this cannot be found within city limits new towns will have to be set up outside.

Greater sensitivity in urban management and control procedures is also called for by the chapter on building codes. This chapter makes the point that most urban housing is built both by and for the urban poor. Yet some overall control is needed, both, of course, on housing location (so that non-divisible services can later be provided and some urban renewal and upgrading undertaken) and on such matters as ventilation (for health), load and stress bearing (for safety) and combustion, fire being a common danger in poor urban settlements. Urban builders may not be fully aware of all the implications of their finished artefacts for their own, let alone their neighbours', welfare. Yet building codes often have only the effect of separating legal from illegal housing and, as Cook notes, in some instances have thwarted the intention of the planners of sites and services projects to reach low income households. A transformation of building codes is suggested (with examples of which materials and means of construction might be "deemed to satisfy" certain "higher level" norms, rather than imposing designs and materials) and also a transformation of building departments and the role of building inspectors. The last should become a helpful extension service able to advise on methods and materials and promote self-help.

The chapter on transport points out that while the urban poor often do not travel so far or so regularly as the less poor (either because they cannot afford to or because they must necessarily live where they work) they nevertheless spend a large share of their income on transport. The most effective way to meet their travel needs seems to be by encouraging, or permitting, a competitive system of public transport probably in private hands and avoiding municipal transport monopolies, which have certainly proved highly inefficient in many places. There is, however, some evidence that in certain developing countries, particularly in Africa, there is official opposition to plans discouraging private cars or public transport corporations in favour of minibuses. Municipal administration has certainly also to remember the needs of those who walk through congested streets, or who would cycle if they felt it safe. Certainly transport and urban congestion present problems that are a tough nut to crack. Vast sums are spent in cities such as Bangkok in allowing office workers to live further out of town and to drive conveniently into the centre. The poor may inherit the inner city and later inherit its problems. However, for the moment what is probably needed is for urban planners to develop a greater awareness of the transport and travel needs of the poor, greater sensitivity towards their problems and some institutional method whereby these needs can be first expressed and then taken into account.

A somewhat different approach is taken in the chapter on human waste disposal. There the discussion relates specifically to immediate and known means of meeting the sanitation needs of the urban poor, exemplifying an incremental approach to the achievement of higher welfare levels. The improved sanitation methods discussed are those that can be, and clearly have been, applied with a minimum extra cost and physical effort. Indeed the most suitable innovations are those which present minor improvements to existing and familiar systems. This chapter then reflects an approach which has often been successful in improving the urban environment: the mobilisation of community and household effort often through non-official channels (or at least by officials extra-curricularly) supported by a modicum of outside financing. Of course, there are easily recognisable limits to such activities, for example, an institutionalised urban authority is necessary to ensure that water flows to the standpipes and solid waste is regularly removed. Furthermore, as the chapter on housing discussed, once such self-help efforts move beyond the immediate goal of acquiring an additional household amenity they are likely to become an element in local politics. They may attract party-political patronage or conversely they may be seen as a threat to existing elected or appointed representatives and liable to upset current party political systems of control and influence. In any event such efforts at larger scale mobilisation of local resources are likely to move out of the arena of self-help and into one of competition and the use, or mis-use, of the local power system to acquire scarce and rationed resources and commodities.

But the immediate problem in this field of upgrading household sanitation remains that of

disseminating knowledge of the techniques which are
available and stimulating personal effort to make use
of them. Non-official bodies so often appear to play
a major role here, perhaps because no official
government or municipal department seems obviously
responsible for their promotion (official public
health services appear always secondary to the
provision of personal health care in terms of
prestige, resources and promotion) and because, by
their nature, bureaucracies cannot inspire people to
commit themselves to personal effort. Perhaps a
different sort of out-reach, extension service, tied
in with the primary health care concept and using
trained and enthusiastic field level staff might
succeed where traditional systems have failed. But
such a service has yet to be institutionalised and,
of course, might not survive institutionalisation.

As noted above the discussion of major water
supply systems has to consider issues of pricing, of
the behaviour of long run average cost curves, of
loan repayments and the institutional problems of
collecting water rates and seeking as well as
repaying international loans. The chapter
demonstrates how the massive paraphernalia which
accompanies World Bank lending can still totally miss
the World Bank's anti-poverty objectives and that, in
the examples discussed, most new project loans
strengthen existing water supply systems and ipso
facto improve the service enjoyed by existing
beneficiaries. No doubt municipal and other water
supply agencies are better equipped to implement a
few large-scale rather than many small-scale
projects. Perhaps it is also administratively simpler
to rely, as many countries do, on major contractors
to lay new city water systems and open new supply
sources than to organise local supplies for low
income settlements. Different institutions and
implementing agencies may be involved with no
co-ordination between them. Of course, the World Bank
is well aware that existing beneficiaries may be both
highly vocal, and demand a higher standard of
service, and more reliable payers. Nevertheless it is
hardly easy to structure major urban project lending
so as to assist low income groups and to satisfy more
traditional urban bureaucracies. International
development finance is, of course, a major weapon of
persuasion for projects and programmes to be
undertaken which will be more sensitive to the needs

of the poor. In this, of course, it differs from the
private international lending which financed so much
urban development in North and South America one
century back. But it is nonetheless a very blunt
instrument to use to achieve anti-poverty objectives
if urban institutions and urban management have not
the sophistication needed to translate laudable
objectives into simple programmes.

One overall conclusion to be drawn from the
chapters in this study must be one of both optimism
and pessimism. Optimism because a large number of
means are clearly known to exist by which the welfare
levels of the urban poor can be raised, probably
without great financial cost. Achieving higher
welfare levels, through the provision of better
sanitation, drainage, health care, improved housing
conditions and the like is important both in itself
and because of the positive effects which can be
expected to follow for income generation and
employment in the medium and longer run. Of course,
reaching fuller and more highly remunerated levels of
employment is crucial to personal well-being, both
material and mental. But it is not so crucial that
everything else has to wait until it has already
happened. Programme and project management can be
improved before higher levels of GNP are reached.
However, the general conclusion must also be
pessimistic because, with exceptions, urban
management (understood here as the management of all
programmes which affect the urban poor, not only
infrastructural but also health and education) does
not appear to be responsive nor perhaps always want
to be responsive to the needs of the urban poor.
Probably the difficulties involved in readjusting the
planning and implementation of urban projects and
programmes to make them more sensitive to basic needs
satisfaction are often underestimated. Perhaps staff
can be better trained but perhaps their motivation
cannot be stimulated further. Hierarchy and
bureaucracy are themselves obstacles to improved
urban management. And, of course, there are
straightforward problems of competing claims by the
urban poor and non-poor on all government resources
and attention.

One point which needs to be stressed in these
conclusions concerns the self-reinforcing nature of
many of these programmes. Thus health care programmes
will themselves be more successful if adequate

shelter is provided and if adequate sanitation is available. Adequate sanitation under environmentally unfavourable conditions can pose complex problems and is more easily provided to a literate and more educated community. Thus action needs to be taken on a number of fronts together, leaving out one element may jeopardise the success of other programmes.

The role of the private sector in providing communal services has been mentioned in a number of chapters. In housing small scale private sector enterprises help a lot in squatter and later sites and services development. Larger companies, of course, work under contract to the government. In transport it was strongly argued that private operators can provide a cheaper service. It can be questioned whether some routes may be unprofitable for the private operators to handle but still beneficial to the urban poor. The answer is probably not that the need for transport in some areas is so low as to be commercially unprofitable as that the money demand for transport is low. Rather than running and subsidising a loss-making transport service the local or central government might then consider some form or subsidy to private operators along specific routes.

One somewhat different problem is posed by larger public utilities, the more important in this case being water supply and distribution agencies. They are not usually private concerns and probably should not be, however, they are generally urged to be self-financing. Self-financing is naturally likely to have economic advantages, it should increase operational efficiency and reduce the subsidy burden on the government budget, which may otherwise by financed by regressive fiscal means. Yet the utility may then behave more or less as would a private enterprise, the complete opposite of say the provider of education or health programmes. One solution might be to split up the utility into a profit making section serving those who could pay and a service providing section for those who cannot. However, the simplest solution seems to be that discussed in the chapter on water, namely establishing higher water charges for amounts above the minimum, thus effectively achieving cross-subsidisation in the average unit costs paid by rich and poor. Nevertheless this will be of limited value unless some higher authority can order the water utility to expand and improve its coverage of poorer areas. The existence of this authority should be precisely a consequence of having public rather than private utility companies. However, governments may have more frequently considered that the advantage of public utilities was that they could be more easily ordered to keep rates down, with effects often inconsistent with the goals of poverty alleviation.

There are two other general issues emerging from the chapters of this study on which specific comments can be made. One concerns the "highjacking" of benefits intended for the poor, by the less poor (a subject mentioned in more than one country context in the chapter on housing) and the other, the relative levels of satisfaction of basic needs (and prospects for the satisfaction of basic needs) in cities or parts of cities with older or more recent housing stock, water pipes and sewerage systems, etc.

"Highjacking" can occur at different stages. Clearly, as the chapter on water supply demonstrates, it may occur at the planning stage, so that appropriate delivery services to suit the needs of the poor are never constructed or even developed. In housing highjacking may occur after the housing stock has been completed, especially if its location is more acceptable to the less poor than the poor. In health and education services highjacking is not an issue since so often the quality of the service officially provided varies in step with the household income of the beneficiaries. Thus, in principle, the poor require a higher standard of health and education merely to compensate for their low household incomes and other disadvantages. Of course, highjacking would then no doubt be stimulated. Once housing policies have passed the planning stage the form of intervention which is least susceptible to having its benefits diverted to other income groups is slum and squatter area upgrading (including the provision of drinking water, sewerage, etc.). However, as noted, this form of upgrading cannot in fact guarantee any increase in the number or quality of dwellings. Nevertheless in terms of equity it is a very desirable measure.

Apart from the high-jacking issue there is also the possibility that inevitably the measures intended to help the poor will also help the non-poor. Of course, there are external economies always present in eliminating disease or fire hazards affecting the poor directly but from which the non-poor would also benefit indirectly. However, it is also possible that eg. measures taken to ease the mobility problems of the poor could also be enjoyed by the rich, if only because they can afford to consume more of the new service provided.

The other issue concerns differences between older and newer cities, or more realistically, since virtually all cities are growing, between older inner-city areas and newer areas on the periphery. This distinction has been referred to in terms of locational preference given that jobs and other opportunities to make a living are more likely to be situated in the inner city. In fact, of course, the inner city probably has other advantages. Settlements are usually not irregular but legal, centralised services, such as hospitals, are probably close and water and other services, although of a poor quality, are generally available. In more peripheral settlements access to all of these items is usually more time-consuming and requires more effort. Inner city areas, however, have a far higher population density, may be unhealthier and generally more unpleasant. However, the only real distinction may be that one form of settlement is multi-storey and the other single storey. No doubt in the long run achieving better urban welfare is associated with lower population densities and, indeed, satellite town development. In the short run, however, this is not obviously so. Upgrading multi-storey slums is technically difficult, not least because they are so often privately owned. However, conceivably it could be cheaper to raise levels of basic needs satisfaction precisely in older areas.

The final irony perhaps is that the urban poverty problems of Asia are almost always open to full scrutiny by professionals from the urbanised West who can see many opportunities to apply the lessons of their own experience and history (and who are often supported in this by the availability of foreign loans). Hence we can always suggest means by which urban management in Asia and elsewhere can be made more technically efficient (as the World Bank has competently done in many technical fields) and how more "social engineering" can be beneficially undertaken. But the institutional and participatory framework of most Asian cities is not usually that of the West. Firstly municipal government in Asia is generally less powerful in relation to the central government (or fewer initiatives, revenue sources and responsibilities are devolved from the latter to the former) than in the West. Urban education and health programmes, for example, are often a division of an overall, national department. Local bureaucracies may have simply less room for manoeuvre in responding to the needs of the urban poor. Major utilities supplying e.g. water or electricity may be institutionally completely unrelated to urban, local government and derive their authority directly from the central government. Thus local government leaders cannot directly control and may in fact have no influence at all on a whole range of projects and programmes which directly impinge on their constituents' welfare. Secondly large numbers of the urban poor may be unregistered for voting purposes (if they are squatters or perhaps indecisive rural-urban migrants).

The question whether stronger local government is an essential or desirable step in strengthening the effectiveness of anti-poverty and basic needs programmes is a contentious one. Any form of decentralisation of authority away from the central government risks increasing the power of the local elite, which may be less sensitive to the needs of the poor (whether urban or rural) than the national leaders. The latter may be more susceptible to national political movements and to international pressure. Of course, it can also be argued that local government has the detailed local knowledge and can make better informed decisions. The central government, however, is unlikely to give up a large measure of control over the capital city since events there will reflect ill or well on the government's own prestige.

Probably the advantages of decentralised local government are not great (since the resources for all programmes and projects will be almost entirely raised or channelled through the central government) unless there are genuine and effective institutionalised means for the urban poor to express their priorities. Of course, even with central government control this is desirable. As many of the chapters describe, the poor often seem to be living in an institutional vacuum. They can only react to the measures taken by a water supply company or by outside well-wishers who seek to raise their levels of sanitation. One major conclusion therefore is that participation of the urban poor in all forms of democratic exercise must be encouraged and that if possible they should form their own community organisations. These organisations, as was noted in the chapter on health, should contribute to introducing an element within each government or agency activity which ensures that the service provided is appropriate to the values, norms and culture of the society. Under those circumstances greater local government responsibility will be desirable so that changes in programme design and implementation can be made.

What is the outlook for the fuller satisfaction of basic needs in Asian (and, for that matter, North African or Middle-Eastern) cities for the next twenty years or so? Presumably some real income growth will continue since, on average, city incomes will hardly grow more slowly than the national average. Whether urban income inequality will worsen depends largely on the structure of employment. Here perhaps the outlook is not so bad. Over the 20-year period 1951-71 the share of manufacturing workers in the working population of Bombay and Calcutta Municipal Councils (combined) rose from 30 to 37 per cent and that in "other services" fell from 31 to 22 per cent. In Hong Kong from 1961-81 the share of workers in manufacturing rose from 38 to 42 per cent and those in agriculture fell from 7 per cent to 2 per cent. If such increases in the share of employment in manufacturing are common in large Asian and other cities then the structure of employment may be turning away from the least paid sectors with possibly equalising effects on urban income distribution. This in turn would boost the household resources available to improve levels of nutrition, health, housing and other forms of environmental welfare and should clearly have positive effects on basic needs satisfaction.

However, it is highly doubtful whether, over the next 20 years, many major Asian cities will grow to resemble Singapore with its high housing, environmental and education standards. However, some progress can be expected as governments become both more sensitive to the problems of the urban poor and more adept at handling urban projects and programmes.

In slower growing countries such as India, Nepal, Bangladesh and Sri Lanka some progress towards basic needs satisfaction in urban areas can be expected as knowledge on means to upgrade welfare levels is gradually disseminated and urban management improves. However, there will still no doubt be ample scope to deplore the persistence of low levels of health, education and environment into the next century.

Tables and figures are indicated respectively by the abbreviations (T) and (F) following the page reference.